𝔗𝔥𝔢 𝔍𝔫𝔣𝔦𝔫𝔦𝔱𝔦𝔳𝔢

The gerund and the participles of the
English verb

H. Poutsma

Alpha Editions

This edition published in 2020

ISBN : 9789354040719

Design and Setting By
Alpha Editions
www.alphaedis.com
email - alphaedis@gmail.com

As per information held with us this book is in Public Domain.
This book is a reproduction of an important historical work.
Alpha Editions uses the best technology to reproduce historical
work in the same manner it was first published to preserve its
original nature. Any marks or number seen are left intentionally
to preserve its true form.

THE INFINITIVE,
THE GERUND AND THE PARTICIPLES
OF THE ENGLISH VERB

BY

H. POUTSMA
ENGLISH MASTER IN THE MUNICIPAL GYMNASIUM OF AMSTERDAM

P. NOORDHOFF   1923   GRONINGEN

III

BOOKS AND TREATISES CONSULTED.

Abbot	"A Shakespearean Grammar", Macmillan and Co., London, 1888.
Akerlund	A Word on the Passive Definite Tenses, Englische Studien, XLVII, 3.
Alford	"The Queen's English", George Bell and Sons, London, 1889.
Aronstein	Die Periphrastische Form im Englischen, Anglia, XLII.
Birger Palm	The Place of the Adjective Attribute in English Prose, Ph. Lindstedts Universitetsbokhandel, Lund, 1911.
Bradley	The Making of English, Macmillan and Co., London, 1904.
Curme	History of the English Gerund, Englische Studien, XLV, 3.
	The Gerund in Old English and German, Anglia, XXXVIII, III.
Deutschbein	System der neuenglischen Syntax, Otto Schulze, Cöthen, 1917.
Dubislav	Beiträge zur historischen Syntax des Englischen, XIV.
Earle	"The Philology of the English Tongue", Clarendon Press, Oxford, 1892.
Ellinger	Vermischte Beiträge zur Syntax der neueren englischen Sprache, Alfred Hölder, Wien und Leipzig, 1909.
	Zu dem Gebrauche des Infinitivs nach *to dare*, Englische Studien, XXI.
Einenkel	Zur Geschichte des englischen Gerundiums, Anglia, XXXVII, III.
	Die Entwickelung des englischen Gerundiums, Anglia XXXVIII, I.
	Zur Herkunft des englischen Gerundiums, Anglia, XXXVIII, III.

IV

EINENKEL — Geschichte der englischen Sprache, II, Historische Syntax, Trübner, Strassburg, 1916.

EYKMAN — De Uitgang *ing*, De Drie Talen, VI.
De Vertaling van de Onbepaalde Wijs met *te*, Bedrijvend in Vorm, Lijdend in Beteekenis, De Drie Talen, XXXI, 8—12; XXXII, 2.

FIJN VAN DRAAT, Rhythm in English Prose, Anglia XXIV, 1.

FOWLER — The King's English, Clarendon Press, Oxford, 1906.

FRANZ — Shakespeare Grammatik², Carl Winter, Heidelberg, 1909.

DEN HERTOG — Nederlandsche Spraakkunst, Versluys, Amsterdam, 1892.

HODGSON — Errors in the Use of English, David Douglas, Edinburgh, 1906.

HORN — *I intended to have written*, Herrig Archiv, CXIV, 370.

JESPERSEN — A Modern English Grammar, II, Carl Winter, Heidelberg, 1909.
Growth and Structure of the English Language, Teubner, Leipzig, 1912.
Tid og Tempus, Oversigt over det Danske Videnskabernes Selskabs Forhandlinger, 1914, No. 5—6.
De To Hovedarter av Grammatiske Forbindelser, Det Kgl. Danske Videnskabernes Selskab, Historisk-filologiske Meddelelser, IV, 3, Bianco Lunos Bogtrykkeri, København, 1921.
Negation, id., I, 5, id., id., 1917.
Dare, use and *need* als präteritum, Englische Studien, XXIII.

KELLNER — Historical Outlines of English Syntax, Macmillan and Co., London, 1902.

KRÜGER — Syntax der englischen Sprache, C. A. Kochs Verlagsbuchhandlung, Dresden und Leipzig, 1914.
Vermischte Beiträge zur Syntax, id. id., 1919.
Die partizipiale Gerundialfügung, ihr Wesen und ihr Ursprung, Englische Studien, XXXVII, 385 ff.

V

Kruisinga	A Handbook of Present-day English, Kemink en Zoon, Utrecht, 1915.
Mason	English Grammar, Bell and Sons, London, 1892.
Matzner	Englische Grammatik, Weidmannsche Buchhandlung, Berlin, 1875.
Murray	A New English Dictionary, s. v. *ing*. Dropping of the final *g* of the Present Participle, Notes and Queries, 1890, 406—7.
Onions	An Advanced English Syntax, Swan Sonnenschein, London, 1905.
Paul	Prinzipien der Sprachgeschichte, Max Niemeyer, Halle, 1898.
Poutsma	A Grammar of Late Modern English, Noordhoff, Groningen, 1905.
	Hendiadys in English, Neophilologus, II, 3—4.
Sarrazin	*I dare* als Praeteritum, Englische Studien, XXII
Sattler	Noch einmal *(te) dare*, Englische Studien, XXVI.
Schmidt	Shakespeare Lexicon, s. v. *have*, I.
Stoett	Middelnederlandsche Spraakkunst, Martinus Nyhoff, 'S Gravenhage, 1909.
Stoffel	Studies in English, Thieme and Co., Zutphen, 1894.
	The book is being printed, Taalstudie, III.
	I intended to have written, Taalstudie, IX.
Storm	Englische Philology, Reisland, Leipzig, 1896.
Sundén	The Predicational Categories in English, Edv. Berling, Uppsala, 1916.
Swaen	*To dare*, Englische Studien, XX
	Dare als Praeteritum, Englische Studien, XXIII.
Sweet	A New English Grammar, Clarendon Press, Oxford, 1898.
Willert	Vom Gerundium, Englische Studien, XXXV. Vom Substantivischen Infinitiv, Englische Studien, XLVIII.
Wilmanns	Deutsche Grammatik, Trübner, Strassburg, 1906.

THE INFINITIVE

ORDER OF DISCUSSION.

Grammatical Nature of the Infinitive	§ 1
The Use of *to* before the Infinitive	§§ 2–53
Introductory Observations	§§ 2–5
Practice after Verbs and Group-verbs forming a kind of unit with the following Infinitive	§§ 6–33
Practice after Verbs governing an Accusative + Infinitive or allied construction	§§ 34–41
Practice after the Conjunctions *but, as* and *than*	§§ 42–46
Practice in Elliptical Sentences	§§ 47–50
Repetition and Non-repetition of *to*	§§ 51–53
Tense and Voice of the Infinitive	§§ 54–87
Introductory Observations	§§ 54–56
Tense-shifting in Infinitive Constructions	§§ 57–65
The Passive Infinitive in detail	§§ 66–87

GRAMMATICAL NATURE OF THE INFINITIVE.

1. Like the gerund, the infinitive is a substantival form of the verb, that is to say it has partly the character of a verb, partly that of a noun.

   a) It shows its verbal character by its capacity of:
   1) taking the ordinary verb-modifiers, objects and adverbial adjuncts, e. g.: *He promised to write the letter; He pretended to listen to me; He intended to rise early*. Further discussion or illustration is not necessary.
   2) showing, at least in part, the distinctions of tense and voice.
       It will be no crime to have been Cato's friend. Addison, Cato, IV 1
       I am worthy to be scorned. Thack., Pend., I, Ch. XXVII, 291.
       For detailed discussion see below, 54 ff.

   b) It shows its substantival character by its capacity of filling the same functions in a sentence as an ordinary noun. As such it largely varies with the gerund, one or the other being preferred or required in some cases, or either being applied without any appreciable distinction. In Ch. XVIII of my *Grammar of Late Modern English* the multifarious applications of the infinitive as an element of the sentence have been amply discussed. The area of incidence of the two rival substantival verbals have been submitted to close investigation in Ch. XIX. Under these circumstances there seems, therefore, to be no need to revert to these subjects in this place.

   In this connexion it should, however, be observed that the infinitive differs materially from the gerund in that, unlike the latter, it does not admit of being modified by adnominal modifiers. This distinctive feature of the gerund has been done full justice to in the following treatise. It is also worth mentioning that the above limitation does not attach to the infinitive in either Dutch or German.

   c) As will be shown in the following treatise (46 ff), the gerund is in many applications in no way distinguished from the noun of action. From what has been observed above, under b), it follows, therefore, that the infinitive also bears a strong affinity to the noun of action, substitution of the one for the other being, indeed, in many cases only prevented by requirements of idiom. Nay it would not be difficult to collect a goodly number of sentences in which either of the alternative forms would be admissible without much detriment to idiomatic propriety. We must confine ourselves to a few examples.

He is desirous *of being admired.* MASON, Eng. Gram.³¹, § 397. (= *of admiration,* or *to be admired.*)
To doubt his *originality,* in the creation of poetic phrases would be to show the extreme of poetical incapacity. A. C. BRADLEY. Com. on Ten.'s In Memoriam, Ch VII, 75 (= *doubting his originality,* or *doubt of his originality.*)
Life alone at twenty-six is — lonely. HOPE, Intrusions of Peggy, 44). (= *living alone,* or *to live alone.*)

Similarly nouns denoting a state or quality are essentially equivalent to word-groups consisting of the verb *to be* + corresponding adjective. Thus substitution of the latter for the former would be possible in:

Caution is not always good policy. W. PHILLIPS, Speeches, VI, 139²).
Boldness in business is the first, second and third thing. Prov.
Content is more than a kingdom. id.

Note. Although it has been shown to be highly probable that the infinitive has descended from a verbal noun of which two case-forms have been preserved in Old English (3, Obs. I), its substantival character is now at all prominent only when it stands without any modifier as in *To err is human, to forgive divine.*
In all other cases the verbal character prevails over the substantival to the extent that little or no trace of the latter is discernible, at least, in the English infinitive.

THE USE OF *TO* BEFORE THE INFINITIVE.
Introductory Observations.

2. The infinitive is now mostly preceded by the preposition *to.* An infinitive with *to* is called by SWEET (N. E. Gr., § 321) supine, by MASON (Eng. Gram.³¹, § 196) gerundial infinitive. By some German grammarians it is called **gerund**. For reasons which hardly require comment, none of these terms can be pronounced to be particularly apposite, and since there

---
¹) JESPERSEN, Mod. Eng. Gram., 12.09.
²) MURRAY.

is no need for any special name for the infinitive with *to*, not any of them will be used in the following discussions.

3. Obs I. In Old English *to* was only used before a dative form of the infinitive ending in *enne* or *anne* (*onne*). It denoted chiefly a relation of purpose, as it still does in such sentences as *I came to tell you*. *This house is to let.* This meaning of *to* is distinctly discernible in:

Sóðlice út éode se sáwere his sǽd tó sáwenne. Matth., XIII, 3. (Author Vers.: Behold a sower went forth to sow.)

Gadriað ǽrest þone coccel, and bindað sceáfmǽlum *to forbærnenne*) ib., XIII, 30 (Author Vers. Gather ye together first the tares, and bind them in bundles *to burn* them)

Eálá þu freond, ne do ic ðe nǽnne teonan: hú, ne come þú tó me tó wyrceanne wið ánum peninge) id., XX, 3 (Author Vers Friend, I do thee no wrong: didst thou not agree with me for a penny.)

The dative form was mostly rigidly distinguished from the common-case form, which ended in *an*.

Nim þæt þin ys, and gá, ic wylle þysum ýtemestum syllan eall swá mycel swá þé. Matth., XX 14⁷) (Author Vers Take that thine is, and go thy way: I will give unto this last even as unto thee.)

ða cwæð se Hǽlend tó hyre, Syle me drincan. Jons, IV, 7⁵) (Author Vers.: Jesus saith unto her, Give me *to drink*.)

The uninflected infinitive without *to* seems to have been used occasionally where the dative infinitive with *to* would be expected. Thus in:

Heofona rice ys gelic þám hiredes ealdre, þe on ǽrnemergen, út éode áhýrian wyrhtan on his wingeard Matthew, XX 1¹) (Author Vers. The kingdom of heaven is like unto a man that is an householde, which went out early in the morning *to hire* labourers into his vineyard.)

Compare also Curme, E. S., XLV, III, 375.

In the Middle English period the suffixes gradually wore off, with the result that the dative infinitive and the common-case infinitive became identical. Thus *to writenne* (or *writanne*) → *to writene* → *to writen* → *to write*; and *writan* → *writen* → *write*.

There appear to be no instances in any period of the English language of the infinitive being placed in the genitive, corresponding to the practice represented in Dutch by such formations as prijzenswaardig, levensmoe or the German liebenswurdig.

II. "In process of time (the) obvious sense of the preposition became weakened and generalized, so that *to* became at last the ordinary link expressing any prepositional relation in which an infinitive stands to a preceding verb, adjective, or substantive. Sometimes the

---

¹) Sweet, Anglo-Saxon Reader³, 51 f.
²) Sweet, Anglo-Saxon Read.⁴, 51 f.
³) The Belles Lettres Series.
⁴) Sweet, Anglo-Saxon Reader³, 51 f.

relation was so vague as scarcely to differ from that between a transitive verb and its object. This was especially so when the verb was construed both transitively and intransitively. There were several verbs in Old English in this position, such as *onginnan* (to begin), *ondrǣdan* (to dread), *bebéodan* (to bid), *bewerian* (to forbid, prevent), *ȝeliefan* (to believe), *þencan* (to think, etc.); these are found construed either with the simple (accusative) infinitive, or with *tó* and the dative infinitive. From these beginnings, the use of the infinitive with *to* in place of the simple infinitive, helped by the phonetic decay and loss of the inflexions, and the need of some mark to distinguish it from other parts of the verb and from the cognate substantive, increased rapidly during the late Old English and early Middle English period, with the result that in Modern English the infinitive with *to* is the ordinary form, the simple infinitive surviving only in particular connexions where it is intimately connected with the preceding verb. To a certain extent, therefore, i e. when the infinitive is the subject or direct object, *to* has lost all its meaning, and has become a mere 'sign' or prefix of the infinitive. But after an intransitive verb, or the passive voice, *to* is still the preposition. In appearance there is no difference between the infinitive in *he proceeds to speak* and *he chooses to speak*; but in the latter *to speak* is the equivalent of *speaking* or *speech*, and in the former of *to speaking* or *to speech*. In form *to speak* is the descendant of Old English *tó specanne;* in sense, it is partly the representative of this and largely of Old English *specan."* MURRAY, s. v. *to*, B, History.

According to ONIONS (Adv. Eng. Synt., § 157, 4, Obs.) *to* is not found with the Nom.-Acc. form (i. e. the common-case form) of the Infinitive before the twelfth century.

III. When it had become usual to put *to* before the infinitive irrespective of its grammatical function, the want may have been felt for another expedient to express the notion of purpose. This may have given rise to the use of *for to* before the infinitive. MURRAY's earliest instance of this practice is dated 1175. It appears to have been quite common in Middle English, in which it seems to have served the same purpose as the Dutch o m t e and the German u m z u. But it soon came to be used before an infinitive also when no notion of purpose was implied, in like manner as in colloquial Dutch o m t e is often used in the same connexion, where there is no occasion for it.

The use of *for to* before the infinitive, either with or without a notion of purpose, was still vigorously alive in Early Modern English, but has been constantly losing ground since. In Present English it survives only in dialects and in the language of the uneducated. For discussion see also Ch. XVIII, 24, Obs. IV; and compare STOF.,

Stud., A, VII, 48 ff; Curme, Hist. of the Eng Ger., E. S., XLV, 376; Stoett, Middelned. Spraakk., § 283.

i. And specially, from every shires ende | Of Engelond, to Caunterbury they wende, | The holy blisful martir *for to* seke. Chauc., Cant. Tales, A, 15—17.
Vertue gives her selfe light, through darkenesse *for to* wade. Spenser, Faery Queene, I, I, XII
We will solicit heaven and move the gods | To send down Justice *for to* wreak our wrongs. Shak., Tit. Andr., IV, 3, 51.
For he had healed many; insomuch that they pressed upon him *for to* touch him, as many as had plagues. Bible, Mark, III, 10.
And after the uproar was ceased, Paul called unto him his disciples, and embraced them, and departed *for to* go into Macedonia. ib., Acts, XX, 1.
You've not come here *for to* make me suppose he wants to marry her. Thack., Van. Fair, I, Ch. XXIV, 244.
Miss Arabella wondered why he always said he was going *for to* do a thing. G. Eliot, Scenes, I, Ch. II, 14.
You needn't come *for to* give such advice to any girl of mine. Flor. Marryat, A Bankrupt Heart, II, 45. T.
You see I cannot get started on a speech without saying things like, 'In rising *for to* make a few remarks'. J. M. Barrie, What Every Woman knows, I, (13).
My cousin Thorolf wouldn't go *for to* kill a man. Masefield, The Locked Chest, (56).

ii. And if you lyketh alle; by oon assent, | Now *for to* stonden at my jugement. Chauc., Cant. Tales, A, 779.
Hir othes been so greete and so dampnable, | That it is grisly *for to* here hem swere. ib., C., 473.
We'll teach you *for to drink* ere you depart. Shak., Haml., I, 2, 175. (The Folios have: *to drink* deep.)
It is not lawful *for to put* them (sc the silver pieces) into the treasury. Bible, Matth. XXVII, 6.
By the laws, mamma, you make me *for to laugh* Goldsmith, The Stoops, III, (201).
We don't choose *for to part* with her. Fanny Burney, Evelina, Ch. XV, 48.
Sir, you don't dare *for to breathe* a word against my Lady Maria Thack., Virg., Ch. XXXIV, 407.
I did'nt think *for to get* married so soon. Mrs. Gask., Cranf., Ch. XIV, 262.
I could put them into the Ecclesiastical Court, if I chose *for to* do so. G. Eliot, Scenes, I, Ch. III, 29.
I'm afraid you didn't intend *for to go* and see your mother, Peter. Jacobs, Odd Craft, A, 17.

In the following quotation the use of *for to* + infinitive after *for* + pronoun strikes us as particularly clumsy:

There's no need *for you for to put* in your oar. Fanny Burney, Evelina, XIV, 45.

It will be observed that the infinitive in other Germanic languages, Dutch, German, Danish, differs from that in English in that in these languages it admits of being preceded by other prepositions besides the ordinary te, zu and til.

IV. In Middle English the use of *to* before the infinitive was still more or less variable and in some respects different from modern practice. The discussion of these fluctuations falls beyond the scope of the present treatise and will not, therefore, be attempted. The student interested in the subject may be referred to EINENKEL, Streifzüge, 229 ff; id., Hist. Syntax, § 4.

Some survivals of antiquated constructions in which *to* is dispensed with contrary to ordinary Modern English practice will be mentioned in due course.

V. In some few cases, especially those in which the use of *to* before the infinitive has remained unsettled in Modern English, its employment or omission is, to some extent, conditioned by considerations of metre or rhythm. See FIJN VAN DRAAT, Rhythm in Eng. Prose, Angl. Forsch., § 44 ff. For illustration see 13, Note; 20; 33, c, Note; 35, Obs. I; 39, c; 41, a; 42, a; 45, a; 51, c.

In verse we meet with repeated instances of *to* being dispensed with for the sake of the metre, where this would be inadmissible in ordinary prose. Practically all the instances of irregular practice cited by FRANZ (Shak. Gram.², § 650) will bear this explanation.

How long within this wood intend you *stay?* SHAK., Mids., II, 1, *138*.
He left his bed, he trod the floor, | And 'gan in haste the drawers *explore,* | The lowest first, and without stop | The rest in order to the top. COWPER, The Retired Cat, *88*.
Yet not Lord Cranstoun deign'd she *greet,* | Though low he kneeled at her feet. SCOTT. Lay, V, *398*.
His pensive cheek and pondering brow | Did more than he was wont *avow.* BYRON, Bride of Abydos, II.

Instances of the opposite practice appear to be less frequent. See also 5, Obs. II.

It is better holde thy tonge stille than *to speke.* CHAUCER¹).
By heaven I had rather coin my heart, | And drop my blood for drachmas, than *to wring* | From the hard hands of peasants their vile trash | By any indirection. SHAK., Jul. Cæs., IV, 3, 73.

VI. Sometimes *to* appears to be omitted simply to impart terseness to the style.

Kill or be killed, *eat* or be eaten, was the law. JACK LONDON, The Call of the Wild, Ch. VI, *129*.

If the omission of *to* before the infinitive in the following quotation is not due to carelessness on the part of the writer or the compositor, there seems to be no alternative but to ascribe it to the same desire of terseness.

Do you mean *go* alone — in the dark — with a witch in the house? SHAW, The Man of Destiny, (*243*). T.

---

¹) EINENKEL, Hist. Synt., § 4, K.

VII. There is not, apparently, much use in discussing the question whether, in case the infinitive is connected with a full verb, i. e. one which does not form a kind of unit with it (Ch. I, 15), as in *He came to see me; I intend to come again*, etc., the preposition is felt to belong to the former or the latter.

Jespersen (Growth and Structure², § 211) finds in constructions with what he calls pro-infinitive *to*, such as *Will you play? — Yes, I intend to* (Ch. XXXII, 31), "one amongst several indications that the linguistic instinct now takes *to* to belong to the preceding verb rather than to the infinitive, a fact which, together with other circumstances, serves to explain the phenomenon usually mistermed the split infinitive." But there can be no doubt that other grammarians lean to the alternative view, and consider *to* to be more closely connected with the infinitive than with the preceding verb. This view is, of course, inapplicable to the case of the infinitive standing after a verb governing a prepositional object with *to*, as in *to listen to, to talk to*, etc. The fact that such a verb may form a kind of compound gerund with the preposition is sufficient proof that *to* does not belong to the infinitive so much as to the preceding verb. See Gerund, 41.

You will never read anything that's worth *listening to*. Shaw, Critic, I, 1, (443).
The Prime Minister went for him in a letter, and gave him a good *talking to*. Eng. Rev., No. 106, 264.

Nor does it seem very important to consider the grammatical function of *to* before the infinitive in sentences in which it is the subject, the nominal part of the predicate, or the non-prepositional object of the sentence, e. g. in *To err is human, to forgive divine; To advertise in a small way is to throw away your money; She entreated us to remain.* Kruisinga (Handbook², § 212, footnote) finds it "useful to consider *to* before an infinitive (in connections like the above) as an inseparable part of the infinitive," but he fails to tell us where the usefulness comes in.

The prepositional force of *to* is, of course, unmistakable when the infinitive is connected with a word (verb, adjective or noun) ordinarily construed with *for* or *to*, as in: *I longed to escape to glorious Italy; This apple is not fit to eat; I don't feel any vocation to be a governess; Nothing will induce him to believe this; I am not inclined to go that length; There may be a disposition to exaggerate the peril.*

Thus also when the infinitive stands in an adverbial or adnominal clause implying a relation of purpose, as in: *He toils to earn a living; She gave him the letter to post.*

But in many adverbial and adnominal clauses the meaning of *to* is vague and weak, often to the extent of being hardly discernible. Thus in *Scrooge hung his head to hear his own words quoted by the spirit; I rejoice to see you; You're in luck to come to-day; To hear him, you would think he had passed half his life in Australia; She was old enough to be his mother; He was slow to sympathise with the sufferings of others; Scrooge was not a man to be frightened by echoes; These people have a narrow margin on which to subsist; Our militia was not a body to be proud of.*

Practice after Verbs and Group=verbs forming a kind of unit with the following Infinitive.

4. In Modern English the infinitive stands without *to* after certain verbs which form a kind of complex predicate with it, i. e.:

   a) after any auxiliary of mood or tense, e. g.:

   May you *be* happy in the life you have chosen! He *will* soon *withdraw* from the concern.

   a) after any of the defective verbs *can, may, must, shall* and *will*.

   He *can (may, must, shall, will) come* to you this evening.

   c) after *to do*.

   I *do* not *understand* this.

5. Obs. I. *Will* as a regular verb requires *to* before the following infinitive. See also Ch. I, 48, Obs. II.

   When the soul wills *to remember* anything, this volition, causing the pineal gland to incline itself in different directions, drives the (animal) spirits towards different regions of the brain. HUXLEY, Method and Result, Ch. V, 214.
   I willed *to stay* on yet awhile on my native continent. THACK., Virg., Ch. XC, 969.

   II. *Ought* now almost regularly stands with an infinitive with *to*. MURRAY (s. v. *ought*, III, 5, b) quotes several instances with the bare infinitive from writers belonging to the Middle English period, and a few drawn from Modern English. In the following quotations the absence of *to* is, apparently, required by the metre:

   You *ought* not *walk* | Upon a labouring day, without the sign | Of your profession. SHAK., Jul. Cæs., I, 1, 3.
   How *ought* I *address* thee, how *ought* I *revere* thee? BROWNING, Aga= memnon, 796.

   III. Also when the infinitive is, for emphasis, placed in front=position, which is only possible when it is connected with any of the above verbs, it now regularly stands without *to*.

   Beg he must. LYTTON, My Novel, VII, Ch. XV, 467.

   In Middle English it was frequently preceded by *to*. See EINENKEL, Synt., § 4, λ.

Occasional instances of this practice may be met with in Early Modern English.

To belie him, I will not, and more of his soldiership I know not. SHAK., All's Well, IV, 3, 299.

6. As to the use of *to* before the infinitive after *to need* in the sense of *to be required, to be under a necessity or obligation*, usage is variable.

Before starting on an exposition of the prevailing practice, it seems desirable to advert to the use of *to do* in connexion with this verb, and to some anomalies in its conjugation.

The unsettled nature of some syntactical features in this verb is, no doubt, due to its occupying an intermediate position between a full verb and one which, like *must*, etc., is felt to form a kind of unit with the following infinitive.

7. *To need* dispenses with the use of *to do*, apparently regularly, in questions with inverted word-order. See also 9, a; and 12, a.

   i. *Need I tell my reader that so innocent a girl as Susan was too high-minded to watch the effect of her proceeding behind the curtains?* READE, It is never too late to mend, I, Ch. VI, 72. T.
Need I say more? WILK. COLLINS, The Traveller's Story.
Need he ever know? GALSWORTHY, Saint's Prog., II, V, 1 § , 138.

   ii. *Why need we always play for such high stakes?* FLOR. MARRYAT, A Bankrupt Heart, II, 45. T.
Why need she herself be so scrupulous? GALSWORTHY, Beyond, III, Ch. XII, 333.

b) in negative sentences with *not*, 1) mostly in the present tense, the suffix *s* (or *eth*) of the third person singular being usually suppressed. See also 9, b; and 12, a.

You needn't mind sending up to me if the child cries. DICK., Ol. Twist, Ch. I, 21.
You must rise with the sun and ride with the same | *Until, the next morning he riseth again;* | *And then your grace need not make any doubt,* | *But in twenty-four hours you'll ride it about.* King John and the Abbot of Canterbury.
That need not be! MRS. WOOD, The Channings, Ch. III, 14.

Constructions with *to do* are, however, by no means rare. See also ELLINGER, Vermischte Beiträge, 66, where many instances are given.

Rich baronets do not need to be careful about grammar, THACK., Van. Fair, I, Ch. VIII, 78.
I do not need to leave the rotunda. FRANKF. MOORE, The Jessamy Bride, Ch. VII, 60. T.
You don't need to tell me. WILLIAMSON, Lord Loveland, Ch. XXVIII, 252.
You do not need to be rich to invest in State securities. Eng. Rev. No. 109, Adv.

Substitution of the periphrastic for the simple construction in the phrase *It needs not +* passive infinitive appears to be very rare. Thus it would hardly be admissible in:

> It needs not to be said that much which is true of our country at that time is also true of others. MARY BATESON, Mediæval England, Pref.

With the above quotation, in which *it* represents the subordinate clause, compare the two following in which *it* stands for the infinitive with its objective enlargement. Usage may be equally divided between the periphrastic and the simple construction.

> i. It needs not to tell what she said and promised on behalf of Nelly. BESANT, All Sorts and Cond. of Men, Ch. XLVIII.
> ii. It does not need to take everything Lord Charles Beresford says without a grain of salt. Eng. Rev., 1912, Sept. 284.

2) almost regularly in the preterite indicative, in subordinate clauses, especially statements, the tense-suffix being suppressed. See also 11, a; and 12, b.

> He told me that I need not make myself at all uneasy about his daughter's unhappiness DICK., Cop., Ch. XXXVIII, 276 a.
> Mr. Freely meant her to have a house so pretty and comfortable that she need not envy even a wool-factor's wife. G. ELIOT, Brother Jacob, 394.

It is but rarely that *needed not* (or *did not need*) is employed instead of *need not*.

> She saw that she needed not to fear me. BLACKMORE, Lorna Doone, Ch. XVI, 96.

Except for subordinate clauses the construction with *to do* is the usual one in the preterite indicative, *needed not* appearing only as a literary variant.

> i. They did not need to speak much to each other. G. ELIOT, Felix Holt, I, Ch. VI, 130.
> He did not need to be a hatter to see that is was a very good Panama. PAUL CHISWICK, In the Land of Dreams, Ch. II.
> She did not need to see his face. GISSING, A Life's Morn., Ch. XIX, 265.
> You do not need to have a straight eye for that. BEATR. HAR., Ships, I, Ch. XV, 84.
> ii. John needed not to reply. MRS. CRAIK, John Hal, Ch. XXXVI, 393.

3) apparently regularly in the preterite conditional followed by a perfect infinitive, the tense-suffix being ordinarily suppressed, and the whole word-group expressing the fact that an action for which there was no necessity has yet come into fulfilment. See also 11, b; 12, c; and 58, b.

> i. He need not have done it after all. MEREDITH, Ord. of Rich. Fev., Ch. XI, 71.
> You need not have told me that. FLOR. MARRYAT, A Bankrupt Heart, I, 20. T.
> ii. He needed not to have undertaken an arduous march of 260 miles. SOUTHEY, Penins. War, II, 630.[1]

---

[1] MURRAY.

8. The anomalies in the conjugation of *to need* are twofold, viz:
   a) the dropping of the ending *s* (or *eth*) in the third person singular of the present indicative,
   b) the suppression of the tense-suffix *ed* in the preterite indicative and conditional.

9. a) The omission of the personal ending in the third person singular of the present indicative appears to be almost regular in questions. See also 7, a; and 15, c.

   What *need she be* acquainted? Shak., Com. of Er., III, 2, 15.
   What preacher *need moralize* on this story? Thack., The Four Georges, III, 86. T.

   b) The dropping of the personal suffix is distinctly the rule, 1) in sentences or clauses containing a negative word; i. e. *not, never* or *no*, or a word implying a negative, i. e. *but* (or *only*) or *hardly* (or *scarcely*). See also 7, b; and 15, c.

   i. Tell the housemaid she *need not light* the dining-room fire to-day. Alford, The Queen's English, § 46.
   How Miss Sharp lay awake thinking, will he come or not to morrow? *need not be told* here. Thack., Van. Fair, I. Ch. IV, 37.
   Valour *need never pray* to Fortune. Lytton, Rienzi.¹)
   He who is down *need fear no* fall. Wait. Besant, The Bell of St. Paul's, I, Ch. I, 10 f.
   The gunner *need be* under *no* fear that in sparing one of these swans he is possibly missing an opportunity. Westm. Gaz. No. 6177, 4c.
   After all, *no one need know*. Hugh Walpole, Jeremy, Ch. X, 2, 248.
   ii. Aunt Olive has kindly written to tell you exactly why I am here, so that my letter *need only be* a supplement to hers. Sarah Grand, The Heavenly Twins, I, 109.
   John is so vain that he thinks he *only need propose* to the highest princess to be instantly accepted. Tit-Bits.
   It is a matter of comparatively common knowledge that metals are subject to diseases. Lead, it *need scarcely be said*, is not immune. Il. Lond. News, No. 3857, 330.

   2) in subordinate clauses when the head-sentence contains a negative or negative-implying word, and also when the complex, though containing no negative, has a negative import.

   i. "This house *ain't* so exactly ringing with merry-making", said Miss Nipper, "that one *need be* lonelier than one must be. Your Toxes and your Chickses may draw out my two front double teeth, Mrs. Richards, but that's *no* reason why *I need offer* 'em the whole set". Dick., Domb., Ch. III, 22.

---
¹) Mätzn., Engl. Gram., III, 5.

There is *nothing* in this decision which *need cause* us the slightest uneasiness. Westm. Gaz. No. 5030, 1 b.

ii. That is all that *need be said*. El. Glyn, The Reason Why, Ch. VII, 70. (*all* has the value of *the only thing*.)
All that our lady *need do* is to make a neat list of her needs. Westm. Gaz., No. 7477, 11 b.

iii. This completes what *need be said* about principal sentences. Fowler, The King's Eng., 140. (Underlying notion: No more need be said...)
A pleasant room it was as any party *need desire* to muster in on a cold November evening. G. Eliot, Scenes, II, Ch. IV, 101. (Underlying notion: No party need desire a pleasanter room...)
Poor young man, he seems to come oftener than he *need*. Bar. von Hutten, Pam., Ch II, 15. (Underlying notion: He need not come so often. The infinitive has to supplied from the context.)

Exceptions seem to be mostly due to the preposition *to* being placed before the infinitive (for the sake of the metre or rhythm), the preposition destroying, in a manner, the closeness with which *to need* is connected with the infinitive and, to a certain extent, re-establishing its independence and, consequently, its regular conjugation. See also 13.

He that is well hanged in this world *needs to fear* no colours. Shak., Twelfth Night I, 5, 6.
I am not wont to be battled in my enterprises, nor *needs* a Norman noble scrupulously *to vindicate* his conduct to the Saxon maiden whom he distinguishes by the offer of his hand. Scott, Ivanhoe (Bell's Reading-Books, 112).
The parents want the child's help and care, the child is bound to give it; that is all it *needs to know*. Mrs. Ward, Rob. Elsm., I, 196. T.

In the following quotation *needs* is used although the following infinitive is not preceded by *to*.

I see a man here *needs not live* by shifts. Shak., Com. of Er., III, 2, 187.

The personal ending appears to be regularly preserved in the expressions *it needs not*, *it needs only*. See also 7, b.

It needs not to tell what she said and promised on behalf of Nelly. Walt. Besant, All Sorts and Cond. of Men, Ch. XLVIII, 318.
It needs not to be said that much which is true of our country at that time is true also of others. Mary Bateson, Mediæval England, Pref.
It needs only to turn over a page or two of Ray's collection of English proverbs to become convinced that many of our homely adages are coarse enough.[1])

Similarly in *there needs*, which appears to be usually divided from the infinitive by the subject.

There needs no ghost, my lord, come from the grave | To tell us this. Shak., Haml., I, 5, 125.
There needs be no beggar in countries where there are many acres of unimproved improvable land. Eng. Rev., No. 90, 470.

¹) Scot., Handl. III, § 108.

c) When under no negativing influence, *to need* normally retains the personal suffix.

> A statesman *needs to view* problems from an entirely different and much wider platform than was necessary half a century ago. V. Seymour Bryant, The Public School System, Ch. VI, 72.
> To be a poet a man *needs to be* advantageously *placed* in the world. Tom Hood, Eng. Versific., VI.
> Something *needs to be said* as to the extent and character of the Congo atrocities. Athen., No 4452, 211 c.
> The old is done with; and the Tree of Life *needs to be* well *shaken* before the new fruit will drop. Mrs Ward, Cous. Phil., Ch. VI, 98.

Note. α) Excepted are certain phrases, viz.: α) *he (she or it) need be* when approximately equivalent to *he (she or it) may in all fairness, be expected to be* (considering), Dutch dat mag hij (zij or het) dan ook wel; β) as *need be*, in which the anticipating *it* is dispensed with (Ch. II, 18, b), the suppression of the personal suffix being, perhaps, due to the analogy of *if need be*, in which *need* is a noun and the subject of the subjunctive *be*. See the treatise on Mood, 37, and Addenda and Corrigenda; compare also 11, c, Note.

i. "It's only about young Twist, my dear", said Mr. Sowerberry, "a very good looking boy that, my dear". — "*He need be*, for he eats enough", observed the lady. Dick., Ol. Twist, Ch. V, 57.

ii. I fall as deep *as need be* in love with a young lady. Shak., Riv. III, 4.
The staircase was as wooden and solid *as need be*. Dick., Little Dorrit, Ch. IV, 22 a.
Compare: What happened to her own heart did not matter so long as he was happy, and had all that he wanted with her and away from her — *if need be* — always away from her. Galsworthy, Beyond, IV, Ch. IX, 411.

β) Finally it may be observed that the suffix of the second person singular *est*, is never suppressed.

> Thou *needest* but keep that countenance. Shak., Cymb., III, 4, 14.
> Thou *need'st* not be gone. id. Rom. and Jul., III, 5, 16.

10. The dropping of the tense-suffix may be due to the *d* of *need* being felt as the ending of the preterite (Storm, Eng. Phil.², 1038), but, more probably, to the haplology which has given existence to numerous shortenings, such as *England* (from Old English *Englaland*, i. e. the land of the Angles), *eighteen* (from Old English *e(a)htatýne* or *tene*), *humbly* (instead of *humblely*), *wed* (instead of *wedded*), etc. Compare Abbot, Shak. Gram.³, § 342; Jespersen, E. S., XXIII, 461.

It must also be observed that the substitution of *need* for *needed* often makes for an improved rhythmical flow of the sentence.

11. The dropping of the tense-suffix is chiefly met with in negative contexts.

  a) It is distinctly the rule in the preterite indicative in subordinate clauses, especially statements. See also 7, b, 2.

  Grimm could not help interrupting her with a pleasant laugh and the assurance that she *need* not be uneasy about her debt any longer, STOR., Handl., I, 56.

  Exceptions are not unfrequent.

  This soon convinced me that I *needed to use no* precautions as to my safety on his account. DEFOE, Robinson Crusoe, 210.
  She saw that she *needed not to fear me*, BLACKMORE, Lorna Doone, Ch XVI, 96.
  They promised with the eyes what they *needed not to promise* with the tongue. A. HOPE, The Chron. of Count Antonio, Ch. III, 82. T.

  In principal sentences suppression is usual only when another verb shows the tense, but *needed not* is in ordinary language replaced by *did not need*. See also 7, b, 2.

  i. Thirty years ago *you needed but* to be a Milor Anglais travelling in a private carriage, and credit was at your hand whenever you chose to seek it. THACK., Van. Fair, II, Ch. I, 9
  They *needed to say no more*. TEMPLE THURSTON, The City of Beaut. Nons., III, Ch. VI, 260.

  ii. John *needed not to reply*. MRS. CRAIK, John Hal., Ch. XXXVI, 393.
  One *did not need to be told* that. KINGSLEY, Herew., Ch. III, 26 b.

  iii. Mr. Weston *need not spend* a single evening in the year alone if he did not like it. JANE AUSTEN, Emma, Ch. I, 12. T.
  There was play, certainly — all the world played... But *nobody need play* who did not like; and surely *nobody need have* scruples regarding the practice. THACK., Virg., Ch. XLIX, 724.
  Nothing was impossible for Ropsley and he *need only try* to succeed. W. MELVILLE, Interpreter, I, Ch. VII, 67.
  If you didn't want to learn, you *needn't*. WELLS, Kipps, III, Ch. I, § 2, 132.

  b) The dropping of the tense-suffix is practically regular in the preterite conditional followed by a perfect infinitive, the complex predicate expressing the fact that an action or state for which there was no necessity has yet come into fulfilment. See also 7, b, 3; 12, c; and 58, b.

  You *needn't have been* so sharp. DICK., Domb., Ch. IV, 29.
  You *need not have told* me that. FLOR. MARRYAT, A Bankrupt Heart, I, 20. T.
  The world knows that Paris *need never have fallen*, could France only have produced one mediocre military genius in this her moment of need. MERRIMAN.[1])

  The following quotations exhibit exceptional practice:

  He *needed not to have undertaken* an arduous march of 260 miles. SOUTHEY, Penins. War, II, 630.[2])

---

[1]) WENDT, Synt. des heut. Eng., 29.
[2]) MURRAY.

She hardly *needed to have asked* this question. Mrs. Gask., Life of Ch. Bronte, 209.

c) In non-negative contexts the full form *needed* is the rule.
The ladies Devenish were not disposed to make her life any easier than it *needed to be*. Flor. Marryat, A Bankrupt Heart, 230. T.
M. Charles Rivet ... in an arresting study entitled The Last of the Romanofs, sets forth many things that *needed to be said*. Punch, No. 4005, 240a.

Note. But the suffix is regularly suppressed in the phrases α) *I (you, etc.) need be* in the sense of *I (you, etc.) had need be*, and β) *as need be*, in which there is a suppression of the personal pronoun *it*. Compare Ch. II, 18, b; also 9, c, Note 2.

i. "Is yours a strong constitution?" inquired Tozer. Paul said that he thought not. Tozer said that he thought not also, judging from Paul's looks, and that it was a pity, for *it need be*. Dick., Domb., Ch. XII, 105.
ii. They would be as happy among themselves *as need be*. Dick., Ol. Twist, Ch. VI, 64.
On they went as briskly *as need be*. id., Pickw. Ch. XIX, 165.

12. a) *To* is dispensed with after *need* as a present indicative,
  1) regularly in questions. See also 7, a; and 9, a.
    i. Then live, Macduff: what *need I fear* of thee? Shak., Macb., IV, 1, 82.
    ii. Who *need go* hungry with such kind friends ready to feed him? Westm. Gaz., No. 8373, 6a.

  2) mostly in negative contexts, including such as imply a negative although containing no negative word. See also 7, b; and 9, b.
    i.° What an amazing place London was to me when I saw it in the distance. I *need not stop* here to relate. Dick., Cop., Ch. V, 36a.
    "Thank God," said the Dean at breakfast, "we *needn't cast down* our eyes and slink by when we meet a Frenchman". W. J. Locke, The Rough Road, Ch. IV, 46.
    °° Heaven knows we *need never be* ashamed of our tears. Dick., Great Expect., Ch. XIX, 192.
    If we are careful we *need never cease* to be attractive. Sarah Grand, Our Manifold Nature, 103.
    You *never need urge* clemency on me. Mrs. Wood, Orv. Col., Ch. IV, 5e.
    °°° While I live you *need have* no fear for Doggie. W. J. Locke, The Rough Road, Ch. XIV, 171.
    ii.° Only the closing or the opening *need be heard* for the ear to distinguish the sound. Rippmann, Sounds of Spok. Eng., § 21.
    Attention *need only be drawn* to the fact that, while the price of the book has been lowered, the matter contained in it has been augmented by thirty-two closely-packed pages. Annandale, Conc. Dict. Pref. to Sec. Ed.
    °° I *need hardly say* that I shall be grateful for any criticisms and suggestions. Sweet, N. E. Gr., Pref., 16.
    We *need scarcely emphasize* the point that naval strength is at present chiefly estimated by those ships generally called Dreadnoughts II. Lond. News No. 3852, Sup. IV.

iii. It is not at all in this bargain that you *need become* attached to my child, or that my child *need become* attached to you. Dick., Domb., Ch. II, 15.
On the whole I don't think people *need keep* awake at nights worrying about us. Westm. Gaz. No. 8373, 6 b.
iv. Very little appears to have happened that *need be kept* secret. ib. No. 8467, 3 a.
" It is only for that that we *need postpone* the marriage. Gissing, A Life's Morn., Ch. VI, 88.
" Of course that is not all, but it is all I *need speak* of. ib., Ch. IV 56. (ill has the value of *the only thing*.)
" They made the prettiest, quaintest groups you *need think of*. Westm. Gaz., No. 5185, 45 a.

Note. In SHAKESPEARE and his contemporaries *to* is frequently retained in negative contexts, not only in verse, but also in prose.

i. For what I have I *need not to repeat*. Rich. II, III, 4, 17 (verse).
You *need not to fear* the bawd. Meas. for Meas., II, I, 247 (prose).
You *need not to have pricked* me. Henry IV, B, III, 2, 125 (prose).
As for triumphs, masks, feasts, weddings, funerals, capital executions, and such shows, men *need not to be put in* mind of them. Bacon, Es. XVIII, Of Travel (51).

ii. The boy never *need to understand* any thing. Merry Wives, II, 2, 132 (prose).
Never excuse; for when the players are all dead, there *need none to be blamed*. Mids., V, 364 (prose).

Late Modern English instances appear to be rare.

i. You *need not to think* ... that you're a neglected man of science. Ch. Brontë, Shirley, I, Ch. V, 78. T.
You *need not to suppose* that your class are martyrs. ib.
I *need not to swear* that oath, for I have sworn it long ago. Kingsley, Westw. Ho!, Ch. XXVI, 202 a.

ii. He that would form a lively idea of the regions of the damned, *need only to witness*, for six hours, a scene to which I was confined. Godwin, Cal. Wil., II. Ch. XI, 253.
Reason is faith, faith is reason. That is all we know on earth and that is all we *need to know*. Max Beerbohm, Seven Men, IV, 147.

b) After *need* as a preterite indicative *to* appears to be regularly suppressed in negative contexts. See also 7, b; and 11, a.

i. He told me that I *need not make* myself at all uneasy about his daughter's unhappiness. Dick., Cop., Ch. XXXVIII, 276 a.
Miss Bussey observed, in an indignant tone, that John *need not throttle* the dog. A. Hope, Comedies of Courtship, I, Ch. I, 5.
The victory was so complete that fear *need play* no part in the settlement. Kinsis, Econ. Con. of the Peace, Ch. III, 34.

c) Similarly after *need* as a preterite conditional followed by a perfect infinitive, *to* is regularly dispensed with in negative contexts. See also 7, b, 3; 11, b; and 58, b.

i. He *needn't have taken* the trouble to shrink from Mr. Bumble's glance. Dick., Ol. Twist, Ch. V.

He had spoken late, but he *need not have* spoken at all. Dor. Gerard, Exotic Martha, Ch. XXII, 260, I.
You *needn't have made* an exhibition of yourself in the town if you didn't want to. W. J. Locke, The Rough Road, Ch. XI, 123.

ii. If at that moment he had clasped her and kissed her, instead of sitting there, glaring into space, the rest of this story *need never have been* written. Fl. Gay, The Reason Why, Ch. XX, 184.

d) When the context is not negative, *to* is rarely absent.

i. People *need to* rise early, to see the sun in all his splendour. Dick., Pickw., Ch. V, 58.
You *need to be told* something that your eyes would not tell you. Ch. Kingsley, Herew., Ch. III, 26 b.
It is you who *need to* slink and cower, not we. Grant Allen, Hilda Wade, Ch. XI, 329.
How is it, then, that we *need to* dig our souls so deeply to ensure good crops? Westm. Gaz., No. 8461, 16 a.
Englishmen *need to* think very seriously about the situation into which the Government's policy has led them. ib., No. 8527, 2 b.

ii. I know my duty. I *need know* it, I am sure. Dick., Barn. Rudge, Ch. XIX, 74 a.
You *need have* good cards, sir. id., A Tale of Two Cities, III, Ch. XIII, 336.
We *need analyse* it into such parts as these. Prof. Whitney.[1])

Note. The absence of *to* is regular in the phrases *I (you, etc.) need be* in the sense of *I (you, etc.) had need be*, and *as need be*, in which the anticipating *it* is dispensed with. For illustration see 9, c, Note *e*; and 11, c, Note.

In SHAKESPEARE *to* is sometimes retained.

I was as virtuously given as a gentleman *need to be*. Henry IV, A, III, 3, 17.

13. After the finite forms *needs* (or *needeth*), *needest* and *needed* the infinitive almost regularly stands with *to*. See also 9, b, 2.

i. Blank verse ... *needs to be relieved* by the greatest intensity of thought and expression. Academy, 1891, 498 a.
The officer *needs to be* exceptionally spry to get through his multifarious duties in a satisfactory manner. Graph., 1892, 759.
Hall's Distemper *needs only to be seen* to be admired. Ill. Lond. News, No. 3858, 420 b.

ii. He never *needed to ask* what they were about. Lyton, Paul Clif., Ch. XXII, 262.

Note. The following quotations exhibit exceptional practice, mostly due to the requirements of metre or rhythm:

i. Nor *need'st* thou much *importune* me to that Whereon this month I have been hammering. Shak., Two Gent., I, 3, 17.
Thou *need'st* say no more. Scott, Ivanhoe, Ch. XXIV, 224. T.
Thou *need'st* no longer *fear* me. ib., 232.

ii. This incident ... *needed be* no surprise to him. Hume, Hist. Eng. III.

---

[1]) Stof., Handl., III, § 107.

14. After the verbals, i. e. the infinitive, the gerund and the participles of *to need*, the infinitive is almost regularly preceded by *to*. See also 7, b, 2.

   i. One would *need to be learned* in the fashions of those times to know how far in the rear of them Mrs. Glegg's slate-coloured silk gown must have been. G. Eliot, Mill, I, Ch. VII, 45.
   You *don't need to be* mad to do that. Mrs. Ward, The Mating of Lydia, I, Ch. III, 59.
   Free institutions may *need to be suspended* if not destroyed in the interests of distant empire. Daily Chron.
   The dictionary will *need to be supplemented* for the requirements of our posterity. Athenæum.
   ii. You will soon feel how your tongue moves without *needing to look* at it. Rippmann, Sounds of Spoken Eng., § 9.
   iii. The favourite seat of Byron in the churchyard on Harrow Hill has *needed to be guarded* by an iron cage from the poet's admirers, who were carrying it away piecemeal. Edw. E. Morris, Intr. to Byron's Childe Har., 12.

   In the following quotation *to* is dispensed with to satisfy the requirements of the metre.
   I shall not *need transport* my words by you. Shak., Rich. II, II 3, 81.

15. a) *To need* is used not only in the meaning of *to be required*, but also in that of to *require*, i. e. the notion it expresses may be not only that the operation of a demand is directed to a person or thing, but also that it proceeds from a person or thing. The latter meaning is indubitable in the verb when it has a (pro)noun for its object, as in *I need your assistance;* and also when it is construed with an accusative with infinitive. Thus in:

   I don't *need you to tell* me what you think. Frank Swinnerton, Nocturne, I, Ch. II, II, 74.
   Under the very nose of John was the best place for that secret bottle of pills, had she *needed* it to be seen. Temple Thurston, The City of Beaut. Nons., III, Ch. VII, 278.

b) Also when followed by an infinitive, especially a passive infinitive, *to need* may have the second meaning, but in this combination there is mostly some uncertainty as to the interpretation to be put upon the verb. It is particularly the verbals which, when followed by an infinitive, frequently lean to this interpretation.

   i. I know all I *need to know* about her. Hichens, The Fruitful Vine, Ch. II, 24. (If *need* were to be understood in the first meaning, it would, most probably, have rejected *to* before the infinitive (12, a, 2).

And you have done this for us, Crichton, because you thought that — that father *needed to be kept* in his place. G. M. Barrie, The Admirable Crichton, I, 47.

ii.* One *did not need to be told* that. Kingsley, Hereward, Ch. III, 26 b.
The night air is chill, and you must *need to eat* and rest. Bram Stoker, Dracula, Ch. II, 17.
Things she would formerly have understood at a half-word she now affected *to need to have explained* to her. Gissing, A Life's Morning, Ch. XV, 219.
Or a chariot! to carry us up into the sky, where the lamps are stars and don't *need to be filled* with paraffin oil every day. Shaw, Candida, II, 155. F.

** I am sitting here with some vanity in me, *needing to be scolded*. G. Eliot, Fel. Holt, II, Ch. LI, 353.

*** I have never *needed to use* the catheter again. Il. Lond. News.

c) There would, however, be no reason for insisting on the second meaning of *to need*, if it were not for the fact that it seems to account satisfactorily for a grammatical peculiarity which, otherwise, would be rather baffling. Thus, contrary to the practice ordinarily observed with *to need* in the first meaning, we find it in the second meaning taking the personal ending of the third person in the present indicative. See 9, a and b.

i. Who *needs to be told* that if a woman has a will, she will assuredly find a way? Thack., Van. Fair, I, Ch. XVI, 164.

ii. Vice to be hated, *needs but to be seen*. Pope, Es. on Man, II, 218.
It was an ugly story of low passion, delusion, and waking from delusion, which *needs not to be dragged* from the privacy of Godfrey's bitter memory. G. Eliot, Sil. Marn., I, Ch. III, 25.
I consider the ode beyond the scope of those for whom it is intended and it *needs not to be discussed* on that account. Tom Hood, Versification, 43.
The immense part that sensation has played in the evolution of the drama hardly *needs to be elaborated*. Hor. Hutchinson, (Westm Gaz. No. 8579, 10a).
A prosperous country is found to be compatible not only with Free Trade in foreign agricultural produce, but with the taxation of other commodities which the farmer *needs to buy*. Westm. Gaz., No. 6193, 2a.

d) After *to need* in the second meaning the passive infinitive varies with the gerund, which is regularly kept in the active voice. See Gerund, 26, b.

The conflicting states of mind one passes through about work are among the things which most *need making allowance for*, Rossetti, Let. to Swinburne.
The statement contains at least two assumptions which *need looking into*. Westm. Gaz., No. 8373, 7a.

16. Also before proceeding to discuss the variable practice regarding the use of *to* before the infinitive after *to dare*, it seems advisable to draw the student's attention to the use of *to do* as connected with this verb, and to some anomalies in its conjugation.

Like *to need*, *to dare* is felt partly as a full verb, partly as a verb forming a kind of unit with the following infinitive. Hence the vacillation in some of its syntactical features.

17. a) In questions *to do* is mostly dispensed with, questions of the second kind (Ch. VII, 3) being, apparently, regularly constructed without *to do*. Note the frequent *How dare you?* See also 21, a.

   i. *Do you dare to think that we are to blame after that?* WILKIE COLLINS, After Dark, 167.[1])
   Did he dare set himself up to be finer clay than that common soldier? W. J. LOCKE, The Rough Road, Ch. IX, 100.

   ii. *What! dares the slave come hither?* SHAK., Rom. and Jul. 1, 5.
   Darest thou come betwixt me and mine enemy? SCOTT, Kenilw., Ch. IV, 50.
   Dare I trust thee? id., Ivanhoe, Ch. XXIV, 231.
   Dare you suspect me whom the thought would kill? BYRON, Don Juan, I, CXLII.
   Dare you promise to come to me in ten years and tell me with complete frankness what you think of — a certain step? GISSING, A Life's Morn., Ch. XIV, 201.
   Dare I go to her, Wilfrid? ib., Ch. XXVI, 347.
   He walked slowly along the river. *Dared he speak?* GALSWORTHY, Beyond, III, Ch. V, 273.
   He was sitting there, prodding at the gravel, a nervous twittering in his heart, and that eternal question: *Dare I speak?* asking itself within him. ib., 273.

   ii. *How dare you think your lady would go on so?* BYRON, Don Juan, I, CXLVI.
   How dared you read it? GODWIN, Cal. Wil., II, Ch. III, 63.
   How dare you insult me like that? FLOR. MARRYAT, A Bankrupt Heart, I, 42, T.
   How dare you say such a thing? SHAW, Cand., II, (145). T.
   How dare men be so effeminate? GALSW., Beyond, I, Ch. IV, 39.
   How dared you interrupt my service in the way? Westm. Gaz., No. 8438, 9a.

b) In negative sentences or clauses with *not* the written language apparently prefers the simple, the spoken language the periphrastic construction. Thus DEAN ALFORD (The Queen's Eng.', § 52) observes, "I imagine that every one would write *he dared not*; I am sure that every one would say *he didn't dare* — ". The first part of the Dean's statement is not borne out by what we find in the printed language, *didn't dare* appearing frequently enough in diction which does not strike us as colloquial. See also 28.

¹) ETTINGER, Verm. Beitr., 76.

i. Though I was hungry, I *dared not eat* my slice. Dick., Great Expect., Ch. I, 14.
I *daren't* go to him alone. Bexis Har., Ships, I. Ch. XV. 87.
ii. I didn't think Miss Creakle equal to little Emly in point of beauty and I didn't love her (I *didn't dare*). Dick., Cop., Ch. VII, 46a.
I *did not dare do so*. Lytton, Night and Morn., 35. T.
I *didn't dare* leave him for an instant to wake the Laird and send for a doctor. Du Maurier, Trilby, II. 125. T.

Note. In the rather unusual imperative the simple construction seems to be confined to literary language. See also 25.

i. *Dare not to return* hither a fourth time. Scott, Antiquary, 401.¹)
Dare not to say it is. id., Fort. of Nig.¹)
ii. "Shall I ask him to come to you, madam?" "No, *don't dare to do* it, if you love me." G. Eliot, Fel. Holt, II. Ch. I, 345.
Don't you dare call my wife a monster! Shaw, Overruled (Eng. Rev. No. 54, 1911).

18. The anomalies in the conjugation of *to dare* consist in the frequent suppression of the personal suffix in the third person singular of the present indicative, and of the tense-suffix in the preterite.

19. a) The absence of the personal ending is due to the verb being one of the preterite-present verbs, of which the extant present is an original preterite or perfect. (See my treatise on Tense, S, e.) The original form *dare*, like its preterite *durst*, remained undisturbed until the modern period. But early in the sixteenth century the new forms *dares* and *dared* appeared in the South. The form *(he) dares* was already quite common in the seventeenth century, and is now more frequent than *(he) dare*, at least before an infinitive with *to* (25). According to A. Schmidt (Shak. Lex., s. v. *dare*) Shakespeare uses *dare* and *dares* indiscriminately.

Curses not loud, but deep, mouth-honour, breath, Which the poor heart would fain deny, and *dare not*. Shak., Mach., V, 3, 28.
The poor Amy is now greater than she *dare* name. Scott, Kenilworth, Ch. IV, 45.
It is a thing so terrible that one *dare not think* of it. Graph., No. 2691, 770a.
She *dare not say* his name. J. M. Barrie, The Admirable Crichton, III, 109.

Note. The original form *dare*, instead of the modern *dares*, seems to have been regularly preserved in questions.

Dare any soul on earth *breathe* a word against the sweetest of young women? Thack., Van. Fair, I, Ch. XVIII, 188.

---
¹) Swaen, E. S., XX., 290.

b) MURRAY (s. v. *dare*, Note) observes that "the northern dialects generally retain *he dare, he durst*, and writers of northern extraction favour their retention in literary English when followed by the simple infinitive without *to*". SHAKE= SPEARE has only *durst*, and also BUNYAN seems to have used no other form. Throughout the eighteenth century *durst* appears to have been more generally used than *dared*, but as we approach more modern times, the latter form is more and more preferred, *durst* gradually becoming unusual in Standard English. According to MURRAY (s. v. *dare*, B, I, 1, c), *none dared to speak* is more emphatic than *none durst speak*.

Longer I *durst not stay*. MILTON, Comus, 577.
How *durst* thou then thyself approach so near ! As to make this relation? ib., 617.
I could not sufficiently wonder at the intrepidity of these diminutive mortals, who *durst venture* to mount and walk upon my body. SWIFT, Gul., I, Ch. I (116b).
None ever *durst attack* him. FIELDING, Jos. Andrews, I, Ch. XII, 29.
He *durst* not *strike* them for fear of their uncles, the uncles *durst* not *kill* him, because of their nieces. SHER., Critic, III, 1.
Why does he haunt this house, whispering through chinks and crevices as if there was that between him and you which neither *durst* so much as speak of. DICK., Barn. Rudge, Ch. VI, 24b.
You'd be everybody's master, if you *durst*. id., Great Expect., Ch. XV, 137.
I *durst not*, alas! *tell* the truth. KINGSLEY, Alton Locke, Ch. III, 36.
It was only one glance that I *durst take*. STEVENSON, Treas. Isl.
Sunday was the day he always gave to Beatrice. But he *durst not think* of that now. GISSING, A Life's Morn., Ch. XXIII, 319.

In Early Modern English *durst* is also used as a preterite conditional. This practice survives only in the language of the illiterate, where *durst*, however, is mostly felt as a present indicative, in like manner as *ought* or *should*. Compare FRANZ, E. S., XII; FIDZEDWARD HALL, Mod. Eng., 228—9; STORM; Eng. Phil.², 766.

I *durst*, my lord, *to wager* she is honest. SHAK., Oth., IV, 2, 12.
I have no desire, and besides, if I had, I *durst not*. STERNE, Tristram Shandy, III, XX.
"Come down and undo the shop-window, that I may get in that way." — "I *durstn't* do it, Simmun", cried Miggs. DICK., Barn. Rudge, Ch. IX, 38a.
If hennyone was to orffer to bet a thousan poun that youll hend by bein a bishop yourself, I *dussent* take the bet. SHAW, Candida, I, (128). T.

Sometimes it is uncertain whether *durst* is to be apprehended as a preterite indicative or preterite conditional.

Many a vile plan dwelt with him, which he knew he *durst not put* into practice. GISSING, A Life's Morn., Ch. XIII, 184.

c) Besides *dared* and *durst* we also find *dare* as a preterite indicative, chiefly in connexion with *not*. The substitution of *dare* for *dared* in connexion with *not* is, apparently, due to phonetic decay, the *d* of the three successive point-consonants in *dared not* naturally falling out in unaffected speech. Compare the analogous substitution of *usen't* for *used not*, and *musn't* for *must not*, as in:

i. "I am not one of her admirers." — "I *usen't* to be, but I am now." Osc. Wilde, Lady Wind. Fan, III, (102).
I used to be great on material forces, *usen't* I? Ethel Rolt-Wheeler, The Edge of the World (Eng. Rev., No. 52, 599).
ii. You *musn't* delay me. Shaw, The Man of Destiny, (235). T.

The preterite indicative *dare*, although condemned by Murray (s. v. dare, A, 1, c) as careless, is frequent enough in writers of unquestionably pure English. Compare Jespersen, E. S., XXIII; id., Negation, 124; Sarrazin, E. S., XXII, 354; Swaen, E. S., XX; Storm, Eng. Phil., 766; Hoppe, Sup. Lex.², s. v. *dare*. See also 24.

A sense of awe, weakness, all but fear, came over him. He *dare not* stoop to take up the wood at his feet. Kingsley, Hyp., Ch. II, 2a.
Orestes knew well enough that the fellows must have been bribed to allow the theft; but he *dare not* say so to men on whose good humour his very life might depend. ib., Ch. XX, 105a.
I *dare not* ask my mother for books, for I *dare not* confess to her that religious ones were just what I did not want. id., Alton Locke, Ch. II, 29.
He sat with his head bent forward... a tattered, haggard, hopeless wretch, so broken down that one *dare not* reproach him. Conway, Called Back, 242.
How should I break it to Cora? What should I say to her? Tell her the truth, I *dare not*. Sims, My Two Wives, 49.

The use of the preterite *dare* without *not* is, as yet, very uncommon.

For none of all his men: *Dare* tell him Dora waited with the child. Tns., Dora.
Could he, *dare* he, confess to him the whole truth? Kingsley, Hyp., Ch. I, 2b.

Instances of *dare* as a preterite conditional appear to be very rare.

If I were not chained to the floor, you *dare* as well eat your fingers as use such language. Godwin, Cal. Wil., II, Ch. XIV, 272.
He *dare* not keep you waiting if you were at liberty. Shaw, The Man of Destiny, (203). T.
Do you think that if I wanted those despatches only for myself, I *dare* venture into a battle for them? ib., (220).

d) Since the sixteenth century *to dare* has also been used as an ordinary transitive verb in various shades of meaning. As such it has always been conjugated regularly: *dares*, *dared*.

20. The use of *to* before the infinitive after *to dare* has been the subject of a good many painstaking investigations. Especial

mention should be made of those instituted by SATTLER (E. S., XXVI), SWAEN (E. S., XX and XXIII), ELLINGER (E. S., XXI and Vermischte Beiträge, 75 ff), FIJN VAN DRAAT (Rhythm in Eng. Prose, Angl. Forsch, 29). The last-mentioned scholar has made out a strong case for the use of *to* depending in large measure on the requirements of metre or rhythm.
It is partly on the results obtained by the above scholars that the following exposition is based.

21. *Dare* as a present indicative is followed by an infinitive without *to*,
    a) mostly in questions with inverted word-order. Instances of the alternative practice appear to be uncommon. See also 17, a.
    > i. O Rebecca, Rebecca, for shame! ... How can you — how dare you have such wicked revengeful thoughts? THACK., Van. Fair, I, Ch. II, 10.
    > How dare you call him by such a name? FLOR. MARRYAT, A Bankrupt Heart, I, 122. T.
    > But after what I have said, dare you accuse me again of being ignorant of housemaids? Punch, No. 3721, 349 a.
    > ii. How dare you to insinuate that you don't know any character better than your words imply? DICK., Cop., Ch. IV, 25 a.

    b) mostly in negative contexts.
    > They (sc. the officials) dare not stir outside the Castle walls, except in armoured cars. Westm. Gaz., No. 8379, 2 b.

    c) occasionally in contexts which are neither interrogative nor negative.
    > i. I dare be sworn for him, he would not leave it (sc. the ring). SHAK., Merch. of Ven., V, 1, 172.
    > If you dare utter a word against me, you will find that, as I am the last to care for a threat, so I am the first to resent an injury. LYTTON, Night and Morn., 153. T.
    > ii. "Mr. Copperfield", returned my mother, "is dead, and if you dare to speak unkindly of him [etc.]." DICK., Cop., Ch. I, 4 a.
    > I will never love you again, if you dare to go. KINGSLEY, Hyp., Ch. XII, 62 a.
    > It seems to me that those who dare to rebel are they who make life possible for those whose temperament compels them to submit. SARAH GRAND, The Heavenly Twins, I, 125 b.
    > And then you, who know all this, who have known us so many years, you dare to come here and insult me! FLOR. MARRYAT, A Bankrupt Heart.

22. a) Obs. In the phrase *I dare say* in the sense of *I have no doubt, I am ready to admit,* or *I do not wonder,* the bare infinitive is however, practically fixed.
    > Don t let us despair, I dare say things will all, somehow or other, turn out for the best. WASH. IRV., Dolf Heyl (STOF., Handl., I, 149).

I dare say I gave myself airs as editor of that confounded "Museum". Thack., Ch. I, 9.
"I should be quite amused to know what you did talk about." — "*I dare say*, you would." Blair Hyk., Ships, I, Ch. III, 13.

b) As the phrase is sometimes represented as an isolated expression, it seems desirable to state here that variations are not particularly uncommon; not only so far as we may take the place of *I* in editorial statements, but also, in reported speech, as regards the ordinary possibilities of person or tense.

i. Arabella repaired to her place of destination wherever it might have been — *we dare say* Mr. Winkle knew, but we confess we don't. Dick., Pickw., Ch. XXX.
We dare say this aspect of the matter has been emphasized by that section of the Unionist canvassers. Westm Gaz., No. 6228, 1c.

ii. *He* (sc. the poor relation) *dare say* (sic) you must find a great convenience in having a carriage of your own. Ch. Lamb, Last Es. of El., Poor Relations, (294).
The lady of the store and apron will reply that peas have been out for ten days or more, but that, if you give her time, and don't mind the money, *she dares say* she might manage to get you, say, a saucer full. Punch, Roundabout Readings, 1896, 15 Aug., 81.

iii. "I have always defended you, and said, I didn't think you so ugly by any means." — "Thank you." — "And *I dared say* you'd make a very good sort of a husband." Sher., School for Scand., III, 1, (48).
To this Mrs. Nickleby only replied that *she durst say* she was very stupid. Dick., Nich. Nick., Ch. LV, 366a.
Missis was, *she dared say*, glad enough to get rid of such a tiresome ill-conditioned child. Ch. Bronti, Jane Eyre, Ch. III, 24.
He dared say that at the docks they had a certain number of Irishmen at work. Westm. Gaz., No. 6441, 2 b.

c) Even instances of the infinitive being preceded by *to* are not entirely wanting.

Molly *dared to say* Mrs. Barter would let his honour see the house. Trol., Virg., Ch. I, 11.
It is announced that our cavalry are on the heels of the Hun. How many of our troopers are engaged on this work? Just detachments employed in maintaining touch with the enemy's rearguards, who are in process of orderly withdrawal to a deliberately prepared new alignment. And so, *I dare to say*, will be the task that our own and the French mounted arm will still find imposed on them when these pages appear in print. Eng. Rev., No. 101, 377.

d) In the meaning of *I venture to assert* the expression is now rarely, if ever used; but the negative *I (or we) dare not say* in the sense of *I will not venture to say* seems to be current English.

I daren't say I know, but here are some impressions. Westm. Gaz., No. 6564, 12 b.
We dare not say it is untrue. ib., No. 7011, 1a.
We dare not say as yet that the rout (of the Italians) is stopped. ib., No. 7607, 1a.

e) In conclusion we call attention to such variants of *I dare say* as *I dare answer, I dare swear*, which also appear to dispense with *to* before the following infinitive.

> Hyst. Then you're no friend to the ladies, I find, my pretty young gentleman? — Tony. That's as I find 'um. — Hyst. Not to her of your mother's choosing, *I dare answer*. Goldsmith, She Stoops, II, (194).
> *I dare swear* the truth of the matter is, Maria heard you were here. Sher., School for Scand., I, 1, (366).
> *I dare swear* he will do both (sc. look after the place and marry). Marj. Bowen, The Rake's Progress, I, Ch. I, 6.

23. *Dare* as an imperative seems to require *to* before the following infinitive, but this use of the verb is an uncommon one. See also 17, b, Note.

   i. Berf. Death and hell! | *Dare to speak* thus when you come out again. Torr. *Dare to provoke* me thus, insulting man! Dryden, Span. Friar, II, 1, (139). You bring me, to-morrow morning early, that file and them wittles... You do it, and you never *dare to say* a word or *dare to make* a sign concerning your having seen such a person as me. Dick., Great Expect., Ch. I, 8. Go —, and never *dare to speak* to this man again! Rider Haggard, She, 182.¹) Never you *dare to darken* my doorstep again! Du Maurier, Trilby, II, 60. If you want a great casus belli, | If you would be thumped to a jelly, | Just *dare to suggest* | That the greatest and best | In the world is not Marie Corelli | Punch, 1896, 9 May, 221.
   ii. Look at me, Sir, and *dare tell* me there is any reason why I should take your word. Harper's Mag., No. 7, 182.²)

24. *Dare* as a preterite indicative is rarely, if ever, followed by an infinitive with *to*. See also 19, c.

   > I *dare not ask* my mother for books, for I *dare not confess* to her that religious ones were just what I did not want. Kingsley, Alton Locke, Ch. II, 29.

25. Both *dares* and *darest* mostly stand with the bare infinitive. In fact hardly any instances of the alternative practice have come to hand up to the moment of writing.

   i. And all the world to nothing, that he *dares ne'er come* back to challenge you. Shak., Rom. and Jul., III, 5.
   Let me hear now who *dares call* him profligate. Shr., School for Scand., IV, 2, (406).
   It being bright daylight, however, Peter soon plucked up heart, knowing that no ghost *dares show* his face in such clear sunshine. Wash. Irv., Dolf Heyl., (Stor., Handl., I, (149).
   One often fancies in reading him (sc. Swi't) that he *dares not be* eloquent when he might. Thack., Eng. Hum., I, 16. T.
   No one *dares say* that this sum is in fact what has been demanded. Westm. Gaz., No. 8420, 2a.

---

¹) Swaen, E. S., XX, 290.
²) Fijn van Draat, Rhythm, 90.

Yonder is the enchanted manor, and the dragon, and the lady, all at thy service, if thou *darest venture* on them. Scott, Kenilw., Ch. II, 26.
Darest thou *appeal* to it (sc. the cross)? id., Ivanhoe, Ch. XXIV, 229. |
But there be deeds thou *darest not do*. Byron, Bride of Ab., I, V.
ii. What art thou that *darest to echo* my words? Scott, Ivanhoe.¹)

26. *Dared* as a preterite seems to govern a pure infinitive regularly when negatived by *not*. In other negative connexions there appears to be some predilection for the prepositional infinitive. For the rest the infinitive rarely stands without *to*, the preposition being indispensable when the two verbs are divided by another element of the sentence. It will be observed that the practice observed mostly makes for a rhythmical flow of the sentence.

i. He *daredn't refuse* Miss Crawley anything. Thack., Van. Fair, I, Ch. XIV, 138.
This woman, who loved rule, *dared not speak* another word of attempted persuasion. G. Eliot, Fel. Holt, I, Ch. X, 175.
I *dared not contradict*. Ch. Bronte, Villette, Ch. XXIII, 324.
She *dared not leave* the house. Fior. Marryat, A Bankrupt Heart, II, 279. T.
Whatever pangs of self-pity he felt ... he *dared not express* them to a living soul around. W. J. Locke, The Rough Road, Ch. XIV, 163.
His fiercest torment was the thought that he *dared not fulfil* the menace. Gissing, A Life's Morn., Ch. XIII, 184.

ii. No one *dared attempt* to stop him. Lamb, Tales, XII, 201. T.
I never *dared say* so before ... I love you with my whole heart and soul. Lytton, My Novel, II, X, Ch. XXV, 242.
If only I *dared tell* her now. Beatr. Har., Ships, 81.
"He's a darling", she said in a whisper. — "And so are you", he thought, "if only I *dared say* it". Galsw., Saint's Prog., IV, II, 361.
The disillusion was so complete, that some of those who had trusted most hardly *dared speak* of it. Keynes, Econ. Cons. of the Peace, Ch. III, 35.
(Here) no spectre *dared to show* his face. Wash. Irv., Sketch-Bk., XXXII, 349.
Nobody *dared to annoy* one whom he honoured with his countenance. Dick., Cop., Ch. VII, 46.a.
Neither side *dared to strike* the first blow. Mac., Hist., I, Ch. II, 257.
No admiral, bearded by these corrupt and dissolute minions of the palace, *dared to do* more than mutter something about a court-martial. ib., Ch. III, 298.
Nobody *dared to separate* them. Fior. Marryat, A Bankrupt Heart, I, 79.
I hardly *dared to ask* her. E. F. Benson, Dodo, 33.
Hood scarcely *dared to utter* the words which came into his mind. Gissing, A Life's Morn., Ch. V, 83.
There were times when he scarcely *dared to take* in his own that fine-moulded hand. ib., Ch. XXVI, 344.

iii. I would not have her think, he *dared to love* her. Dryden, Span. Friar, II, I. (138)

---
¹) Swaen, E. S., XX.

30

My mother immediately began to cry, and I wondered how Peggotty *dared to say* such a thing. DICK., Cop., Ch. VIII, 56 b.
The noble wanderer (sc. Lord Byron) put boldly out to sea with his fortunes, and *dared to hope* for consolation on distant shores. LYTTON, Life of Lord Byron, 23 a.
It was very little that she *dared to say* on business. G. ELIOT, Fel. Holt, I, Ch. VIII, 161.
What he *dared to do*, he would. GISSING, A Life's Morn., Ch. XIII, 184.
And that girl *dared to say* he was wasting himself. GALSW., Beyond, IV, Ch. IV, 375.
She *dared to feel* that, because she *dared to believe* in the endless mercy of God. HICHENS, The Garden of Allah, II, 136, T.
Who dared, I want to know, *to make* us suffer so? THACK., Virg., Ch. LXXV, 797.

27. *Durst* almost regularly stands with a bare infinitive. See the quotations in 19, b. The only instances of the alternative practice that have come to hand are the following, in which the use of *to* is, apparently, due to some other element of the sentence intervening between the two verbs.

I durst, my lord, *to wager* she is honest. SHAK., Oth., IV, 2, 12.
Nor durst they for a while *to knock* any more. BUNYAN, Pilg. Prog.¹)

28. After the infinitive *dare* the use of *to* is the rule, but constructions without *to* are by no means unfrequent. They are especially common after *do* (or *did*) *not dare*, but occur also after other complex predicates with *dare*. Some intervening element of the sentence being placed between the two verbs entails the use of *to*. When *dare* is not part of a complex predicate i. e. when it is itself preceded by *to*, usage is variable. See also 17, b.

²) I did not dare *to interrupt* him. SWEET, N. E. Gr., § 148 d.
She almost did not dare be affected by the hymn the children sang. THACK., Van. Fair, I, Ch. XII, 114.
Here lies the coward who did *not dare forgive*. LYTTON, Rienzi, V, Ch. I, 194.
I did not dare ask. DU MAURIER, Trilby II, 231, T.
I did not dare show my face at Court for a month. OSC. WILDE, Dor. Gray, Ch. II, 38, T.
She did not dare go out. FLOR. MARRYAT, A Bankrupt Heart, II, 47, T.
You don't dare sit there and tell me coolly youre a married man! SHAW, Overruled (Eng. Rev., No. 54, 183).
That I should dare *to remain* thus alone in darkness, showed that my nerves were regaining a healthy tone. CH. BRONTË, Villette, Ch. XXIII, 321.
A fellow you wouldn't dare *to ask* a question of. G. ELIOT, Felix Holt, I, Ch. XXI, 328.
He would admire her hands and feet, and delight in looking at their beauty, and long, yet *not dare to kiss* them. ib., I, Ch. XV, 256.

¹) SWEET, N. S. XX.

I should like to see the man who *would dare to insult* me in Iltracombe's presence. Flor. Marryat, A Bankrupt Heart, II, 62, T.
May I *dare to present* my two comrades? W. Locke, The Rough Road, Ch. XIII, 149
⁹⁹ I *shall not dare show* my head. Thack., Pend., I, Ch. I, 15.
Young men of the present day who find their greatest pleasure in associating with women whom they *would not dare introduce* to their mothers and sisters, are apt to become rather dumb when they find themselves in respectable company. Flor. Marryat, A Bankrupt Heart, I, 53, T.
Perhaps their more fettered brethren *would* then *dare step* outside the suggestions of the Inspectorate. Ninet. Cent., No. 592, 687.
Who *will dare question* the tradition of Shakespeare's deeply religious cast of thought towards the end of his life. James Walter, Shak's True Life (Lit. World, 1891, 3e).
iii. I *shall not dare openly to say* so. Temple Thurston, Traffic, V, Ch. III, 269.
iv. The mother . . . seemed only thus *to dare gaze* in the face of her exceeding joy. Mrs. Craik, John Hal., Ch XXXIX, 422.
⁶⁶ (This) stimulated Joe *to dare to stay* out half an hour longer on Saturdays than at other times. Dick., Great Expect., Ch. X, 94.

29. After *daring*, whether as a gerund or a present participle, the infinitive does not, apparently, tolerate the absence of *to*.

i. Without *daring to seem* to understand them. Scott, Fort. of Nigel, 286.¹)
ii. I got down after the lady who was like a haystack, not *daring to stir*, until her basket was removed. Dick., Cop., Ch. V, 36b.
He had gone to the Savoy, not *daring to show* his face at the familiar Sturrocks's. W. J. Locke, The Rough Road, Ch. VII, 74.

30. The past participle *dared*, although usually governing an infinitive with *to*, is occasionally found with a bare infinitive.

i. Look what Orestes *has dared to send* me. Kingsley, Hyp., Ch. IV, 189.
They *had not dared to meddle* with me. Blackmore, Lorna Doone, Ch XII, 255.
He was not the kind of man whom a servant would ever *have dared to express* any sympathy with. Sarah Grand, The Heavenly Twins, I, 88.
Mrs. Hood *has not dared to hint* at the truth. Grand, A Life's Morn., Ch. XV, 224.
ii. Two months ago I should have scouted as mad or drunk the man who *had dared tell* me the like. Rud. Kipl., The Phantom Rickshaw, 9.
How I wish Iltracombe had been at home to protect me from your cowardly sentence. You *would not have dared utter* it, had he been standing by. Flor. Marryat, A Bankrupt Heart, I, 43, T.
Hugh was not the only one she *would have dared tell* her story. ib., II, 21.
Who *had dared upset* his darling? Gyp., Beyond, I, Ch. II, 20.
Doggie would no more *have dared address* him in terms of familiarity, than he *would have dared slap* the Brigadier-General on the back. W. J. Locke, The Rough Road, Ch. XXIII, 286.
The whole mob of Paris would have turned on us for having arraigned him, for *having dared lay* hands upon his sacred person. Bar. Orczy, I will repay,

¹) Swaen, E. S., XX, 275.

31. Obs. In passing attention is drawn to the fact *to dare* seems to admit of being construed with a gerund or a noun of action. The following are the only instances that have come to hand, these constructions being, apparently, very rare.

i. Burke had decided to keep himself in hand until the time should come when he *should dare risking* a declaration in form. Bar. v. Hutten, Pam, IV, Ch. I, 158.
ii. Deronda *dared no movement*. G. Eliot, Dan. Der., III, VII, Ch. LI, 121.

32. *To* is mostly absent before the infinitive standing after *had better*, *had as soon*, *had need* and similar locutions, in which *had* is a preterite conditional, although often understood as a present or preterite indicative. For discussion of other aspects of these phrases see Ch. II, 27; also Stof., Taalst., VIII, 216 ff; Jespersen, Prog. in Lang., § 180; Fitzedward Hall, Americ. Journ. of Phil., Vol. II, No. 7; Storm, Eng. Phil.^{2}, 708; Murray, s. v. *have*, 22; and especially v. d. Gaaf, Transition from the Impersonal to the Personal Construction in Mid. Eng.; id., The Origin of *would rather* and some of its analogues, E. S., XLV, 381 ff.

Had better. Instances of the infinitive standing with *to* appear to be rare.

i. By the Lord, if ever I come up with him, he *had better be* in Greenland, that's all! Smol., Rod. Rand., Ch. III, 19.
You *had better tell* me. Reade, It is never too late to mend, I, Ch. VI, 63.
ii. If any man is of that humour, he *had better to cut* himself up, ... before he meets me again. Kingsley, Westw. Ho! Ch. I, 4a.
He *had better not to speak* to me, unless he is in love with gaol and gallows. ib., Ch. VII, 52 b.

Note. With *I had better* compare the practically equivalent *I should do better*, which regularly takes *to* before the following infinitive.

I was standing looking at this house and wondering whether I *shouldn't do better to go* right back home there and then. A. Bennett, The Great Adventure, I, 1, (19).

were better. Rare in Late Modern English. The construction with the bare infinitive seems at all times to have been the normal one.

i. Poor lady she *were better love* a dream. Shak., Twelfth Night, II, 2, 27.
You *were better speak* first. id., As you like it, IV, 1, 75.
After your death you *were better have* a bad epitaph than their ill report while you live. id., Haml., II, 2, 549.
Thou *wert better dally* with a lioness than with Elizabeth. Scott, Kenilworth.
Were we not better... send him on to the court? id., Mon., Ch. XVI, 114.
ii. I *were better to be married* of him than of another. Shak., As you like it, III, 3, 85.
I *were better to be eaten* to death with a rust than to be scoured to nothing with perpetual motion. id., Henry, IV, B, I, 2, 245.

You were better to go down, and see after poor Lucy. — KINGSLEY, Westw. Ho! Ch. XXVII, 208 a.

Note. On the analogy, perhaps, of *I (you, etc.) were better*, the infinitive sometimes stands without *to* after *(it were) better*. Instances are especially met with in verse, the omission of *to* being required by the metre.

i. *Were it not better sleep and wake no more?* — SCOTT, Mon., Ch. XVII, 195.
  °° *Better be with the dead, | Whom we, to gain our peace, have sent to peace | Than on the torture of the mind to lie | In restless ecstasy.* — SHAK., Macb., III, 2, 20.
  Better have none | Than plural faith which is too much by one. — id., Two Gent., V, 4, 51.
  Better dwell in the midst of alarms | Than reign in this horrible place. — COWPER, Alex. Selk., 1.
ii. *Better to wear out than to rust out.* — Proverb.
  Better to be anxious for others than only for thyself. — KINGSLEY, Hyp., Ch. XI, 56 b.

ad **best**. Distinctly uncommon and now, apparently, vulgar. Not in SHAKESPEARE. No instances with the prepositional infinitive have come to hand.

I had best lose no time in getting to my post. — SHER., Duenna, I, 1, (310).
I'd best go and talk to the hermit. — THACK., Van. Fair, I, Ch. VI, 57.
I'd best, if you please, inspect the premisis, and will think you to allow your young man to show me the pantry and kitching. — id., A Little Dinner at Timmins's, Ch. v., (325). (*think* vulgar for *thank*.)

were best. Now distinctly rare. SHAKESPEARE seems to use the two constructions indifferently.

i. *You were best stick her.* — SHAK., Two Gent., I, 1, 108.
  Thou wert best look to't. — id., As you like it, I, 1, 134.
ii. *Your ladyship were best to have some guard about you.* — id., Twelfth Night, III, 4, 13.
  You were best to call them generally, man by man, according to the scrip. — id., Mids., I, 2, 2.
  We're the Squire's tenants here, and we're best to keep the right side of him. — RICH. BAGOT, Darneley Place, I, Ch. II, 25, 1.

Note. In SHAKESPEARE we also find instances of *(it were) best* + bare infinitive, the omission of *to* being required by the metre.

Best first go see your lodging. — Twelfth Night, III, 3, 20.
This butcher's cur is venom-mouth'd, and I | Have not the power to muzzle him; therefore best | Not wake him in his slumber. — Henry VIII, I, 1, 121.

Observe also the absence of *to* in:

It is best | Put finger in the eye, an she knew why. — Taming of the Shrew, I, 1, 78.

had liefer (or *liever*). Apparently not in SHAKESPEARE, though much earlier instances are given by MURRAY, s. v. *lief*, A, 1, d. Instances with a prepositional infinitive have not been found. The phrase is now distinctly archaic and literary, *had rather* and *had sooner* ordinarily taking its place.

I *had liefer* twenty years | *Skip* to the broken music of my brains | Than any broken music thou canst make Tys., Last Tourn., 257.
Far *liever* by his dear hand *had I die* | Than that my lord should suffer loss or shame. id., Ger. and En., 927.

had rather. The construction with the bare infinitive is now practically the only one. In Early Modern English the infinitive with *to* seems to have been less unusual. MURRAY cites two instances. SHAKE‑SPEARE's practice does not materially differ from the present, there being only one instance of a prepositional infinitive in his works.

i. I'd *rather have been shot* myself. MRS. WOOD, ORV. COL., Ch. III, 44.
ii. I *had rather to adopt a* child than get it SHAK., Othello, I, 3, 191.
I *had much rather to do* it than say it. CARL ORRERY, St. Let., II, 311.[1])

had sooner. Of comparatively recent date: not in SHAKESPEARE. In colloquial English more frequent than had rather. No instances with the prepositional infinitive have come to hand.

I'd *sooner cut* my tongue out. SHER., Riv., I, 2
I'd *sooner kill* a man than a dog any day. DICK., Barn. Rudge, Ch. XXI, 82a.
I'd *sooner stay* in prison all my life. ANSTY, Tinted Venus, 171.

had as good. Not in SHAKESPEARE, but frequent enough in writers of the eighteenth century. Now somewhat unusual. Only instances with the bare infinitive have come to hand.

Well, I see one *had as good go* to law without a witness, as break a jest without a laughter on one's side. WYCH., Country Wife, I, 1.
You *had as good come* along with me to the jubilee now. FARQUHAR, Const. Couple, V, 3, (132).
You *had as good make* a point of first giving away yourself. GOLDS., Good‑nat. Man, II.
I perceive . . . that none of you have a mind to be married, and I think we *had as good go back again.* id., Vic., Ch. XXXII, (489).
He *had as good mind* his own business. DICK., Bleak House, Ch. LVII, 477.

had as lief (or *lieve*). Now archaic and literary, *had as soon* being its ordinary substitute. Apparently the phrase is regularly construed with the bare infinitive.

I *had as lief take* her dowry with this condition. SHAK., Taming of the Shrew, I, 1, 135.
I'd *as lieve let* it alone. SHER., Riv., V, 3.
I'd *as lieve stand.* DICK., Chuz., Ch. XIII, 118a.

had as soon. Of comparatively recent date: not in SHAKESPEARE. Apparently construed only with the bare infinitive.

I'd *as soon undertake* to keep Portocrero honest. VANBRUGH, False Friend, II, 1.

---

[1]) MURRAY, s. v. *rather*, II, 9, d.

had as well. Not in Shakespeare and altogether rather unusual. Apparently regularly construed with the bare infinitive.

You *had as well* come to the window. Scott, Mon., XIV, 16.

had need. Formed on the analogy of *had better* (rather, etc.) *Need* is now adverbial in grammatical function, but originally it was a noun, being used as such with the indicative of *to have* from the earliest periods, and followed by a final infinitive with *to*. The construction without *to*, however, appears already in Middle English, Murray's earliest instance being drawn from the Paston Letters (1461). In Present English both the bare and the prepositional infinitive are met with, the latter less frequently than the former. See also Stoffel, Taalstudie, VIII, 230.

i. Thou *hadst need* send for more money. Shak., Twelfth Night, II, 3, 199.
Fred *had need be* careful. G. Eliot, Mid., VIII, Ch. LXXX, 614.
He'd *need have* a big fortune that marries her. id., Felix Holt, I, Ch. XXII, 340.
I *had need have* you always to find fault with me and teach me. id., Mill, VI, Ch. VII, 383.
I *hadn't need keep* y'out. id. Adam Bede, I, Ch. XIV, 124.
I *had need be patient* with him. Miss Braddon, Lady Audley's Secret, II, Ch. XIII, 268. T.

ii. But if thou art chief of such a clan, | And art the son of such a man, | And ever comest to thy command, | Our wardens *had need to keep* good order. Scott, Lay, III, XX.
The man who reviews his own life ... *had need to have been* a good man indeed, if he would be spared the sharp consciousness of many talents neglected. Dick., Cop., Ch. XLII, 301 b. (This may be the usual practice with the perfect infinitive.)
If the bad-tempered man wants to apologise, he *had need to do* it on a large public scale. G. Eliot, Theophr. Such, Only Temper.
My driver was profuse with his apologies, as, indeed, he *had need to be*. Aunt Jane at the Seaside, Ch. I.

Note. *a*) *Had need* in a similar meaning is also met with after weak *there*.

Nan suggested there was something besides ancestry to be reckoned with "*There had need be*", Miss Janet retorted. Una L. Silberrad, Success, Ch. II, 33.

β) It will be observed that the substantival function, which originally attached *to need* in this phrase, is still distinctly discernible when an infinitive with *to* follows. This substantival function is unquestionable, when *need* is connected with the indicative of the verb *to have*.

"What *need have* I *to say* more!" — "You *haven't need to say* so much." Dick., Cop., Ch. XXXIX, 275 a.
By God! 'tis he who *has need to prepare* for death. Frankf. Moore, The Jessamy Bride, Ch. XIX, 165.
"I am sorry for myself" — "You *have need to be*." Bernard Capes, The Pot of Basil, Ch. III, 35.

The bells of a city church *have need to be* loud. TEMPLE THURSTON, City of Beaut. Nons., I, Ch. XVI, 123.

Being a noun, *need* may be preceded by an adnominal modifier. Thus frequently by *no*.

i. Thou wast a pretty fellow when thou *hadst no need to care* for frowning. SHAK., Lear, I, 4, 211.
Tom *had no need to direct* that appalling look towards his friend. DICK., Chuz., Ch. XXXVI, 287 a.
It is a private affair, which you *had no need to speak* of unless you thought proper. THACK., Sam. Titm., Ch. XII, 155.
I *had no need to read* "The Laocoon" again. Westm. Gaz., No. 8467, 6 a.
ii. Mary's making him a black silk case to hold his bands, but I told her she'd *more need wash* 'em for him. G. ELIOT, Scenes, II, Ch. III, 205. (Note the curious absence of *to* before the infinitive.)

γ) *Had need* is also found construed with a noun. Of this construction no Late Modern English instances have been found.

But Beauty, like the fair Hesperian tree | Laden with blooming gold, *had need* the guard | Of dragon watch with unenchanted eye, | To save her blossoms, and defend her fruit | From the rash hand of bold Incontinence. MILTON, Comus, 394.
Here *he had need* | All circumspection. id., Par. Lost, II, 413.

In the following quotation the noun-construction is found together with the ordinary construction with a bare infinitive:

I *had need have* it well roasted and good sauce to it, if I pay so dear. MARLOWE, Doct. Faust., I, 4, 12.

33. The verbs *to come*, *to go* and *to help* are sometimes construed with a bare infinitive. In Modern English this construction appears to be practically confined to the infinitive of these verbs, only the imperative of *to go* being occasionally found with the non-prepositional infinitive also. It is even doubtful if the verb after the imperative of *to go* is not in some instances to be apprehended as an imperative as well. No other interpretation is, of course, possible if the two verbs are separated by the comma. For discussion and illustration of the above combinations see also ABBOT, Shak. Gram.³, § 349; MÄTZN., Eng. Gram.², III, 15; ELLINGER, E. S., XXIV; id., Verm. Beitr., § 79 ff; ONIONS, Adv. Eng. Synt., § 165; STORM, Eng. Phil.², 939; EINENKEL, Streifz., 238.

The above verbs are now mostly followed by the prepositional infinitive, sometimes varying with gerund-constructions. Frequently also, especially in colloquial English, the two succesive verbs are, by way of hendiadys, connected co-ordinately by

and. For detailed discussion and illustration of the various possible constructions the student is referred to my Gram. of Late Mod. Eng.:
as regards *to come* see Ch. I, 11; 70, Obs. II; Ch. X, 5, C; Ch. XVIII, 12; 24, Obs. II; Ch. XX, 15, Obs. IV;
as regards *to go* see Ch. X, 5, b; Ch. XVIII, 24, Obs. II; Ch. XIX, 45; 63, Obs. I and III;
as regards *to help* see Ch. XIX, 18, c; 34.
Compare also my paper on Hendiadys in Neophilologus, II, III and IV.

34. a) After *to come* the bare infinitive has become obsolete. MURRAY (s. v. *come*, 3, e) mentions no later instance than one dated 1647. EINENKEL, (Hist. Synt., § 4, *i*) gives an instance from VANBRUGH.

> We'll come *dress* you straight. SHAK., Merry Wives, IV, 2, 84.
> The Hyrcanian deserts and the vasty wilds | Of wide Arabia are as thorough: fares now | For princes *to come view* fair Portia. id., Merch., II, 7, 43.

b) *To go* is found with the bare infinitive in the latest English, but, except for dialects, only archaically. Compare MURRAY, s. v. *go*, 32, a; ABBOT, Shak. Gram., § 349. See also Participles, 6, Obs. VIII.

> i. I'll go *seek* the King. SHAK., Haml., II, 1, 101.
> I'll go *amuse* my aunt with the old pretence of a violent passion for my cousin. GOLDSMITH, The Stoops.
> He went straight from here purposing *to go see* his uncle. MRS. GASK., Mary Barton, Ch. XXIII, 249.
> Let Mary go *find* Will. ib., Ch. XXV, 265.
> I'll go *seek* him. BAR. ORCZY, I will repay (Stories and Sketches, 68).
>
> Note the rather frequent colloquial *go hang*, as in:
>
> As for women she let them *go hang*. W. J. LOCKE, The Glory of Clem. Wing., Ch. II, 16.
> The ordinary girl would have told a living experiment like me *to go hang* long before this. id., The Rough Road, Ch. XXI, 269.
> The reconstruction of the Ministry may *go hang*. H. Lond. News.
>
> ii. Go *work* today in my vineyard. Bible, Matth., XXI, 28
> Go, *tell* him I am here. SHER., Riv., II, 1, (225).
> Go *see* who it is! DICK., Chuz., Ch. XLVI, 358a.

c) The use of the bare infinitive after *to help* is pronounced to be now dialectal or vulgar by MURRAY (s. v. *help*, 5, a), but it is by no means unfrequent in style which is innocent of vulgarity.

Hannah contemptuously forbore to make her come in and *help clear* away.
Mrs. Ward, Dav. Grieve, I, 37.
He has lately got a niece to stay with him and *help look* after the children.
id., Delia Blanchflower, II, Ch. XVI, 136.
And you *help do* all the rooms? Galsworthy, The Silver Box, I, 39. T.
We want you *to help decide* this question. T. P.'s Weekly, No. 472, 663a.
They (sc. the Young Turks) can go to the Army and invite it *to help save*
the sacred city. Sat. Rev. (Westm. Gaz., No. 6135, 1oc).
It would seem to be the patriotic duty of all *to help make* perfect the
scheme. Westm. Gaz., No. 4943, 1c.

Thus even after other forms than the infinitive, the con=
struction without *to* is occasionally met with.

They *helped place* the scenery. Williamson, Lord Loveland, Ch. XXXII, 287.
She *had helped concoct* her grandson's journey to Middelburg. Marj. Bowen,
I will maintain, I, Ch. X, 105.

Note. *c*) According to *Kruisinga* (Crit. Contrib. to Eng. Synt., I,
English Studies, II, No. 8) *to help* may, in dialects, coalesce with
the following infinitive into a kind of compound, so that the in=
flexional ending is attached to the infinitive instead of *to help*, e. g.:
I help loaded the cart.

β Also in the construction in which *to help* is divided from the
infinitive by a (pro)noun, *to* is frequently enough absent in style
which can hardly be suspected of vulgarity. According to Onions
(Adv. Eng. Synt., § 165) the dropping of *to* is especially current
in American English, and "has, no doubt, been furthered by the
regular construction with *hear, feel*, etc." Also rhythmical con=
siderations may not unfrequently have operated towards the sup=
pression of *to*.

The time will come when thou shalt wish for me | *To help thee curse* that
poisonous bunch-backed toad. Shak., Rich. III, I, 3, 246.
If those you seek, | It were a journey like the path to Heav'n, | *To help
you find* them. Milton, Comus, 303.
Help me lift the little sofa near the fire. Dick., Domb. Ch. VI, 55.
I am going *to help them get* the bucket out of the captain's well. Hardy,
Return of the Native, III, Ch. III, 222.
I think I know some one who would be only too happy to be allowed
to help you build it. Flor. Marryat, Open Sesame, I, 34.
Faversham came down *to help him show* his cases. Mrs. Ward, The
Mating of Lydia, I, Ch. V, 109.
Now you shall *help me lay* them (sc. the fern fronds) upon her. John
Oxenham, Great-heart Gillian, Ch. I, 12.
Captain Truman says he will come and *help me put up* curtains, Dolf
Wyllarde, The Story of Eden, I, Ch. I, 27.
You must *help us make* our nests. Bradby, Dick, Ch. IX, 98.
Rosamond I'll *help you find* 'em (sc. the children). Galsw., Beyond, IV,
Ch. XII, 437.
He can stay and *help Dick tidy* up. Williamson, Lord Loveland,
Ch. XXVIII, 247.

Also after other forms than the infinitive the construction without *to* is occasionally met with.

P. Gordon was *helping* Black Dick *put* things to rights. ib., Ch. XXVIII, 246. Mrs Bruhng *helped him pack* a bax. Wells, Mr. Britling, II, Ch. III, § 9, 286.

Practice after Verbs governing an Accusative + Infinitive or an allied construction.

35. After verbs which express a perceiving or discovering the infinitive almost regularly stands without *to*; excepted is only the verb *to be*, which in this connection regularly takes *to*. For illustration, which, for the rest, is easily accessible see Ch. XVIII, 31. Here we may confine ourselves to giving some instances of the comparatively rare construction of *to see* + (pro)noun + *to be*. Observe that in this connection *to see* is used in the meaning of *to find*, denoting a mental as opposed to a physical perception.

I see it *to be* so. BUNYAN, Pilg. Prog. I, 10.
It was a resolve, which had become a habit, that she would never quarrel with this man — never tell him what she saw him *to be*. G. ELIOT, Fel. Holt, I, Ch. IX, 172.
She was truly a high-minded person of that order who always do what they see *to be* right. MEREDITH, Ord. of Rich. Fev., Ch. XLII, 422.
The next person I came across was a dapper little man in a beautiful wig, whom I saw *to be* a barber on his rounds. STEVENSON, Kidnapped, Ch. II (196.
William Morris in his Sagas, like Homer in his Iliad, has so drawn human life that we see it *to be* greater than we knew. Eng. Rev., No. 75, 533.
What is there to show today that Parliament is the normal executive organ for an advanced republic? Do we see it *to be* so in the United States, or in France? FRED. HARRISON, On Society, Lect. III, 64.

36. Obs. I. *To* is sometimes found before the infinitive of other verbs than *to be*, where, in many cases, it apparently appears for the sake of the metre or rhythm. Compare ABBOT, Shak. Gram.³, § 349; FRANZ, Shak. Gram.², § 650 f.; MÄTZN., Eng. Gram.², III, 14.

I had rather hear you *to solicit* that Than music from the spheres. SHAK., Twelfth Night, III, 1, 120.
Methinks I feel this youth's perfections With an invisible and subtle stealth *To creep* in at mine eyes. ib., I, 5, 278.
The multitude wondered, when they saw the dumb *to speak*, the maimed *to be* whole, the lame *to walk* and the blind *to see*. Bible, Math., XV, 31.
But I perceive thy mortal sight *to fail*. MILTON, Par. Lost, XII, 8.
These eyes Which have not seen the sun *to rise* For years. BYRON, Pris. of Chil., II.
The duke observing his eve *to brighten* a little, said [etc.]. LAMB, Tales, Meas. for Meas., 247. T

I've never heard any one *to touch* you. Westm. Gaz., No. 8455, 5 b.
(Observe that *to hear* = *to be told*, and *to touch* = *to equal*.)

In the following quotation the suppression of *to* would improve the rhythm:

I generally observe such men *to retain* a certain freshness. Dick., Cop., Ch. II, 7 a.

11. After *to find* and *to know* in its modified meaning of *to observe* (Ch. XVIII, 34, Obs. V) *to* is not seldom met with, apparently more or less irrespective of considerations of metre or rhythm. So far as appears from the available evidence, the bare infinitive is the rule after *to find*, while the case is reversed after *to know*. The prepositional infinitive seems to be fixed when it is passive.

to find. i. I find the whole neighbourhood *begin* to grow very inquisitive after my name and character. Spect., No. 131.
I did not find those rash actions *answer*. Shek., Critic, I, 2.
I found her *prefer* a plain dish to a ragout. Jane Austen, Pride and Prej., Ch. VIII, 38.
You'll find the lock *go* the better for a little oil. Dick., Chuz., Ch. XXXIX, 310 b.
I find the King's English *express* my meaning better. G. Eliot, Fel. Holt, I, Ch. XVII, 285.
He never cut a chimneysweep if he knew him. And he found it *pay*. Kingsley, Alton Locke, Ch. VI, 71.

ii. The next annoyance that we had was a very bad smell which we found *to proceed* from the drains. Marryat, Olla Podrida.
I found this plan *to tell* through life. Mrs. Craik, A Hero, 8.

to know. i. I have known him *walk* with Tiny Tim on his shoulder very fast indeed. Dick., Christm. Car.b, IV, 98.
These marriages between people of such different rank and age ... are sad things. I have known them *produce* a great deal of unhappiness. Thack., Pend., I, Ch. VII, 85.
I have known her *take* it (sc. green tea) in ignorance many a time without such effects. Mrs. Gask., Cranf., Ch. XIII, 240.
I have known a cat *get up* and walk out of the room on a remark derogatory to her species being made by a visitor. Jerome, Idle Thoughts.
For these seventeen years he had never known her *make* an intimate friend. Mrs. Ward, The Case of Rich. Meyn., I, Ch. VI, 117.
I've known the plainest of women *become* quite good-looking. W. J. Locke, The Rough Road, Ch. XXII, 274.
I have known two hundred words about the acting at the end of an article *take* longer to write than the twelve hundred words that precede them. Westm. Gaz., No. 8597, 6 b.

ii. I had never known him *to pass* the garden-gate before. Dick., Cop., Ch. X, 68 b.
I never knew the Duke *to fail*. Thack., Pend., I, Ch. XXXII, 343.
She thought his diamond shirt-pin (which she had not known him *to wear* before) the prettiest ornament ever seen. id., Van. Fair, I, Ch. XIII, 127.

I have known them *to do* that sort of thing before. Rid. Hag., Mees. Will, Ch. I, 11.
I have known her *to show* impatience when George's name was mentioned. Walt. Besant, St. Kath., Ch 1.
I have seen men suffering the most excruciating agony. I have known them *to be cut, to be lost* utterly from the vulgarity of their wives' connections. Thack., Pend., I, Ch VII, 85.
I have known her *to be thrown* into fainting fits by the king's taxes. Dick., Cop., Ch XI, 79 b.
I have known an imposition of Two Thousand Lines of the Poet Virgil *to be set* in punishment. Payn, Glow-Worm Tales, II, M, 206.

III. Also in the rare case that the infinitive is a perfect, i. e. indicates completed action, it seems to be regularly preceded by *to*.

Mr. Lorry observed a great change *to have come* over the doctor. Dick.[1]) Dickens often gets verbose, rings the changes on a point which he sees *to have caught* his readers. Fr. Harrison.[1])

IV. Mention may here also be made of the collocation *to hear say* (*tell*, or some other verb of a similar import) followed by an objective statement or by *of* (in vulgar language *on*) + (pro)noun, in which the infinitive regularly stands without *to*. The phrase is a concealed accusative + infinitive, the accusative (*people persons* or *somebody*) being suppressed because of its indefiniteness. It used to be common enough, but is now felt to be dialectal or colloquial. See Murray, s. v. *to hear*, 3, c; and compare Ch. III, 24, Obs. II and Ch. XVIII, 9, Obs. I.

I *heard say* your lordship was sick. Shak., Henry IV, B, 1, 2, 118.
I have *heard say* that people may be guessed at by the behaviour of their servants. Farquhar, The Beaux' Stratagem, III, 3, (399).
I *heard tell* she has a power of money. Lytton, My Novel, II, XI Ch. XVIII, 337.
11.? in this house, in the presence of Mr. and Mrs. Crummles, ... are we *to hear talk* of nooses? Dick., Nich. Nick., Ch. XXV, 165 b.
Did you ever *hear tell* of mermaids? id., Barn. Rudge, Ch. I, 6a.
I've *heard tell* of dumb dawgs. Herb. Jenkins, Bindle, Ch. V, 72.
I've *heerd tell* on him. Miss Braddon, Lady Audley's Secret, II, Ch. XIV, 286, 1.

37. The bare infinitive is also the rule after *to have*. For illustration see also Ch. XVIII, 31, b.

Had I a dozen sons, ... I had rather had eleven *die* nobly for their country than one voluptuously surfeit out of action. Shak., Coriol, I, 3, 26.
It is my wish to have my son *make* some figure in the world. Godrow, Vic.

Also the verb *to be* in this connection mostly seems to stand without *to*. The construction is, however, an unusual one.

I would have you *be* on your guard. Jane Austen, Pride and Prej., Ch. XXVI, 145.

---
[1] Windt, Synt. des heut. Eng., I, 45.

I would not have it *be* so. LYTTON, My Novel, II, XI, Ch. VII, 276.
It really grieves me to have you *be* so naughty. Mrs. BEECHER-STOWE, Uncle Tom's Cab., XXV, 239.[1])
I can't bear to have people *be* sorry. BAR. v. HUTTON, Pam, Ch. X, 56.

38. Obs. I. The prepositional infinitive seems to be more common than the bare infinitive after *would have*. SHAKESPEARE appears to use the two constructions indifferently. Compare FRANZ, Shak. Gram.², § 651. Of special frequency is the combination. *I would have you (to) know*.

i. They would not have you *to stir* forth to-day. SHAK., Jul. Cæs., II, 2, 38.
I'd have you *to know*, sir, that I am as knowing as the stars, and as secret as the night. CONGREVE, Love for Love, V, 2, (296).
I'd have you *to know*, the poor man, whosoe'er he is, will have little cause to thank you. WYCHERLEY, Gent. Danc. Mast., I, 1, (139).
Though I was obliged ... to undervalue myself by marrying a poor man, yet I would have you *to know* I have a spirit above all them things. FIELD., Tom. Jones, V, Ch. IX, 54 a.
I suppose you'd have me *to learn* to cut capers. MISS BURNEY, Evelina, XVI, 57. T.
I'd have you *to know* that I don't care a penny, madam, for your paltry money. THACK., Virg., Ch. XXXV, 368.
I would have him *to understand* that her decision is final. ib., Ch. XCII, 991.
I wouldn't have a Queen *to cut* jokes on her throne. id., Newc, I, Chr. XXV, 278.
Mr. Rochester would have me to *come* in. CH. BRONTE, Jane Eyre, Ch. XVI, 191.
What would you have a man *to do?* KINGSLEY, Hereward. Ch. XIV, 60 a.
What would you have me *to do?* READE, The Cloister and the Hearth, Ch. III, 22.
(He) would have him *to stay* supper. ib., Ch. VI, 33.
An idiot is a human being, sir, and has an immortal soul, I'd have you *to know*. MAR. CRAWF., Kath. Land., I, Ch. VI, 103.

ii I would not have my father | *See* me in talk with her. SHAK., Merch., II, 3, 9.
I'd have you *know* I was never afraid of losing my mistress in earnest. WYCHERLEY, Gent. Danc. Mast., I, 1, (137).
I have passions, | And love thee still; therefore, would have thee *think* | The world is all a scene of deep deceit. G. LILLO, Fatal Curiosity, I, 1.
I would not have you *provoke* me to the degree of falling foul. SCOTT, Ken, Ch. I, 17.
I would not have you *think* all I said of him, even now, was strict gospel. ib., Ch. I, 21.
Would you *have your father stop* here, useless and despised? BUCHANAN, That Winter Night, Ch. II, 22.
What *would* you *have me do?* SWEET, N. E. Gr., § 2316.

---

[1]) MURRAY, s. v. *grieve*, 5.

II. The infinitive in the following quotations is best understood as a kind of adverbial adjunct of purpose, so that *to* could not possibly be dispensed with:

> You ought to ..., have your black nurse *to tuck* you up in bed. THACK., Virg., Ch. LXXVI, 802.
> They had him *to dine* with them at the inn. id., Henry Esm., I, Ch. III, 22 (= *to dinner*).
> You will not have him *to dine* with you? G. Eliot, Fel. Holt, I, Ch. VII, 195.
> I can have aunt *to live* with me. Fr. Grys, Refl. of Ambrosine, III, Ch. IV, 307.
> Why do you have disreputable people *to stay* with you? Mrs. Ward, The Case of Rich. Meyn., II, Ch. VII, 150.

Thus also when the infinitive is passive, as in:

> I haven't my fortune *to be settled*, or my wedding dresses *to be made*. Dick., Chimes, I, 23.

39. After the verbs which express a judging, knowing, remembering or declaring, and such as express a revealing or showing, the infinitive, mostly *to be*, regularly takes *to*. For illustration see Ch. XVIII, 31, c and d.

40. The verbs of causing, viz. *to cause*, *to do*, *to make* and *to occasion* show different practice. For illustration see also Ch. XVIII, 31, e.

a) To *cause* and to *occasion* are regularly, or all but regularly, followed by an infinitive with *to*.

> He caused one of his attendants *to mount* his own led horse. Scott, Ivanhoe, Ch. II, 22.
> He caused the troops *to march* onwards. Mason, Eng. Gram., § 597, N.
> She asked Matilda what occasioned Manfred *to take* Theodore for a spectre. Hor. Walpole, Castle of Otranto, Ch. IV, 193.

Instances of the alternative practice are not, however, entirely wanting.

> Setting spurs to his horse, he caused him *make* a demivolte across the path. Scott, Ivanhoe, Ch. II, 17.
> The liberality of the age has caused it *be* very commonly admitted that a Deist may be truly religious. J. S. Mill, Autob., 26.[1]
> She caused men *make* a silver image fair Of me unhappy. W. Morris, Earthly Par., Doom of King Acris., 75a. (Evidently due to the requirements of the metre; substitution of *made* for *caused* being objectionable for reasons of euphony.)

b) Also the verb *to do* when archaically construed with an accusative + infinitive, requires *to*.

---

[1] Fijn van Draat, Rhythm in Eng. Prose, Ang. Forsch., 76.

We ... do thee *to know* that [etc.]. Scott, Fair Maid, Ch. XXXI, 323.

For metrical reasons *to* is suppressed in:
And as she fled, her mantle she did *fall*. Shak., Mids., V, 1, 14.

c) After *to make*, on the other hand, the bare infinitive is the ordinary construction.

It might be pleasant to them to remember upon Christmas-Day, who made lame beggars *walk* and blind men *see*. Dick., Christm. Car.², III, 67.
She made the oldest-established families in the country ... *know* their distance. Thack., Virg., Ch. LXXII, 773.
It is not easy to make a simile go on all fours. Mac., Pilg. Prog., (136 a).
He made me *laugh*. Mas., Eng. Gram³¹., § 195.

The prepositional infinitive, however, is not uncommon. Apart from metrical or rhythmical considerations, it is not unfrequently preferred, α) when the accusative is a lengthy sequence of words, β) when the accusative is represented by a relative pronoun or otherwise leaves its ordinary place and stands after the infinitive, γ) when the infinitive is preceded and modified by so. Sometimes there is no apparent reason for the use of *to*. For detailed discussion and illustration see especially Fijn van Draat, Rhythm in Eng. Prose, § 46 ff, Ang. Forsch., No. 79.

i¹ We will make our leisures *to attend* on yours. Shak., Merch., I, 1, 68.
Down ran the wine into the road, | Most piteous to be seen, | Which made his horse's flanks *to smoke* | As they had basted been. Cowper, John Gilpin, XXXII.
For — Heaven forgive that thought! the while | Which made me both *to weep* and smile — | I sometimes deem'd that it might be | My brother's soul come down to me. Byron, Pris. of Chil., X.
The wild justice of this idea made the blood *to bubble* in his ears. Hall Caine, Manxman, VI, Ch. IX, 180 b.
We cannot relume the extinguished lamp of reason. We cannot make the deaf *to hear*. We cannot make the dumb *to speak*. Graph., 1889, 346.

Interesting from a rhythmical point of view is the alternate use of the bare and the prepositional infinitive in:

Money makes the old wife *trot*, and makes the mare *to go*. Prov.¹)
Amelia's love makes the burning sand *grow* green beneath him, and the stunted shrubs *to blossom*. Carlyle, Life of Schiller, I, 30, T.
ii. To be tapped on the shoulder by a French cook was a piece of familiarity which made the blood of the Pendennises *to boil up* in the veins of their descendant. Thack., Pend., I, Ch. XXVII, 282.
When I see youth going to capsize on virtue, it makes my blood, as a Christian man, *to curdle*. W. M. Bryant, All Sorts and Cond. of Men, Ch. XXXVIII, 260.

¹) M ... s. v. *make*.

The evening gun from the Duke of York's bastion proclaimed the death of another day with a loud report, which made the branches in the tree above us *to shake* and tremble. id., By Celia's Arbour, I, Ch. I, 10. More than any other of his arguments, Mr. Hyndman's preference for the conditions in the States will make any one who knows India *to smile*. Westm. Gaz., No. 8052, 16 a.

iii. He got a premium of four or five hundred pounds with each young gent, whom he made *to slave* for ten hours a day. Thack., Sam. Titm., Ch. II, 1.

" How they pile the poor little craft ... with luxuries that only cloy with pleasures that bore, with empty show that, like the criminal's iron crown of yore, makes *to bleed* and swoon the aching head that wears it. Jerome, Three Men in a Boat, Ch. III, 29.

An occasional trespasser in wellbordered domains makes *to glow* the more brightly the sense of proprietorship. E. F. Benson, Arundel, Ch. III, 55.

iv. Jack the Guardsman and La Tulipe of the Royal Bretagne are face to face, and striving to knock each other's brains out. Bon! It is their nature to — like the bears and the lions — and we will not say Heaven, but some Power or other has made them so *to do*. Thack., Virg., Ch. LXIV, 685.

v. Your innocent smiles made me *to bear up* against my misfortunes. Lamb, Tales, Temp., 14, T.
What made you *to swear* to fatal vows? Thack., Eng. Hum., I, 30, I.
But the circumstance which, more than any other, has made Ireland *to differ* from Scottland, remains to be noticed. Mac., Hist., I, Ch. I, 66.

Note. The bare infinitive is fixed in the expression *make believe* in which the accusative is understood.

He denied it utterly, *made believe* at first to think they were accusing him in joke. Mrs. Wood, Orv. Col.

41. After verbs expressing a desiring or a (dis)liking the prepositional infinitive is now obligatory. For illustration see Ch. XVIII, 31, f, and g. In Early Modern English we sometimes find *to* suppressed, evidently from considerations of metre. Compare Matzn., Eng. Gram.², III, 15.

I would wish you *reconcile* the lords. Marlowe, Edw. II, I, 4.
Sir, I desire you *do* me right and justice; | And *to bestow* your pity on me. Shak., Henry VIII, II, 4, 13. (Observe the varied practice).

42. This seems to be the most suitable place to discuss the use of *to* after verbs of allowing, commanding or requesting, which are often followed by a person=object + infinitive, a construction which bears a close resemblance to the accusative + infinitive. The bulk of these verbs normally stand with the prepositional infinitive. For illustration see Ch. XVIII, 31, h; 38, Obs. I.
a) After *to bid* practice is variable. In verse the choice naturally depends on the metre. In prose the bare infinitive is

distinctly the rule, especially after the monosyllabic forms of the verb, the absence of *to* mostly making for an improved rhythmical movement of the sentence. The prepositional infinitive, however, appears to be the normal construction when the (pro)noun forming the person-object is not immediately followed by the infinitive. For instances of the prepositional infinitive see also ELLINGER, Verm. Beitr., 8.

i.° I would stay ... if you bid me *stay* — or go if you bid me *go*. WALT. BESANT, All Sorts and Cond. of Men, Ch. XIV, 115.

   Bid Rodolph of Saxony *approach!* LYTTON, Rienzi, V, Ch. I, 192. Bid your anger against me *cease!* ib., 195.

   She would bid the girls *hold up* their heads. GOLDSMITH, Vic., Ch. I, (238). I would bid you *stay* because I like your society. WALT. BESANT, All Sorts and Cond. of Men, Ch. XIV, 115.

   The faithful Tinker, having wakened her bedfellow, and bid her *prepare* for departure, unbarred and unbolted the great hall-door. THACK., Van. Fair, I, Ch. VII, 72.
   He had bid them *be* brother and sister. MEREDITH, Ord. of Rich. Fev., Ch. I, 3.
   They would have bid their countrymen *draw* their own inferences as to the true intentions of his Majesty. Times.

   He gives me a stroke on the head with his cane; bids me *carry* that to my master. SHER., Riv. II, 1.

   The good woman bade me *remain* in the apartments we occupied. THACK., Sam. Titm., Ch. XII, 164.

   It was Traddles; whom Mr. Mell instantly discomfited by bidding him *hold* his tongue. DICK., Cop., Ch. VII, 48b.
   (She) shook me by the hand, and bidding me *be* of good cheer, set off with Gus in a coach, to pay a visit to those persons. THACK., Sam. Titm., Ch. XII, 162.

ii.° He bid his horses *to be prepared*. LAMB, Tales, Lear, 155. T.

   We are now poor, my fondlings, and wisdom bids us *to conform* to our humble situation. GOLDSMITH, Vic., Ch. III, (246).
   He bids his followers *to be prepared* for all contingencies. Manch. Guard, V, No. 15, 282c.

   He bade the conductor *to put* him down at the gate of the Upper Temple. THACK., Pend., I, Ch. XXVIII, 303.
   The old butler entering at the summons, Arthur bade him *to serve* that refreshment. ib., I, Ch. XVI, 167.
   His lordship ... bade me *to come* and watch over him. id., Virg. Ch. XXXV, 365.
   We cannot tell what her (sc. Stella's) style was, or what sort were the little letters which the Doctor placed there and bade *to appear* from under his pillow of a morning. id., Eng. Hum., I, 46. T.
   He bade me *to think* well ere I asked him to my house. ANNIE BESANT Autobiography, 177.

iii.° And hereby (I) take farewell, bidding all gents who peruse this, *to b* cautious of their money, if they have it. THACK., Sam. Titm., Ch. XIII, 184.

Have I not bidden you never *to look* upon the face of woman? Kingsley, Hyp., Ch. I, 3a.
Leaving Wooden Sword in the passage and bidding him not *to stir* from there till I saw him again, I went on to the gun-room. Fq. Lawless, A Colonel of the Empire, Ch. VIII.
** I cannot bid the bright star again *sparkle* in the sphere it has shot from. Scott, Kenilw., Ch. IV, 44.

b) After *to let* the prepositional infinitive is very rare. Al. Schmidt (s. v. *let*) registers none in Shakespeare. Murray gives four instances, the latest of which is dated 1678. For discussion see also Konrad Meier, E. S., XXXIII, 327.

i. Would you let any woman you love *be contaminated* by their company? Thack., Pend., II, Ch. XXIV, 264.
ii. These visions will not let them sleep, will not let their tongues *to cease* from bitterness. Gaisw., The Country House, III, Ch. VII, 270. (Note the varied practice.)

c) When other verbs of this description are construed with a bare infinitive, this is, evidently, done from considerations of metre in the majority of cases. This applies to all the instances given by Mätzn. (Eng. Gram.², III, 10), and also to the following:

So loving to my mother That he might not beteem the winds of heaven *Visit* her face too roughly. Shak., Haml., I, 2, 142.
Your betters have endured me *say* my mind. id., Taming of the Shrew, IV, 3, 75.
Tell him, so please him, *come* unto this place. id., Jul. Cæs., III, 1, 140.
But first I beg you, *Thank* me for Frederick's visit. Bridges, Hum. of the Court, II, 1, 1116.

A few prose instances have come to hand.

A host of servants stood around, and begged Heaven *bless* her ladyship. Thack., Virg., Ch. XX, 202.
And now, my Lord Savelli, for my question, which I pray you *listen* to. Lytton, Rienzi, V, Ch. I, 191.
Elementary humanity forbade him *leave* his lame old godmother one moment unattended. Ags. and Eg. Castle, The Lost Iphigenia, Ch. I, 24.

43. a) The infinitive is normally preceded by *to* after the passive voice of any verb; accordingly also after all the verbs which may be construed with an accusative + infinitive. For illustration see Ch. XVIII, 42. The verb *to let* does not make an exception. The regular use of *to* may have been furthered by the metrical and rhythmical advantage it offers.

There's a letter for you, sir, if your name be Horatio, as I am let *to know* it is. Shak., Haml., IV, 6, 11.
We shall be let *to* go home quietly. Thack., Van. Fair, I, Ch. XXXII, 347.

b) *To*, however, seems to be regularly absent in the collocations *(to be) made believe, let go, let fall, let drop, heard drop* and, perhaps, a few others, in which the two verbs form a kind of unit. Compare WENDT, Synt. des heut. Eng., I, 47; KONRAD MEIER, E. S., XXXIII, 327.

    i. Part of the fraud and deception of the slop-trade consists in the mode in which the public are *made believe* that the men working for such establishments earn more money than they do. KINGSLEY, Cheap Clothes and Nasty, (73).

    ii.° The lucky insects are *let go* their way. HOR. HUTCHINSON (Westm Gaz., No. 6228, 4c).

    °° Drop == small platform or trap-door on the gallows on which the condemned stands with the halter round his neck, and which is *let fall* under his feet. MURRAY, s. v. *drop*, 17.
This (sc. felled oak) could be *let fall* in a moment. BLACKMORE, Lorna Doone, Ch. XXXVII, 219.

    °°° The general sentiment was that the incident should be *let drop*. G. ELIOT, Dan. Der., I, Ch. VI, 88.
The smallest pin could be *heard drop*. Lit. World, 1888, 9 Nov. 381.
Not only a pin, even a dead mosquito, might have been *heard drop*. DOR. GERARD, Exotic Martha, Ch. XVIII, 217.

c) For the rest exceptions from the general rule are very rare.
After tea I am *made sing* some fal la la of a ditty. EATON STANNARD BARRETT, The Heroine, Let. I.

Practice after the Conjunctions *but, as* and *than.*

44. The bare infinitive is regularly used after *but* and its synonyms *except* and *save,*

a) after the phrases *I cannot but, I cannot choose but,* and *I cannot help but,* and their variations for tense, number and person. The two last phrases are now more or less archaic or, at least, unusual in ordinary Standard English. For illustration of *I cannot but* + infinitive see also Ch. I, 35, Obs. IV.

    i. I cannot but *admire* his courage. MASON, Eng. Gram.³¹, § 194.

    ii. Yond same cloud cannot choose but *fall* by pailfuls. SHAK., Temp., II, 2, 23.
He cannot choose but *break*. id., Merch., III, I, 120.
I believe that she could not choose but *adore* him with all her heart. DICK., Cop., Ch. VII, 46a.
He could not choose but *love* her. MEREDITH, Ord. of Rich. Fev., Ch. XXV, 186.
Thus also in: You shall not choose but *drink* before you go. SHAK., Taming of the Shrew V, 1, 12.

iii. We could not help but *love* each other. Hall Caine, The Christian, IV, Ch. XV, 282.
He could not help but *see* them. Hugh Walpole, Jeremy, Ch. XI, 2, 272.
A cynic ... couldn't help but *mention* that last Saturday 10.000 people paid £ 50.000 to see a polo game at Hurlingham. Graph., No 2691, 770.a

b) when preceded by a construction with the bare infinitive *do* as part of a complex predicate.

i. What must Amelia do, but *remind* her brother of a promise made last Easter holidays? Thack., Van. Fair, I, Ch. IV, 28.
What does Fanny do, but *fall* into a deep melancholy? id., Virg., Ch. LXXXIV, 894.
Pressed by such arguments as these what could a weak old man do but *yield*? Trol., Barch. Tow., Ch. LII, 456.

ii. I can't do anything hardly, except *write*. Dick., Bleak House, Ch. IV, 28.
There are women ... who can't do a blessed thing except *write* letters W. J. Locke, Stella Maris, Ch. I, 9.
I'll do anything else to show my gratitude except *marry* the daughter Williamson, Lord Loveland, Ch. XIII, 121.

c) when preceded by certain negative collocations with *to do*, such as *he does nothing, he never does anything, there is nothing to be done.*

i. He does nothing but *laugh*. Mason, Eng. Gram.⁵¹, § 117.
He had done nothing but *talk* to his tutor. Thack., Pend. I, Ch VII, 80
You have done nothing but *flirt* with him. Mrs. Wood, East Lynne, I, 181, T.
If I had done nothing else in my life but *bring* them together, I should not have lived in vain. Lytton, Night and Morn., 192, T.
Unless I had taken the life of Trabb's boy on that occasion, I really do not even now see what I could have done save *endure*. Dick., Great Expect., Ch. XXX, 293.

ii. You never did anything in your life except *make* yourself agreeable Mar. Crawf., Kath. Laud., I, Ch. I, 11, T.

iii. There is apparently nothing to be done for the present except *bring* opinion to bear upon the more obstinate of the masters. Westm. Gaz., No 6353, 1c.

Thus also in: He does everything but *attend* to his own business Mason, Eng. Gram.⁵¹, § 535. (= He does not attend to his own business.)

45. a) For the rest the prepositional infinitive is used after *but* practically to the exclusion of the infinitive without *to*. Note that one and the same idea underlies the idioms illustrated by the first four groups of the following quotations:

i. There was something extremely provoking in this obstinately pacific system; it left Brom no alternative but *to draw* upon the funds of rustic waggery in his disposition. Wash. Irv., Sketch-Bk., XXXII, 357

i. He had no alternative but *to state*, boldly and distinctly, that he had been required to eat cold meat. Dick., Pickw., Ch. XXXVII, 344.
ii. She had ... nothing for it but to suffer Joe *to give* her hand a gentle squeeze. id., Barn. Rudge, Ch. XXII, 85 b.
There was nothing for it but *to pay*. Thack., Pend., I, Ch. XX, 210.
There was nothing for it but *to submit*. Mrs. Ward, The Mating of Lydia, I, Ch. II, 31.
iii. I have no choice but *to accept* the fact. Rid. Hag., Mees. Will, Ch. XXI, 225.
M. van Ghent had no choice but *to follow*. Marj. Bowen, I will maintain, I, Ch. XI, 130.
iv. What was left to them but *to drink* and get merry, or to drink and get angry? G. Eliot, Sil. Marn., I, Ch. III, 25.
v. What did she want in life, but *to see* the lad prosper? Thack., Pend., I, Ch. II, 81.
I want nothing but *to lie* here till I die. Wm. Brant, St Kath., Ch. II.
vi. We had no duties provided for us save *to eat* and sleep. Trol. in Oceana, Ch. II, 31.
vii. There remains no more but *to thank* you for your courteous attention. Murray, s. v. *but*.
viii. What could poor Jane expect but *to be married* for her money? Ans. and Ed. Castll, Diamond cut Paste, II, Ch. II, 134.

The following is the only exception that has come to hand:
You have no choice but *marry* Doris now. W. C. Smith, Kildrostan, 77.)

b) Infinitives which are distinctly final in function are, naturally, preceded by *to*.
He hath never spoken a word, save *to ask* for his food and his reckoning Scott, Kenilw., Ch. I, 18.
The landlord apparently is to do nothing except *to sell* such land as he desires to part with. Westm. Gaz., No. 6353, 2 a.

When the notion of purpose is vague, the necessity of placing *to* before the infinitive is not felt. Thus variable practice may be observed in the construction instanced in the following quotations:
i. They have nothing to do but *enjoy* themselves. Murray, s. v. *enjoy*, 2, b.
ii. I am sure we in England had nothing to do but *to fight* the battle out. Thack., Virg., Ch. LXXXIV, 891.
Do you think we have nothing to do but *to eat* your fish? Con. Doyle, Refugees, 305. T.

46. *a)* The infinitive standing after the conjunction *as* is normally preceded by *to*. For illustration see also Ch. XVIII, 28, a, c and d.
I asked the carrier to be so good as *to reach* me my pocket handkerchief again. Dick., Cop., Ch. V, 32 a.

) Murray, s. v. *but*, 4, c.

b) Dickens has a trick of occasionally dropping *to* after *as* as a correlative of *so*. For the rest this practice seems to be exceedingly rare in Late Modern English.

> If you'll be so good as *give* me your keys, my dear, I'll attend to all this sort of thing in future. Dick., Cop., Ch. IV, 24 b.
> If he was to make so bold as *say* a word to me, I should slap his face ib., Ch. VIII, 54 b.
> May I tell her as you doesn't see no hurt in t, and as you'll be so kind as *take* charge on t. Mas r Davy? ib., Ch. IV, 391 b.
> Would you be so kind as *see* me? id., D. se., Ch. XII, 111.
> You chose to be so obliging as *give* it (sc. the money) me. G. Eliot, Sil. Marn., I, Ch. III, 24.

47. *a)* After *than* the infinitive normally stands without *to*, when it corresponds to another infinitive without *to* in the same grammatical function.

> I had rather wink than *look* on thee. Shak., Two Gent, V, 2, 14.
> I will drink a round with your guests with all my heart, rather than be termed a mar-feast. Scott, Kenilw., Ch. I, 20.
> For my part I would rather be damned with Plato and Lord Bacon, than *go* to Heaven with Paley and Malthus. Shelley, Pref. to Prom Unbound.
> I had rather err with Plato than *be* right with Horace. id., Essays, II, 155 (?).
> A man might do worse than *make* happy two of the best creatures in the world. Thack., Pend., I, Ch. XXVII, 289.
> Ilfracombe would die sooner than *part* from me, and I would die a thousand deaths sooner than *part* from him. Flor. Marryat, A Bankrupt Heart, I, 44, T.
> I think you can't do better than *go*. Kingsl., It is never too late to mend, I, Ch. VI, 63, T.
> He would die sooner than *yield*. Swift, N. E. Gr., § 2322.

Thus also when *than* depends on *other* or *otherwise*.

> i. How could I have done other than *accept* him? Trol., Framl. Pars., Ch. XXXV, 350.
> I could not do other than *ask* Miss Roberts to my house. ib., Ch. XLI, 399.
> It seems to us extremely unlikely that the Peers will do other than *reject* the Government's scheme. Westm. Gaz., No. 5466, 2 a.
> ii. We could not do otherwise than *obey* his orders. Norris, My Friend Jim, Ch. VIII, 55.

Instances of the alternative practice, sometimes due to the requirements of metre or rhythm, seem to occur chiefly in the older writers.

> Brutus had rather be a villager | Than *to repute* himself a son of Rome | Under these hard conditions as this time | Is like to lay upon us. Shak., Jul. Cæs., I, 2, 172.

---
[1]) Murray, s. v. *rather*, II, 9, d.

By heaven, I had rather coin my heart, | And drop my blood for drachmas, than to *wring* | From the hard hands of peasants their vile trash | By any indirection. ib., IV, 3, 72.

I had rather be a doorkeeper in the house of my God, than *to dwell* in the tents of wickedness. Bible, Psalm, LXXXIV, 10.

Nothing could touch me nearer than *to see* that generous worthy gentleman afflicted. Farquhar, Recr. Of., II, 2. (269).

I cannot do better than *to try* to give you an idea of our modern industrial system. Bellamy, Looking Backward, 33.

She tried to reconcile herself to the idea that she might do worse than *to accept* for a while the harsh shelter of the work-house. G. Moore, Esth. Waters, Ch. XVIII, 115.

b) When the corresponding infinitive is preceded by *to*, usage is variable, the tendency being, perhaps, rather to use the prepositional than the bare infinitive.

   i. I would advise you to employ an honest and respectable house in London, rather than *to have* recourse to the Oxbridge tradesmen. Thack., Pend. I, Ch. XVIII, 186.

It is better to exceed a little with a friend, than *to observe* the strictest regimen, and eat alone. Lytton, My Novel, II, XI, Ch. III, 263.

It appears to me to be preferable to retain the classic names for these feet rather than *to try* and invent new titles for them. Tom Hood, Versification, 24.

Better to be a lonely woman all your life than *to marry* a man whom you have never loved. Walt. Besant, Bell of St. Paul's, II, Ch. XIX, 107. T.

   ii. Better to dwell on the sand under His law than *fly* to the rock of human trust. Scott, Abbot, Ch. X, 92.

He chose rather to encounter the utmost fury of the storm abroad, than *stay* under the same roof with these ungrateful daughters. Lamb, Tales, Lear, 158.

I thought it better to take the anthem myself than *give* it to a junior, who would be sure to make a mull of it. Mrs. Wood, The Channings, Ch. I, 4.

Sooner than *yield* he resolved to die. Swift, N. E. Gr., § 2322.

Competition is bound to increase rather than *diminish*. West. Gaz., No. 6311, 1 b.

Even when the infinitive expresses some notion of purpose or allied adverbial relation, usage is divided.

   i. Since you are in the humour to talk rather than *to sleep*. Bellamy, Looking Backward, 33.

I have nothing more to do than *to declare* our proceedings terminated. Times.

   ii. The coachman had strict orders to turn into the dirtiest side-street rather than *risk* meeting a funeral. Dor. Gerard, The Eternal Woman, Ch. II.

Do you think I had nothing better to do than *count* Paleface and Redskin, 191.

He is determined to resign sooner than *yield*. Athen, No. 4463, 528 b.

Competition is bound to increase rather than *diminish*. Westm. Gaz., No. 6311, 2 b.

48. a) When there is not a corresponding infinitive in the same grammatical function, the infinitive after *than* normally stands without *to*.

> Age and good living had disabled him from doing more than *ride* to see the hounds thrown off and make one at the hunting dinner. Wash. Irv., Sketch-Bk., X, 98.
> Rather than *disturb* him she went for a light-box and his cigar-case to his bedroom. Thack., Pend., I, Ch. XVIII, 185.
> You were raised from a stock that cast the dust of England from their feet rather than *bow down* to Baal. Cos. Doyle, Refugees, 232. T
> Rather than *remain* in the house John retired to the stable. Croker, Three Advices.
> The Norse bonders ... left Norway rather than *submit* to the overlordship of Harold Harfager. Notes and Queries.
> General Boulanger took to flight rather than *face* the personal risk of trial. Graph.
> One day he was dared by a companion to drink a glass of beer, and rather than *be called* a coward he did so. Punch, No. 3674, 413 b.

Thus also after *else*.

> Since her interview with the signora she had done little else than *think* about Mr. Arabin. Trol., Barch. Tow., Ch. XLVIII, 427.

b) The prepositional infinitive, however, seems to be all but regularly employed after:

1) *further than* in the sense of *except for, beyond*.

> The English Duke took little part in that vast siege of Lille, further than *to cover* the besieging lines. Thack., Henry Esmond, II, Ch. XIV, 275.
> You have nothing to do with the master of Thornfield further than *to receive* the salary he gives you for teaching his protégée. Ch. Bronte, Jane Eyre, Ch. XVII, 196.

2) *to know better than*. For illustration see also Ch. XVIII, 7, Note; 28, e; Ch. XXX, 7 b.

> i. I wonder old Mr. Willet, having been a married man himself, doesn't know better than *to conduct* himself as he does. Dick., Barn. Rudge, Ch. XIII, 53 b.
> They might know better than *to leave* their clocks so very lank and unprotected, surely. id., Crick., I, 4.
> I hope you know better than *to tempt* her to disobey me. R. xor., It is never too late to mend, I, Ch. I, 18.
> They would know a great deal better than *to insult* a sister of mine. Blackmore, Lorna Doone, Ch XXX, 177.
> Sir Roland knew better than *to stop*. Black's Sir Walter Scott Read., Abbot, 50.
> You ought to know better than *to encourage* a child to make herself ridiculous. Shaw, The Philanderer, II, (111).
> When you grow a little older ... you will know better than *to believe* all the gossip you hear. Mrs Ward, The Case of Rich. Meyn, II, Ch. VII, 150.

ii. "There's one of your tradesmen." — "It isn't. They know better than come to my front door." A. Bennett, The Great Advent., III, 1, (103).

Thus, probably, also after the unusual *to learn better than*.
If I let you shriek your abominable little throat hoarse, you'll learn better than *to torment* your uncle. John Habberton, Helen's Babies, 39.

c) Also when the preceding comparative modifies a noun, *than* seems to require the prepositional infinitive.
I hope you have more honour than *to quit* the service, and she more prudence than *to follow* the camp. Farquhar, Recr. Of., II, 1, (267).

Practice in Elliptical Sentences.

49. *To* is often absent before the infinitive in elliptical sentences which have the value of emotional questions.
   a) The omission seems to be regular when the subject is understood, whether the sentence corresponds to a question of the first or the second kind (Ch. VII, 3).
      i. For shame, Tony, you a man, and *behave* so! Goldsmith, She Stoops, II, (193).
      "How?" cried I, "*relinquish* the cause of truth?" id., Vic.
      Not *let* Miss Sharp dine at table! Thack., Van. Fair, I, Ch. XI. 108.
      O fie! it is wicked to talk so. Compare a poor coarse-favoured girl like me with the Queen of Heaven? Reade, The Cloist. and the Hearth, Ch. II, 18.
      What, not *know* me! Swift, N. E. Gr., § 2321.
      ii. Why, then, *wait?* Thack., Pend., I, Ch. I, 14.
      Why not *go* there myself? Swift, N. E. Gr., § 232.

   b) Also when the subject is expressed, the bare infinitive appears to be more common than the prepositional infinitive.
      i. What, I! I *love!* I *sue!* I *seek* a wife! Shak., Love's Labour's Lost, III, 191.
      "Now, madam, will you please to send your maid to fetch it?" — "I *fetch* it! the devil fetch me if I do!" Farquhar, Recr. Of., IV, 3, (320).
      Thou *put* a jape upon me, thou sodden-brained gull? Scott, Kenilw., Ch. IV, 43.
      I *think* the worse of him? Dick., Bleak House, Ch. XVII, 144.
      My nephew *marry* a tragedy queen! Thack., Pend., I, Ch. I, 15.
      A passenger *take* the whole cabin and not *pay?* Gracious mercy, are you a fool, Captain Franks? id., Virg., Ch. I, 3.
      ii. And I *to sigh* for her! *to watch* for her! | *To pray* for her! Shak., Love's Labour's Lost, III, 202.
      Psaw! this fellow here *to interrupt* us! Goldsmith, She Stoops.
      You *to be* low-spirited. You! Dick., Bleak House, Ch. XVII, 145.
      I *to marry* before my brother, and leave him with none to take care of him! Blackmore, Lorna Doone, Ch. XXX, 178.

Note. In non-emotional elliptical questions *to* is not dispensed with, any more than in full questions. Thus it could not possible be omitted in such a sentence as:
What to do at Ventnor? which may be understood to be short for *What are visitors to do at Ventnor?* or *What are visitors recommended to do at Ventnor?* etc.

What *to do* with our boys? Graph., No. 2691, 773.

50. The prepositional infinitive is regularly used in elliptical sentences which have the value of a complex sentence consisting of a subordinate statement and a head-sentence, the latter being understood or represented by a simple word group of an emotional description. The subject is mostly understood, but may also be expressed.

i. Wisdom! *to leave* his wife, *to leave* his babes, | His mansion and his titles in a place | From whence himself does fly? Shak., Macb., IV, 2, 6 (approximately equivalent to: Is it an act of wisdom that he should leave his wife, etc.?).
O, may Heaven's eternal fury light upon him and his! Thus *to rob* me of my child! Goldsmith, Vic., Ch. XVII, (341) (approximately equivalent to: What a heinous offence was it that he should thus rob me of my child!).
Oh God! *to hear* the insect on the leaf pronouncing on the too much life among his hungry brothers in the dust! Dick., Christm. Car., III, 62.
To think of your turning book-hunter! Lytton, Caxt., XVII, Ch. I, 450.
(He) had an objection to dramatic entertainments, and he had never yet seen a play. But Shakespeare! — but *to go* with Mrs. Pendennis in her carriage, and *to sit* a whole night by her side! — he could not resist the idea of so much pleasure. Thack., Pend., I, Ch. VI, 69.
Oh, for shame, Hans! — *to speak* in that way of Mr. Deronda! G. Eliot, Dan. Der., III, VI, Ch. XLVII, 52.
O mother, mother, *to think*, that you should have turned against us! Mrs. Craswl., Kath. Land., I, Ch. VII, 137.
The Pheasant: Fancy reducing me to the level of a rabbit, just as if I were ground vermin! The Fox: And *to talk* about exterminating me! Westm. Gaz., No. 7595, 4.

ii. That dear father, who was once so kind, so warm-hearted, so ready to help either man or beast in distress, *to murder!* Mrs. Gask., Mary Barton, Ch. XXII, 230.

Of especial interest are infinitives of the above description which express what is the subject of an idle wish.

Oh! but *to breathe* the breath Of the cowslip and the primrose sweet! Tom Hood, The Song of the shirt, IX.
Oh! *to be* in England Now that April's there! Browning, Home Thoughts from Abroad, I.
Oh! *to have been* there! Onions, Adv. Eng. Synt., § 42.

51. In elliptical sentences that are co-ordinately related with a preceding sentence with a finite verb, the infinitive may stand with or without *to*.

i. Most senceless man he, that himselfe doth hate | To love another. Lo then for thine ayd | Here take thy lovers token on thy pate. So they *to fight*. SPENSER, Faery Queene, I, VI, XLVII. (The Clar. Press editor changes *to* into *two*.) Five days we do allot thee, for provision | To shield thee from diseases of the world; | And on the sixth *to turn* thy hated back | Upon our kingdom. SHAK., Lear, I, 1, *178*.
But on this condition that she should follow him, and he not *to follow* her. BACON, Adv. of Learn.[1])
"Haven't got your Coke upon Littleton in your waistcoat-pocket, have you?" No, Joseph hadn't; and, him *to be* sitting with us of the Inner Bar! Punch, 1888, 10 Nov., 228 a²) (*him* vulgar for *he*).

ii. Men talk of your being under some special protection; nay, stare not like a pig that is stuck, mon, thou canst not dance in a net and they not see thee. SCOTT, Kenilw., Ch. IV, 41.
Indeed, do not things happen under our eyes, and we not see them? THACK., Virg., Ch. LXI, 734.

For discussion of the above idiom, viewed, however, from a different angle, see also KELLNER, Hist. Outl., § 400; STOF., Stud., A VII, 44 ff; DUBISLAV, Beitr. zur hist. Synt. des Eng. I; EINENKEL, Hist. Synt., § 4.

In passing it may here be observed that the first and the third of the Mod. Eng. passages quoted by KELLNER differ, in grammatical function, from the second (See the Note below). Moreover the quotation from THACKERAY, Virg., IV, 3 (taken, I understand, from the Tauchnitz Edition) is not in harmony with the wording of THACKERAY, according to the version of the Oxford Thackeray, edited by SAINTSBURY, in which the passage in question runs thus, "And the fellow began to roar with laughter, and all the girls to titter". See Ch. LXXII, page 758.

Note. The infinitive is distinctly final in meaning and, accordingly, preceded by *to* in such elliptical constructions as:

Ten years afterwards the caul was put up in a raffle down in our part of the country, to fifty members at half-a-crown a head, the winner *to spend* five shillings. DICK., Cop., Ch. I, 2 a.

52. a) Infinitives stand without *to* when used as a kind of echo of a preceding infinitive, whether bare or prepositional.

i. "Nephew!" returned the uncle, sternly, "keep Christmas in your own way, and let me keep it in mine." — "*Keep* it!" repeated Scrooge's nephew. "But you don't keep it." DICK., Chrisrm. Car., I.
ii. "But the enemy has thought fit to withdraw, I think." — "*Withdraw!* oons, sir, what d'ye mean by withdraw?" FARQUHAR, Recr. Of., IV, 2, (511).

[1] EINENKEL, Hist. Synt., § 4
[2] STOF., Stud., A. VII, § 45.

b) A bare infinitive as a similar expression of excited feelings, not a mere echo, however, of an infinitive, but rather a reflex of the preceding statement, may be seen in:

He was a terrible old fellow, was Lobbs, when his pride was injured or his blood was up. *Swear.* Such trains of oaths would come rolling and pealing over the way, ... that [etc.]. Dick., Pickw., Ch. XVII, 151.

Repetition and Non-repetition of *to*.

53. *To* is often dispensed with before the second of two successive infinitives whose grammatical functions are identical.

   a) This suppression is especially frequent when the two infinitives are connected by *and* and form a kind of unit, or are merely meant to denote different elements of one and the same action or state. In the first case the second infinitive is often, from a logical point of view, related to the first as object or adverbial adjunct, the connexion by *and* being the result of hendiadys. See my Treatise on this subject in Neophilologus, II, III and IV.

   i. Here's a lady possessing a moderate independence, who wants to board and *lodge* with a quiet, cheerful family. Dick., Chuz., Ch. XXXVI, 288a.
   The rest of the world are in a conspiracy against him, which it requires all his wit to battle and *turn* to his own proper aggrandisement and profit. Lytton, My Novel, II, XI, Ch. I, 250.
   Tom told me to be sure and *remember* the rabbits every day. G. Eliot, Mill, I, Ch. IV, 24.

   ii. There cometh one mightier than I after me, the latchet of whose shoes I am not worthy to stoop down and *unloose*. Bible, Mark, I, 7.
   He concluded that his wisest course would be to turn and *face* his pursuers. Goldsmith, Vic., Ch. XXXI, (469).
   On Sundays it was his duty to accompany her and *carry* her bible. Wash. Irv., Dolf Heyl. (Stol., Handl., I, 109.)

   The bare infinitive is practically regular when connected by *and* with certain verbs which in the infinitive and the imperative normally require hendiadys, such as *to try, to write; to call, to come, to go, to send.*

   i. Her business here on earth is to try and *get* a rich husband. Thack., Newc., II, Ch. VII, 81.
   What business had she to be so ungrateful and to try and *thwart* Philip in his thoughtful wish of escorting them? Mrs. Gask., Sylv. Lov., Ch. III, 44.
   Why don't you try and *do* pictures? Mrs. Alex., A Life Interest, I, Ch. II, 42. T.

   ii. That nasty Lightfoot feels it his duty to write and *tell* me what is in reserve for him. Dick., Our Mut. Friend, I, Ch. IV, 55. T

It was settled that I was to write to my father and a*sk* him to come over. Mrs. Gask., Cranf., Ch. XIV, 256.
iii. Tell the boy to call and *see* me in a day or two. Morley Roberts, Time and Thomas Waring, Ch. VII, 70.
iv. Here is a family, ... a quiet cheerful family who want exactly such a lady to come and *live* with them. Dick., Chuz., Ch. XXXVI, 288 a.
It was too far for people to come and *dine* with us. Marryat, Olla Podrida.
If he likes to come to me and *beg* my pardon for his rudeness, that's another matter. Keble Howard, One of the Family, I, Ch. III, 52.
v. The child ... preferred to go and *take* refuge at Pen's knee. Thack., Pend., I, Ch. XXXII, 344.
He passed the door a dozen times before he had the courage to go up and *knock*. Dick., Christm. Car.⁵, V, 108.
My father and mother want you to go and *see* them them for a whole day. Sweet, Old Chap'el.
vi. I should like to send and *get* my sketches. Rudy. Kipl., The Light that failed, Ch. III, 40.
vii. I venture to ask you to stay here, and *aid* me in consulting with Baron Levy. Lytton, My Novel, II, X, Ch. XXV, 243.
I asked you to stay and *aid* us by your counsel. ib., 245.
If one of you gentlemen will stay and *dine* with Mr. Higginbotham, it will greatly assist the effect of his medicine. ib., II., XI, Ch. IV, 263.

b) Suppression of *to* is also the rule when, although distinctly two actions are thought of, the second infinitive is the headsword of another infinitive with *to*.

The main object of practical grammar is to give — or rather, *help* to give — a mastery of foreign languages either living or dead. Sweet, N. E. Gr., § 9.
Passengers are particularly cautioned not to open the door, nor *attempt* to alight from the carriages till the train is at rest at the platform. Notice in London Trains.

c) Sometimes the non-repetition of *to* is, clearly, due to a desire of terseness or rhythm, or to both.

"My friends!" said Mr. Pecksniff in reply, "my duty is to build, not *speak*; to act, not *talk*; to deal with marble, stone and brick, not language". Dick., Chuz., Ch. XXXV, 281 b.
I do not, just now, like to think or *speak* about it. ib., Ch. XXVI, 287 a.
It's dreadful to see death and not *weep*. Sarah Grand, Our manifold Nature, 109. T.
You should hear my poor patient talk of it (sc. the Brent)... — you would not know whether to laugh or *cry*. Lytton, My Novel, II, XI, Ch. IV, 266.

The requirements of metre are, evidently, responsible for the suppression of *to* in:

They love to see the flaming forge | And *hear* the bellows roar. Longi., Vil. Blacks.

d) In a great many cases no reason can be given for the suppression of *to* beyond economy of language, which often becomes manifest in the rejection of what SWIFT (N. E. Gr., § 58) calls form-words, words, that is, which do not convey any idea by themselves. It is only natural that anything like consistency, or uniformity of practice, in the repetition of *to* where it is not needed is far to seek even with one and the same writer. Thus it would be difficult to account for the varied practice observed in the following quotations taken from a few consecutive pages of one and the same composition, in which, however, the cases of non-repetition outnumber those of repetition.

i. She was not prepared to betray the one, and *entrap* the other. LYTTON, My Novel, II, X, Ch. XX, 242.
He had only time to rise and *withdraw* to the window. ib.
All we can do to-day is to remove my sister, and *let* the execution proceed ib., 244.
Shame on me if I could be mean enough to boast of love, and *enforce* a suit, at such a moment. ib., 247.

ii. He wrote a brief line to Levy, charging him quietly to dismiss the execution, and *to come* to Frank's rooms with the necessary deeds. ib., 247.
I have lived to feel the truth of your words, and *to bless* the lesson. ib., II, XI, Ch. II, 256.
I have so much to ask you, and *to talk* about. ib., 258.
Now to gain time, and *to baffle* the usurer. ib., II, XI, Ch. VI, 272.

54. For the rest it may be observed that, when none of the above considerations make themselves felt, there is a tendency to repeat *to*.

He looked earnestly in my face, and began to fancy a resemblance to his sister, and *to think* I might be her child. MARY ANN LAMB, The Sailor Uncle, 2 (The World's Clas.)
Frank, however, did not pause to notice her countenance — *to hear* her dignified salutation. LYTTON, My Novel, II, X, Ch. XXV, 241.
Many a time he (sc. the Prince Consort) must have felt inclined to renounce it (sc. the scheme of the Great Exhibition), or at least *to regret* that he had ever taken it up. MC. CARTHY, Short. Hist., Ch. IX, 108.

Thus naturally in the case of the second infinitive standing in adversative relation to the first.

I came not to upbraid, but *to serve* and *to free* you. SCOTT, Kenilw., Ch. IV, 45
He told Dolf never to despair, but *to throw* physic to the dogs. WASH. IRV. Dolf Heyl. (STOF. Handl., I, 138).

55. a) In a succession of three or more infinitives in identical grammatical function *to* is mostly repeated before each of them. The following quotation may be considered to represent normal practice:

The Tories must come into office free to raise taxation, *to defend* our own markets, and *to meet* the great Dominions in their demand for reciprocal trade. Eng. Rev., No. 32, 624.

b) It is only natural that for rhetorical reasons this practice is not seldom deviated from.

To thrust on his boots — *change* his dressing-robe for a frock-coat — *snatch* at his hat, gloves and cane — *break* from Spendquick — *descend* the stairs — a flight at a leap — *gain* the street — *throw* himself into a cabriolet; all this was done before his astounded visitor could even recover his breath enough to ask "What's the matter?" LYTTON, My Novel, II, X, Ch. XXIV, 240.

TENSE AND VOICE OF THE INFINITIVE
Introductory Observations.

56. Like the gerund and the present participle, the infinitive is capable of expressing the distinctions of tense and voice.

57. The infinitive shows the distinction of tense only when its time-sphere differs from that of the predication with which it is connected.

   a) In the case of its time-sphere being anterior to that of the latter, this is now done by the auxiliary *to have*, mutative verbs using *to be* for this purpose in earlier stages of the language: Imperfect Infinitive: *to give;* Perfect Infinitive: *to have given.*

   In our island the Latin appears never *to have superseded* the old Gaelic speech. MAC., Hist., I, Ch. I. 4. T.
   It was the misfortune of my friend, however, *to have embarked* his property in large speculations. WASH. IRV., Sketch-Bk., IV, 26.

   The tense of the infinitive is not affected by a change of time-sphere in the predication with which it is connected. Compare Gerund, 9, Obs. II; Participles, 3, Note β. See also Tense, 12, c.

   He toils (toiled *or* will toil) *to earn* a living.

   b) The ordinary auxiliaries of the future tense, *shall* and *will*, having no infinitive, relative futurity is mostly left unexpressed.

   I was afraid *to sleep*, even if I had been inclined. DICK., Great Expect., Ch. II, 20.
   And there, in daily doubt | Whether *to live* or *die*, for many a week | Hid from the wide world's rumour by the grove | Of poplars with their noise of falling showers, | And ever-tremulous aspen-leaves, he lay. TEN., Lanc. and El., 519.

Note. It stands to reason that the numerous secondary expedients to express modified futurity, such as *to be going, to be about, to be near, to be in act,* etc., discussed in my treatise about Tense (68—71), would sometimes be available to supply the want.

The weather seems *to be going to change.*
He seemed *to be about to leave* the room.
The letter seemed *to be about to be dropped* into the pillar-box.

About + infinitive, whether active or passive, occurs rather frequently as a constituent of an undeveloped clause.

No one could have had the slightest foreboding of anything *about to happen.* Mc. Carthy, Hist. of Our Own Times, 2, 92.¹)
A remnant of one (sc. a fleet) *about to be put up* to auction. Ruskin, Time and Tide, 194.¹)

The attributive use of *about* + passive infinitive seems to be very rare.

The *about-to-be-released* prisoner tried to explain that Irish Unionists were loyal to England. The New Statesman, No. 95, 403 b.

58. The distinction of voice is expressed by means of the auxiliary *to be*: Imperfect Passive Infinitive: *to be given*; Perfect Passive Infinitive: *to have been given.*

i. Mrs. Hood begged *to be left* to herself. Gissing, A Life's Morning, Ch. V, 82
ii. Now Joe, examining this iron with a smith's eye, declared it *to have been filed* asunder some time ago. Dick., Great Expect., Ch. XVI, 145.
His crime was *to have been born* in Germany. Gissing, Tatterdemalion, I, IV, 81
She was alleged *to have been dismissed.* Ill. Lond News, No. 3859, 446 a.

Tense-shifting in Infinitive constructions.

59. It is a well-known fact that an Englishman is inclined to say *I intended to have come,* but [etc.] rather than *I had intended* (= *should have intended*) *to come,* but [etc.], i. e. to express the notion of completed action in this combination not in the finite verb, where it logically belongs, but in the following infinitive. This remarkable tense-shifting, as it may be called, is to be observed in a good many similar combinations of very common occurrence and has, naturally, excited the interest of many scholars, and been the subject of not a few grammatical disquisitions. See Stoffel, Taalstudie IX; Hodgson, Errors in the Use of English, 98 ff; Horn, Herrig Archiv, CXIV, 370; A. Schmidt, Shak. Lex., s. v. *have,* 1; The King's English, 154 f; Mätzner, Eng. Gram.³, III, 63 f; Abbot, Shak. Gram.³, § 360.

¹) Jespersen, Mod. Eng. Gram., 15, 89

60. a) Tense-shifting of the above description is unavoidable when the infinitive is connected with any of certain defective verbs which have no past participle and, consequently, no pluperfect conditional, such as *can, may, must, ought* (or *should*).

    i. If I had not been so foolish as to enter into that agreement with Messrs. Meeson, I *could have got* the money by selling my new book easily enough. RID. HAG., Mees. Will, Ch. IV, 38. (with which compare the sequel of this sentence: and I *should have been able* to take Jeannie abroad.)

    ii. They *might have been* great people in the country, they preferred being little people in town; they *might have chosen* friends among persons of respectability and rank, they preferred being chosen as acquaintance by persons of 'ton'. LYTTON.

    iii. It would have been a severe pang to lose you; but it *must have been*. You would have thrown yourself out of all good society. I *must have given you up*. JANE AUSTEN, Emma, Ch. VII, 51. T.
But for him I *must have died* abroad. DICK., Chuz., Ch. XLIII, 337 b.

    iv. I *ought to have married*; yes I *should ha' married* long ago. GISSING, A Life's Morn., Ch. IX, 137.

    Note. α) When the present indicative *must* is followed by a perfect infinitive, there is, of course, no tense-shifting.

    The spirit *must have heard* him thinking. DICK., Christm. Car.
Experience, no doubt, served him there; but he *must have had* an instinct that it was dangerous with one so sensitive. GALSW., Beyond, Ch. IV, 42.

    β) In passing it may here be observed that *could* when followed by a perfect infinitive is always a preterite conditional. Such a sentence as Hij zei dat hij niet had kunnen komen cannot, therefore, be translated by °*He said that he could not have come*, the correct translation being *He said that he had not been able to come*.

b) The same tense-shifting is regularly observed in connection with *will*, whose past participle is used only by way of exception, and *need*, which, as has been observed in 7, resembles, in its grammatical function, the verbs mentioned in a). See also 7, b, 3; 10; 11, b; and 12, c.

He beat me then as if he *would have beaten* me to death. DICK., Cop., Ch. IV, 29 b.
Poor Betty!... she *need not have given* way to tears on the door-step. GALSWORTHY, Beyond, I, Ch. I, 1.

c) Also the construction with the archaic or dialectal *durst* regularly exhibits tense-shifting. For the rest ordinary literary English has the logical construction *had dared* or *should* (or *would*) *have dared* + imperfect infinitive, colloquial English, apparently, favouring *daren't* + perfect infinitive.

i. When Cæsar lived he *durst not* thus *have moved* me. SHAKS., Jul Cæs., IV, 3, 58.

ii.² Two months ago I should have scouted as mad or drunk the man who had *dared tell* me the like. RUDY. KIPL., The Phantom Rickshaw, 9.

*² Hugh was not the only one she *would have dared* tell her story. Flor. MARRYAT, A Bankrupt Heart, II, 21 T.

iii. You know you *daren't have given* the order to charge the bridge if you hadnt seen us on the other side. SHAW, The Man of Destiny, (211) I.

61. Obs. I. It will have been observed that the verb used in connection with the perfect infinitive in the above combinations stands in the conditional. But, as has already been stated in my treatise about Mood (14, Obs. III), the notion of conditionality is apt to get obliterated in the speaker's consciousness when, as is often the case, the protasis of the conditional sentence is understood. As there is no formal difference between the preterite conditional and the preterite indicative, except only in the case of the verb *to be*, this leads to the conditional becoming indistinguishable from the indicative. The verbs *ought* and *should* have even practically ceased to be used as conditionals, unless followed by a perfect infinitive, and this applies more or less to *must* as well.

II. Another point to which attention may be drawn in this connection is that the construction described above, like all pluperfect conditionals, implies non-fulfilment of what is denoted by the main verb of the predicate. When the predicate is negatived, the case is, of course, reversed, fulfilment being, in this case, understood.

III. Tense-shifting never takes place with most words or phrases which often serve as substitutes for the above verbs in some of their various shades of meaning, such as *to be able, to be allowed, to be obliged, to have.*

An important exception is formed by the verb *to be*, which, as has been shown in Ch. I, 29—31, is often used to express some weakened form of coercion or obligation, notions which it has in common with *must* and *ought.* The notion of conditionality not making itself felt, the indicative is used instead of the conditional.

At ten I had an appointment under a certain person's window, who *was to have been looking* at the moon at that moment. THACK., Sam. Titm., Ch. I, 9.

She *was to have dined* with us here the day after her father's death. GISSING, A Life's Morn., Ch. XIV, 203.

She *was to have married* a Member of Parliament, ib., Ch. XXVI, 345. The monument *was to have been surmounted* by an equestrian statue. Times.

Also when the meaning of *to be* is faded to the extent that it is a mere copula, the same tense-shifting may occasionally be observed.

Babie performed her mistress's command with the grace which was naturally to have been expected. Scott, Bride of Lam., Ch. III, 46. (= might (or could) have been expected).

62. *a)* In the second place tense-shifting is unavoidable in combinations in which the infinitive is connected with the phrases mentioned in 32: *I had better (best, liefer or liever, rather or sooner), I had as lief or lieve (as soon, as good, as well), I had need, I were better (best).*

Arthur *had better have taken* a return-ticket. Thack., Pend., II, Ch. XXXVI, 380.
I *had as lief have heard* the night-raven. Shak., Much Ado, II, 3, 84.
I *had almost as well never have been* a child. B. Baxton, Selections, XXVII¹).
The man who reviews his own life . . . *had need to have been* a good man indeed, if he would be spared the sharp consciousness of many talents neglected. Dick., Cop., Ch. XLII, 301 b.

b) The same construction is regularly observed in connection with the more or less archaic phrase *had like*, shaped, on the analogy of *had rather*, etc., from *was like*. See Ch. II, 36, Obs. II. In passing it may be observed that *had like* + imperfect infinitive seems to be non-existent.

I *had like to have been picked* up by a cruiser under false colours. Farquhar, Recruit. Offic., V, 7, (349).
This intrigue *had like to have ended* in my utter destruction. Swift, Gul., I, (128 a).
Poor man, poor man! It *had like to ha' killed* him when she died. G. Eliot, Scenes, II, Ch. I, 82.
It *had like to have cost* the nursery-maid her place. Thack., Fitzboodle, Pref., 209.
I *had like to have burst* out crying. Reade, The Cloister and the Hearth, Ch. IX, 47.

Note. *Was like* + perfect infinitive seems to be very rare: the following is the only instance that has come to hand.

The vivacity of this good lady, as it helped Edward out of this scrape, *was like to have drawn* him into one or two others. Scott, Wav., Ch. LXI, 152 a.

63. The sense-shifting, which is unavoidable with the verbs that have no past participle, is often extended to a good many verbs that are in no way deficient in their conjugation, and accordingly, give no urgent occasion for the anomaly. In the case of some of them, i. e. such as express, or at least suggest, some movement of the human will, the adaptability to the peculiar

¹) Murray, s. v. *have*, 22.

construction may be due to their bearing some analogy to *will*. This, for example, applies distinctly to *to intend, to mean, to want, to wish, to like*. But it cannot be denied that the number includes some others which can hardly be said to express any such notion.

It will be observed that the absence of the notion of conditionality in the speaker's mind mostly causes the construction of the periphrastic conditional with *should* or *would* to be rejected, the verb *to like* being a notable exception. Indeed a strong case might be made out for the preterite, as opposed to the pluperfect, being an indicative.

On the whole the construction with the shifted tense appears to be more in favour with most writers than the alternative. The negative *not*, however, causes the latter to be preferred.

to expect. Mr. Speaker, I *expected* from the former language and positive promises, of . . . the Chancellor of the Exchequer, *to have seen* the Bank paying in gold and silver. WILLIAM COBBETT,[1])

to hope. i. I *hoped to have seen* him on the green to-night. DICK., Old Cur. Shop, Ch. XXIV, 91a.

I *hoped to have left* them in perfect safety, and then *to have quitted* Paris. id., Tale of Two Cities, III, Ch. IX, 347.

He (sc. the Duke of Mayenne) *hoped to have been elected* king. WEBB, Note to Mac., Ivry, 17.

ii. I *had not hoped to see* you again so soon. SHER., Riv., III, 2, (242).

I *had hoped to gather* some traditionary anecdotes of the bard from these ancient chroniclers. WASH. IRV., Sketch-Bk., XXVI, 261.

When he went away, she *had hoped to see* him often again; but she never did. MISS BURNETT, Little Lord.

to intend. i. I *intended* only *to have teased* him three days and a half, and now I've lost him for ever. SHER., Riv., I, 2.

For that reason I *did not intend to have sent* you the following sonnet. KEATS, Let. (Times, Lit. Sup., No. 996, 97d).

I *intended to have written* a line to you. MRS. GASK., Life of Ch. Brontë, 299.

ii. When Harry Warrington was taken by those bailiffs, I *had intended to tell* you how the good Mrs. Lambert, hearing of the boy's mishap, had flown to her husband, and had begged, implored, insisted, that her Martin should help him THACK., Virg., Ch. LI, 525.

The amiable old gentleman . . . *had intended to leave* the whole to the Royal Humane Society. DICK., Nich. Nick., Ch. I, 2a.

I *had intended to go* to London at once. WATTS DUNTON, Aylwin, VII, Ch. III, 254.

to like. i. I *should like to have given* him something. DICK., Christm Car., II, 41.

---

[1]) STOF., Taalst., IX.

I *should like to have been* by to give Lady Clavering my arm if she had need of it. Thack., Pend, I, Ch. XXXVII, 397.
I *should like to have been* Shakespeare's shoeblack — just to have lived in his house, just to have worshipped him — to have run on his errands, and seen that sweet serene face. id., Eng. Hum., I, 6. T.

ii. When they were married, Pitt *would have liked to take* a hymeneal tour with his bride. Thack., Van Fair, I, Ch. XXXIV, 382.
I *should have liked to make* her a little present. ib., I, Ch. XIII, 125.
Pen, being new to the town, *would have liked to listen* to Mrs. Leary. id., Pend., I, Ch. XXVIII, 299.
Would we have liked to live with him? id., Eng. Hum., I, 6.

to mean. i. I *meant to have given* you five shillings this morning for a Christmas box, Sam. I'll give it you this afternoon, Sam. Dick., Pickw., Ch. XXX, 269.
I ought to have been a good son, and I think I *meant to have been* one. id., Bleak House, Ch. XXI, 182.
There was to be a considerable book-sale at a country-house one day's journey from London. Mr. Prickett *meant to have attended* it on his own behalf. Lytton, My Novel, I, VII, Ch. III, 441.
I *meant to have sent* them (sc. the flowers) to your room, but have been interrupted in my work. Beatr. Har., Ships, I, Ch. XV, 85.
I *meant to have gone away* before now, but I've put it off day after day. Gissing, A Life's Morn., Ch. VIII, 124.

ii. I *had meant to be* gay and careless, but the powerlessness of the strong man touched my heart to the quick. Ch. Brontë, Jane Eyre, Ch. XXXVII, 54.
I *had not meant to tell* you. El. Glyn, Halcyone, Ch. II. 19.
Halcyone *had not meant to tell* her aunt anything about Cheiron. ib. Ch. II, 21.
I *had not meant to speak* of it — but your lordship knows that all I receive from my living is given back to Church purposes. Mrs. Ward, The Case of Rich. Meyn., I, Ch. V, 107.
She *had not meant to give* them all to-day, but it seemed dreadful, when she saw how pleased they were, to leave any out, and so the whole ninety-seven had their franc each. Galsw., Tatterdemalion, I, I, 17.

to think. i. I *thought* thy bride-bed *to have deck'd*, sweet maid, | And not *to have strew'd* thy grave. Shak., Haml., V, 1, 267.
They showed her the weapon wherewith he *thought to have acted* it. Bacon, Apothegms, (165).
I ne'er *thought to have thanked* God to see my master weep. Scott, Kenilw., Ch. XII, 143.
I never *thought to have seen* this day. Thack., Van. Fair, I, Ch. XIV, 138.
I never *thought to have had* a scamp for my son, Galsw., The Country House, II, Ch. XII, 206,

ii. I *had not thought to see* thy face. Bible, Gen., XLVIII, 11.

to want. i. I *wanted to have seen* you ever so much, but I did not like to trouble you. Philips, Mrs. Bouverie, 89.

ii. Annie *had wanted to take* biscuits, but I was dead against it. Barry Pain, A Change of Rôle, Ch. I.
A year before a rich man *had wanted to marry* her. Rid. Hag., Mr. Mees. Will, Ch. III, 28.

Also *to long* and *to wish*, which express similar notions as *to want*, may possibly be construed with tense-shifting to the infinitive. No instances have, however, come to hand. The logical construction is, no doubt, the ordinary one.

i. He *would have longed to give* his arm to the fair Blanche. Thack., Pend., II, Ch. I, 8.

ii.° When Harry gave to Lord Castlewood those flourishing descriptions of the maternal estate in America, he *had not wished to mislead* his kinsman. Thack., Virg., Ch. XVI, 158.

°° I *should have wished to go* to France, but must take what I can get. Gaisw., Saint's Prog., IV, I, 354.

64. Obs. I. Besides the above we find various other predicates expressing some form of capability, compulsion or, especially, volition liable to tense-shifting to the following infinitive. Any notion of conditionality is mostly absent, insomuch that, so far as appears from the form of the preceding finite verb, the indicative is used. In the following quotations the underlying notion is one resembling that expressed by:

could + perfect infinitive: We were masters *to have taken* the steamer, instead of the diligence at Civita Vechia. Howells, Italian Journeys, 182.[1])

(It was) a glorious vision to the youth, who embraced it as a flower of beauty, and read not a feature. There were curious features of colour in her face for him *to have read*. Meredith, Ord. of Rich. Fev., Ch. XV, 98.

Those of us who feel we are clever enough *to have succeeded* at the Bar, and regret that we did not choose to pursue the fugitive prizes of that honourable and profitable calling [etc.] Times, Lit. Sup.[2])

ought to + perfect infinitive: He was not slack in testifying his displeasure to the falconer's lad, whose duty it was *to have attended* upon it (sc. his favourite bird). Scott, Abbot, Ch. IV, 41.

would + perfect infinitive: For my part, my lord, | My purpose was not *to have seen* you here; | But meeting with Solanio by the way, | He did entreat me, past all saying nay, | To come with him. Shak., Merch., III, 2, 230.

This train he laid *to have intrapped* thy life. Marlowe, Jew of Malta, V, 4.[1])

There was once a design, hinted at by Oldisworth, *to have made* him useful. Johnson.[1])

The squire was *inclined to have compounded* matters, when lo! on a sudden the wench appeared to be, as it were, at the eve of bringing forth a bastard. Fielding, Tom Jones, IV, Ch. X, 55b.

I was much *tempted to have broken* the rascal's head. Scott, Rob Roy, 9.[1])

It was my earnest wish e'er this *to have returned* to London. Thack., Sam. Titm., Ch. IX, 101.

Leslie was *going to have answered*. Mallock, The New Republic.[1])

"*Were* you *going to have walked?*" she asked presently, after a long, long silence. — "No", said John, "I was going to drive — with you". Temple Thurston, City of Beaut. Nons., Ch. XV, 121.

---

[1]) Stof., Taalst., IX.

[2]) Kruisinga, The Student's Monthly, II, No. 23.

II. Tense=shifting may also be observed in constructions with a sub=
ordinate statement, especially one standing after *to think*.

to expect: I expected, when the Right Hon. gentleman rose, that he *would have stated* what the intentions of the Government are. Westm. Gaz.
to hope: I hoped thou *shouldst have been* my Hamlet's wife. SHAK., Haml., V, 1, 266.
to think: I thought that all things *had been* savage here. id., As you like it, II, 2, 107.
I did not think you *had been* read in these matters. CONGREVE, Love for Love; III, 4, (255).
I thought you *would have been* pleased. DICK., Domb., Ch. III, 23.
I never thought Harry Warrington *would have joined* against us. THACK., Virg., Ch. XCII, 984.
I did not think we *had been* so near Scotland. SWEET, N. E. Gr., § 2247.

In a construction like the following tense=shifting would, of course, be unavoidable:

The earl would rather she *had shown* a little jealousy on the subject. FLOR. MARRYAT, A Bankrupt Heart, I, 197. T.

III. There seems to be no call for the perfect infinitive in the following quotations, no reversing import being implied.

In the meantime she worked on for certain examinations which it would benefit her *to have passed*. GISSING, A Life's Morn., Ch. V, 67.
At last he staggered to the shore, and set her down upon the bank; and he strong man he needed *to have been*, or that wild water he never would have crossed. KINGSLEY, The Heroes, II, II, 115.
The midnight train from town ... enables its travellers *to have stayed* to the very end of most theatrical performances. E. F. BENSON, Arundel, Ch. III, 56.

65. Through what appears to be careless haste, many writers have sometimes been betrayed into the error of placing a perfect infinitive after the pluperfect conditional of a finite verb. See, however, 66, Obs. III. The practice is probably due to an ex= cessive sense of the action or state indicated by the infinitive not having come into fulfilment, and a consequent desire of expressing this in the form of the predication. This redundancy of tense is met with after:

a) *to dare:* Many will feel with the writer of this beautiful passage, who would hardly *have dared to have put* their feeling into words. Mrs. OLIPHANT, The Victorian Age, I, 89¹)

b) *had better* and, probably, others of the phrases mentioned in 62. Instances appear to be very rare.

Give me the ocular proof; | Or by the worth of man's eternal soul, | Thou hadst been better have been born a dog | Than answer my waked wrath. Shak., Othello, III, 3, 362.

c) the verbs mentioned in 63. Instances appear to be rather common, especially after *to like*:

to expect: After such a victory | I *had expected to have found* in thee A cheerful spirit. Coleridge, The Death of Wallenstein, V, 1, (659).
to hope: I *had hoped to have prevailed* upon you to allow I am to accompany me. Dick., Pickw., Ch. XLIV, 408.
I *had hoped to have procured* you some oysters from Britain. Lytton, Pomp., I, Ch. III, 16b.
to like: I *should have liked to have taken* a stroll in the hayfields. Thack., Sam. Titm., Ch. I, 2.
Tom ... *would have liked to have stopped* at the Belle Savage. Hughes, Tom Brown, I, Ch. IV, 65.
He *would have liked to have hugged* his father. ib., I, Ch. IV, 67.
I *would have liked to have given* Miss Abby a good smack for sending him up such places. Em. Lawless, A Colonel of the Empire, Ch. V.
I *should have liked to have shown* you some of my little collections. Mrs. Ward, The Mating of Lydia, III, Ch. XVI, 342.
I *should have liked to have seen* him before I left the Hague. Marj. Bowen, I will maintain, II, Ch. VI, 234.
to mean: He *had meant to have taken* advantage of the unwonted softness of Egerton. Lytton, My Novel, II, IX, Ch. V, 95.
to think: I lack iniquity | Sometimes to do me service: nine or ten times I *had thought to have yerk'd* him here under the ribs. Shak., Othello, I, 2, 5.
I *had thought*, sir, *to have held* my peace, until | You had drawn oaths from him not to stay. id., Winter's Tale, I, 2, 28.
He *had hardly thought to have seen* the young gentleman alive. Thack., Pend., III, 150. T.[1])

Of the same nature is the construction in:

What man is there so much unreasonable, | If you *had pleased to have defended* it | With any terms of zeal, wanted the modesty | To urge the thing held as a ceremony? Shak., Merch., V, 1, 204.

d) nominal predicates such as have been described in 64.

Paul *would have been glad to have told* him that he was glad to see him, if he could have done so with the least sincerity. Dick., Domb., Ch. XI, 104.

66. Obs. I. A similar redundancy of tense may also be observed in constructions with:

a) a subordinate statement: I *should have thought* her duty and inclination *would now have pointed* to the same object. Shak., Riv., IV, 3.

b) an adverbial infinitive: And you, Mr. Justice, *might have been* so civil as *to have invited* me to dinner. Farquhar, Recr. Of., 5, 7, (346).

---

[1]) Storm., Eng. Phil.[2], 757.

c) an accusative with infinitive or a similar construction: What madness could *have induced* you *to have acted* as you have? MARRYAT, Jacob Faithful.[1])
As to measuring her waist in sport, as they did, Young brood, I couldn't have done it: I *should have expected* my arm *to have grown* round it for a punishment, and never come straight again. DICK., Christm. Car., II.
It is one of the controversies which we *had thought to have been settled* for all time. Westm. Gaz., No. 8414, 2a.

II. The use of the perfect tense, on the other hand, is mostly quite justified in an infinitive which in no way forms a kind of unit with the pluperfect conditional in the head-sentence of a complex.

To have taken the field openly against his rival would have been madness. WASH, IRV., Sketch-Bk., XXXII, 355.
I would have given any money *to have been allowed* to wrap myself up over-night and sleep in my hat and boots. DICK., Cop., Ch. II, 14a.
A notoriety he would have done much *to have avoided* was forced upon him. OPPENHEIM, A People's Man, Ch. XXVII.[2])
Indeed, after all that had happened, for Burns *to have deserted* Jean and married another would have been the basest infidelity. PRINCIPAL SHAIRP, Burns, 86.[3])
Mrs. Ambrose seemed to be very obtuse, and the vicar would have been the last *to have spoken* of his suspicion, even to the wife of his bosom. MAR. CRAWF., A Tale of a Lonely Parish. Ch. IX.

III. In the head-sentence of the following quotation the pluperfect seems to have been used in preference to the preterite to colour the utterance with some additional emotion. Compare my Treatise on Tense, § 147; SWEET, N. E. Gr., § 2247.

I *had hoped* you had done for ever with that deluder of youth. LYTTON, My Novel, II, XI, Ch. V, 269.

The following cutting from the Saturday Westminster Gazette (No. 8402, 22b) showing, as it does, the emotional colouring which, in the opinion of some Englishmen, the redundant perfect tense in the Infinitive, may impart to the sentence, will, most probably, interest the student:

The Pluperfect Infinitive.

To the Editor of the "Saturday Westminster".
Sir — Your criticism of Mr. Devonald Fletcher for writing *should not have allowed* T. S. M. *to have said* recalls an incident recounted by a young friend, who had been visiting some elderly relatives, and which illustrates an adroit use of the perfect infinitive to serve a subtle purpose. On the breakfast-table were two eggs, which were appropriated by his uncle and aunt respectively. During the marmalade stage the aunt turned to her nephew and exclaimed: "*Oh, Arthur, would you not have liked to have had an egg?*" Note the cautious pawkiness of the construction — it guards against any rash supposition that an egg is forthcoming in the

---
[1]) MALMSTEDT, Stud.
[2]) KRUISINGA, The Student's Monthly, II, No. 23.
[3]) MALMSTEDT, Stud.

near future. It merely bids the inadequately fed youth to contemplate the radiant repletion of his elders, and to admit that under happier conditions (now ruthlessly relegated to the tense of the irrevocable past) he would have found equal satisfaction. For the question, like the examples in the Latin Grammar, clearly expects the answer "Yes". A negative would have been scarcely polite! It was, in short, a refined, if roundabout, means of conveying the popular but rude gibe, "*Don't you wish you may get it?*"

67. In conclusion attention is drawn to the rather common practice in Early Modern English of dropping the *have* of the perfect infinitive after *I would have had*, and its variations for person. This leaves a past participle which strikes the modern reader, who is not aware of the tense-redundancy underlying the practice, as an erroneous substitute for an infinitive. The suppression is, no doubt, due to a reluctance to burden the sentence with an excessive number of forms of the verb *to have*. See especially STOFFEL, in Taalstudie IX, from which all the following quotations have been taken.

My men would have had me given them leave to fall upon them at once. DEFOE Rob. Crusoe.

D'Avenant would fain have had me gone and drink a bottle of wine at his house hard by. SWIFT.

He would have had us taken a road which was full of those people we were so much afraid of. JOHNSON, Voy. to Abys., 41.

The same construction has also been observed after such expressions as *I had like, I had liever,* etc.

This aversion, heightened by a vast ambition ... had like to broke out in the reign of Antoninus Pius. JER. COLLIER.

The Passive Infinitive in detail.

68. When the relation of an infinitive to the (pro)noun it refers to is understood to correspond to that of predicate to object, in other words, when the infinitive has a distinctly passive meaning, it is now normally placed in the passive voice, irrespective of its grammatical function.

I am worthy to be scorned. THACK., Pend., I, Ch. XXVII, 291.

The Allies do not mean to be trifled with any longer. Times, No. 2301, 9 s d.

They are very much in earnest about one thing, which is that they will not submit to be treated as inferior races. Westm. Gaz., No. 8603, 5 a.

69. In the oldest English, when the infinitive still partook considerably of the nature of a noun of action (1, Note), it was,

naturally, neutral as to voice. Its dative preceded by *to* often had a passive meaning.

þá þing þe tō dōnne sind. Sweet, N. E. Gr., § 2325.

We have seen (3, Obs. I) that in course of time both the dative and the common=case form of the infinitive lost their suffixes. As this process went on, the infinitive lost some of its sub= stantival nature, and assumed more and more the character of a verb. The change was the occasion of the passive voice of the infinitive coming to be employed in most of the cases in which this form was used of the finite verb. Thus the above example became *the things which are to be done*. Compare, however, 71, a.

From various causes which it is not always easy to ascertain, the older form has maintained itself in not a few cases which admit or, at least, suggest interpretations which render the use of the passive voice unnecessary. For instances of active in= finitives in Shakespeare, which in Present English would be replaced by passive infinitives see also A. Schmidt, Shak. Lex. s. v. *to*, 3.

70. The infinitive with a passive meaning is now almost regularly placed in the passive voice when it is used in the function of nominal part of the predicate after the copulas *to be* and *to remain*. See also Wilmanns, Deutsche Gram., III, I, § 88, 5.

i. Such a letter was not *to be soon recovered* from. Jane Austen, Pers., Ch. XXIII, 246.
Was it really all to *be believed?* Temple Thurston, Mirage, Ch. V, 36.
He is not *to be found* anywhere. Sweet, Spoken Eng., 43.
It is hardly *to be wondered at* if Germans generally feel a little sore. Rev. of Rev., No 196, 335 a.
A sum of from 80 to 100 millions is not *to be sneezed at*. Westm. Gaz. No. 8227, 2 a.

ii. It remains *to be seen* whether the squire has a heart to appeal to. Mrs. Ward, Rob. Elsm., II, 80. T. (== Dutch Het staat te bezien...)
Glideless combinations remain *to be considered*. Sweet, Sounds of Eng., § 165.
All our main problems remain *to be solved*. Westm. Gaz., No. 8267, 1 b.

Compare with the above the following quotation, in which *yet* + *to be* has the same value as *to remain*:

Treby had prospered without baths, and it was yet *to be seen* how it would prosper with them. G. Eliot, Fel. Holt, I, Ch. III, 67.

Also *to fall* and *to stand* when faded in meaning, so as to come near to copulas, may be followed by a passive infinitive. According to

MURRAY (s. v. *fall*, 32, b) this use of *to fall* is especially common in northern dialects.

i. In speeches that are full of fresh facts and new thoughts not a word *is to be lost*, while the repetition of old ideas and the elaboration of familiar arguments *fall to be* entirely discarded or *to be* summarized in a dozen lines. Good Words.
The deputation ... said appropriately what falls *to be said* on such an occasion. Westm. Gaz., No. 5573, 2b.

ii. The Government has been wavering between the politically attractive idea of hitting the profiteers and the strong objection of its supporters, not a few of whom *stand to be hit* on that ground. ib., No. 8408, 1a.

71. Obs. I. It may be observed that *to be* in the above connexion, although essentially a copula, implies some weak secondary notions, varying as to the general purport of the sentence, i. e.:

a) some form of necessity, approximating to that more explicitly and emphatically expressed by *should* (or *ought*) or *must*.

Why he was *to be pitied* Jeremy did not know. HUGH WALPOLE, Jeremy, Ch. XII, I, 297.
It is very much *to be hoped* that their counsels will prevail. Westm. Gaz., No. 8420, 2b.

b) some form of capability, approximating to that more explicitly expressed by *can* or *may*.

Jaggers would do it if it *was to be done*. DICK., Great Expect., Ch. XX, 197.
This was not *to be endured*. SHAW, The Four Pleas. Plays, Pref., 5, T.
I think Jeremy *is to be trusted*. HUGH WALPOLE, Jeremy, Ch. XI, 3. (Compare: After some hesitation it was decided that Jeremy *might be trusted*. ib.)
Dr. Nansen strove with them (sc. the Allies) till the going down of the sun to avert this collapse and stultification of so much honourable pride and so many real sacrifices. But the Powers *were not be moved*. Manch. Guard., 5, No. 14, 263a.

In the following quotations *to be* has the first secondary notion in connexion with the first infinitive, the second in connexion with the second infinitive:

Human life is everywhere a state in which much *is to endured* and little *to be enjoyed*. JOHNSON, Ras., Ch. XI, 69.
It was much *to be regretted*, but still it was not *to be helped*. DICK., Great Expect., Ch. XVII, 154.

II. Sometimes there is an adjective, often one in *able* or *ible*, which has approximately the same meaning as the passive infinitive. This goes far to show that the main function of *to be* as used in the above connection is that of a copula.

It is a trite but true observation, that examples work more forcibly on the mind than precepts; and if this be just in what is odious and

blameable, it is more strongly so in what is *amiable* and *praiseworthy*. FIELD., Jos. Andr., I, Ch. I, 1.
Of late a great improvement in this respect is *observable* in our most popular writers, COLERIDGE, Biog. Lit., Ch. XVI, 157.
Much capital is not *realisable* or *divisible* at all. Westm. Gaz., No. 8086, 2 b.

III. The above *to be* should be distinguished from another *to be*, which expresses a stronger form of necessity, and is especially used to represent a person, animal or thing as being acted upon by the will of a person other than either the speaker or the person spoken to, or as under the force of an arrangement or a dispensation of Providence. See Ch. I, 29—32.

Thus: You *are to give* this to John. We *were to go* in a carrier's cart. The day broke which *was to decide* the fate of India.
Or passively: This *is to be given* to John The day broke on which the fate of India *was to be decided*.

It cannot be denied, however, that this *to be* in one of its many other applications, i. e. when it appears as a weak *to have*, sometimes hardly differs from *to be*, which is to be set down as a copula. Thus in the example cited higher up *Human life is everywhere a state in which much is to be endured and little to be enjoyed* there is nothing to prevent us from understanding *much is to be endured* as slightly weaker than *much has to be endured*.

A good instance of *to be* + infinitive and *to have* + infinitive being sometimes indistinguishable is afforded by the following quotation:

All was preparation. Fresh sand *had to be strewn* in the arena. New tapestry hangings *were to deck* the galleries, the houses and balconies to be brave with drapery, the fountain in the market-place *was to play* Rhine-wine. YOUNGE, Dove in the Eagle's Nest, II, I.

Compare also NESFIELD (Hist. Eng. and Deriv., § 219, (2), who observes that *I am* or *was to go* and *I have* or *had to go* "mean much the same thing".

It may be added that the active voice never takes the place of the passive after *to be* when it is to be understood as a weak *to have*.

Then sure You know what *is to be done*. SHER., Riv., III, 4, (252).

72. The older practice of leaving the active voice of the infinitive in the function of nominal part of the predicate undisturbed, notwithstanding its undubitably passive meaning, has, to a certain extent, maintained itself to the present day.

a) Thus in Present English we still meet with instances of this active voice, if the infinitive is one of the following verbs:

to blame. Probably the active voice is still more common than the passive.

i. My dear, I am not *to blame.* Field., Jos. Andr., I, Ch. XII, 31.
I do not know if I am *to blame.* Galsw., Saint's Prog., III, II, 2 §, 227
For the delay the Great Powers are largely *to blame.* Manch. Guard., V. No. 18, 343 b.

ii. Yet learning is not *to be blamed.* Imit. Christi, I, Ch. III, 23.
Defoe is scarcely *to be blamed* for using his new-found art upon gross themes. W. J. Dawson, The Makers of Eng. Fict., Ch. I, 10.

In the following quotation both the active and the passive voice are met with:

They are not *to be blamed* for desiring to see us weak and disunited, or for trying to take away as much of the employment of our people as they can. But we are much *to blame* if we do not strain every nerve to frustrate their schemes. Times.

According to Murray (s. v. *blame,* 6) "In the 16—17th century the *to* was misunderstood as *too,* and *blame* taken as an adjective = blameworthy, culpable". Thus in:

Blush and confesse that you be *too too blame.* Harington, Epigr. I, 84 b.

The misapprehension may, at least in part, be responsible for the retention of the active voice.

to compare. To all appearance the active voice is still rather common, although Murray marks it as obsolete.

I don't think you are any more *to compare* to her than a can of small beer to a bowl of punch. Congreve, Love for Love, III, (251).
An imitation of the best Authors is not *to compare* with a good Original. Addison, Spect., No. 160.
I do not know any English women who are *to compare* to such Americans in brilliancy and fascination. Et. Glyn, Halcyone, Ch. X, 88.

ii. All the things thou canst desire are not *to be compared* unto her. Bible, Prov., III, 15.

Note. It should be observed that *to compare* is one of the numerous transitive verbs that may be used intransitively through assuming a passive meaning. Comment on this remarkable feature of English idiom must be reserved for another paper. The following quotations must suffice for the present occasion.

i. There is no bird in England can *compare* with the sweetness of his (sc. the blackcap's) voice. Temple Thurston, The Open Window, I, 6.
As a strengthening stimulating beverage no ordinary meat extract can *compare* with bovril. Ill. Lond. News.

ii. Mr. Swinnerton has written four or five other novels before this one, but none of them *compare* with it in quality. Wells, Pref. to Swinnerton's Nocturne.

iii. Pen's healthy red face *compared* oddly with the waxy debauched little features of Foker's chum. Thack., Pend., I, Ch. V, 53.
She *compares* favourably with Evangeline. Sarah Grand, Our man. nat., 66.

to do. Except for such a combination as *What is to do*, for which see b), the active voice is now obsolete.

I do not know | Why yet I live to say, "This thing's *to do*". Shak., Haml., IV, 4, 44.
The best is yet *to do*. id., As you like it, I, 2, 102.

ii. "And à propos, Moses, have you been able to get me that little bill discounted?" — "It was not *to be done*, indeed, Mr. Trip." Shrr., School for Scand., III, 2, (395).

to learn, in the sense of *to receive instruction, to be taught* or *told*. In this meaning the verb is now well-nigh obsolete, at least in Standard English, and the active voice does not, therefore, strike us as anything out of the common. In fact, *I am yet to learn* appears to the modern reader as a variant of *I have yet to learn*. Compare Stof., E. S., XXIX.

i. But how I caught it (sc. my sadness), found it, or came by it, | What stuff 'tis made of, whereof it is born, | I am *to learn*. Shak., Merch., I, 1, 5.
If there is any difference between the pronunciation of 'see' and 'sea', I am yet *to learn* wherein it lies. Notes and Quer., 1894, Nov. 3, 355 b.

ii. It turns out girls who are systematic and orderly, but I have yet *to learn* that it turns out girls that are resourceful. Lit. World, 1898, May 6, 404 a.

The following quotation with to *learn* indubitably in the above meaning will, no doubt, be acceptable to the student:

She ain't half bad, ... but if she knows her letters it's the most she does — and then I *learned* her. Dick., Our Mut. Friend, I, Ch. III. 27. T.

to let. The passive voice is now, perhaps, rather more frequent than the still common active voice. It is, of course, unavoidable in the combination *to be sold or let*.

i. I went into a cottage that I saw was *to let*. Dick., Cop., Ch. XXXVI, 259 a.
I see the house is *to let*. Galsworthy, Saint's Prog., III, XIII, 1 §, 340.

ii. This desirable Mansion is *to be Let* Furnished. Hardy.[1])

Note. In passing we may here point out he difference between *The house is to be sold* (= It has been determined to sell the house) and *The house is for sale* (= The house is in the market).

to seek, in the sense of *to be in request*.

A work of this kind is still *to seek*. Webst., Dict.
Houses are still *to seek*. Westm. Gaz., No. 8267, 1 b.

Note. The predicative *to seek* is found in a few other interesting shades of meaning, in which 'however, the notion of passivity is more or less 'to seek', i. e. hardly to be recognized. These shades of meaning may be defined to be those of:

1) *deficient:* We find his economical reasoning sadly *to seek* in cogency and grasp. Times.

---

[1]) Günth., Man., § 585.

2) *at a loss*: For if you reduce usury to one low rate, it will ease the common borrower, but the merchant will be *to seek* for money. BACON, Es., Of Usury, (115). (In Elizabethan English usury had not the unfavourable meaning it has now, but simply denoted the practice of taking interest for money borrowed.)
For the details of our itinerary, I am all *to seek*. STEVENSON, Kidnapped. Ch. XX.

3 *unskilled, inexperienced, deficient in knowledge* (or *skill*) *of*: I do not think my sister so *to seek*, | Or so unprincipl'd in virtue's book ... As that the single want of light and noise ... | Could stir the constant mood of her calm thoughts. MILTON, Comus, 366.
He is unacquainted with the maxims and manners of the world; he is *to seek* in the character of individuals. HAZLITT, On the Ignorance of the Learned. (PARDOE, Sel. Eng. Es. 233).
It is in his dialogue that he is, perhaps most *to seek*. Lit. World, 1893, March 3, 196 c.

b) Rather common is the active voice of the predicative infinitive, especially of *to do*, when it has such a subject as *much, a great deal, something, what*, etc.; e. g.: *Much is yet* (or *remains*) *to do. What is to pay?*
This practice is, perhaps, due to the analogy with constructions in which the verb *to be* as an intransitive verb is accom≠panied by weak *there*, and the infinitive has the value of an undeveloped clause. In these, as we shall see below (76), the active voice is quite commonly retained. Compare MURRAY, s. v. *do*, 33, a.

i.° Little is *to do*. SHAK., Macb., V, 7, 28.
What's *to do*. id., Twelfth Night, III, 3, 17.
She looked at him rather frightened, and wondering, and asked him what was *to do*. MRS. GASK., Cranf., Ch. VI, 109.
A great deal certainly is yet *to do* in the non=Aryan fields of language. Lit. World, 1894, 229 a.
∞ Worthy Macduff and we | Shall take upon's what else remains *to do*. SHAK., Macb., V, 6, 5.
Much hath been done — but more remains *to do*. BYRON, Cors., II, IV.
An hour when your servants are in bed is to be preferred for what will then remain *to do*. STEVENSON, Dr. Jekyll, Ch. IX, 83.
Clive had pointed out to him what had already been done and what remained *to do*. A. and C. ASKEW, The Lurking Shadow, Ch. XVI.[1])

The active infinitive even bears no replacing by the passive in the archaic phrase *What's here to do?* in the sense of *What is up here?*

What's here *to do?* CONGREVE, Love for Love, III, 1 (239).
What's here *to do?* DICK., Barn. Rudge, Ch. III, 14 b.
Compare: One maid among three of us. *What's to be done?* J. M. BARRIE, The Admirable Crichton, 1, 33.

---

[1]) De Drie Talen, XXXI, No. 11.

The practice appears to be rare with other verbs.
Much remains *to sing*. Ch. Lamb, Es. of Elia, The South-Sea House.

c) Sometimes the active voice seems to owe its preservation to the fact that the passive voice would convey another meaning. Thus sometimes after *still* or *yet*.

i. His wife ... had maintained all through that this Miss Mountstephen was absolutely innocent, and that the guilty person was still *to find*. L. C. Davidson, The Great Dynover Pearl Case.[1]) (= was still *the subject of the quest*. The passive *was still to be found* would mean *could still be found*, which is here impossible.)
The fortunes of the Allies, certain as the issue is, are yet *to make*.[2]) Daily News and Lead.

ii. Persecution and revenge, like courtship and toadyism, will not prosper without a considerable expenditure of time and ingenuity, and these are not *to spare* with a man whose law-business and liver are both beginning to show unpleasant symptoms. G. Eliot, Scenes, III, 247. (= *in plenty*: compare *to have time, money*, etc. *to spare*. *To be spared* would mean *to be left over or unused*.)

d) In some cases the retention of the active infinitive may be owing to a tendency of mentally supplying such a phrase as *for me (you, us, somebody, some person* etc.) before the infinitive, the (pro)noun in these phrases representing the logical subject of the infinitive.

The cards of address alone remained *to nail on*. Ch. Brontë, Jane Eyre, Ch. XXV, 336. (= for me to nail on.)
"What are all these books for?" — "They are *to read*." El. Glyn, Halcyone, Ch. I, 8. (= for you to read.)
This book it *to read* and not *to tear*. Abbot, Shak. Gram.[8], § 405.

e) The passive meaning of the predicative infinitive is sometimes doubtful owing to the fact that the verb admits of two interpretations, i. e. as an intransitive as well as a transitive verb. Compare what has been observed about *to compare*.

They all knew by now that she was a cypher, — that she was not *to count*. Mrs. Ward, The Mating of Lydia, Prol., Ch. II, 25.

73. a) Closely akin to the infinitives discussed in the preceding sections are those which are to be regarded as constituents of adnominal undeveloped clauses (Ch. XVIII, 16 ff). Also in these the active voice has mostly been changed into the passive voice when they are related to the (pro)nouns they modify as predicate to object.

---
[1]) De Drie Talen, XXXI, No. 10; [2]) ib., No. 12.

> The great calamity which had fallen on Argyle had this advantage, that it enabled him to show, by proofs *not to be mistaken*, what manner of man he was. MAC., Hist., II, Ch. V, 130.
> The dangers *to be braved* were such as could neither be knocked down nor throttled. G. Eliot, Sil. Marn., I, Ch. III, 22.
> He could only think of one thing *to be done*. Hardy, Under the Greenwood Tree, I, Ch. IX, 80.
> The interior of the room is not like anything *to be seen* in the east of Europe. Shaw, Arms and the Man, I, (25). T.

b) An attributive adnominal infinitive, when passive in meaning, is regularly placed in the passive voice. The infinitive often enters into combination with another word. For illustration see also Ch. VIII, 102; and Jespersen, Mod. Eng. Gram., II, 14.41.

> For my own part, I confess that I do not think I have ever read ... a more decided specimen of the *to-be-damned* doggrel, than was then exhibited by Lord Byron himself. Lytton, Life of Lord Byron, 15b.
> It was perhaps the *not-to-be satisfied* satisfaction of a morbid mind ... which first induced him to turn his thoughts upon marriage. ib., 20a.
> It was a *much-to-be-longed-for* place. El. Glyn, The Reason Why, Ch. X, 86.
> The events which are taking place in the eastern theatre may well hasten the *much-to-be-desired* retirement of German troops from French territory. Westm. Gaz., No. 6648, 1b.
> The *about-to-be-released* prisoner tried to explain that Irish Unionists were loyal to England. The New Statesman, No. 95, 403b.
> Her writing reminds me of those *least-to-be-forgotten* evenings of my life when [etc.]. Punch, No. 3836, 40a.

74. The use of the active voice in this function is, however, far more common than in that of nominal part of the predicate. This is, probably, owing to the fact that the distinctly final meaning of the infinitive considerably weakens its adnominal relation to the (pro)noun it refers to. This renders the use of the passive voice uncalled-for, the more so because a (pro)noun in the subjective relation to it is mostly readily suggested by the context. Compare Ch. XVIII, 17, Obs. II, and also Onions, Adv. Eng. Synt., § 173.

75. This is distinctly the case when the infinitive modifies the thing-object, whether non-prepositional or prepositional, of the sentence. The logical subject of the infinitive is then felt to be denoted by:

  a) the subject or the person-object of the sentence

> i°. He has so much *to say* for himself. Sher., Riv., IV, 2, (259).
> Mr. Martin, I imagine, has his fortune entirely *to make*. Jane Austen, Emma, Ch. IV, 29. T.

The gardener was picking fruit *to send* to market. THACK., Van. Fair, I, Ch. VIII, 82.

Mr. Jesse Collings will have nothing *to say* to intoxicants. Tit*bits, No.1291,387a.

If you've got money *to fling about*. A. BENNETT, The Great Adventure, I, 2, (53).

Take this book *to read* on your way. ONIONS, Adv. Eng. Synt., § 164. (The subject is implied in the imperative.)

He longed for worlds *to conquer*. ib., § 173.

Note. In such sentences as *I have a letter to write, I have no end of calls to make*, the active voice is all the more natural, because they often bear a close resemblance to those in which *to have* appears as a synonym of *must*, and the infinitive precedes its object, e. g.: *I have to write a letter, I have to make no end of calls*.

The Lord Mayor has a host of duties *to discharge*. E. SCOTT, England, Ch. V, 64.

There he resumed that struggle for life which is hell to most of those who have it *to fight*. J. E. PATTERSON, Stephen Compton, Ch. IV, 9.

ii.° I gave him bread *to eat* and water *to drink*. MEICKLEJOHN, The Eng. Lang., 39.

Let me have something *to eat*. MASON, Eng. Gram.³¹, § 362, 3, Note.

°° The rest we may leave to the tribes *to accomplish*. GRANT ALLEN, The Tents of Shem, Ch. XVIII.

She had dictated the letter to his father *to write*. TEMPLE THURSTON, The City of Beaut. Nons., I, Ch. XVI, 128.

Also in such a construction as *Mary had pleaded letters to write* (HOPE, Quisanté, 79), mentioned by JESPERSEN (Mod. Eng. Gram., 15, 852), the active voice is justified by the expansion it naturally suggests: *letters that she had to write*.

b) a (pro)noun in a prepositional phrase with *for*, which is understood because it is not necessary for the right under= standing of the sentence. Compare 74, Obs. IV.

It remains to be seen whether the squire has a heart *to appeal to*. MRS. WARD, Rob. Elsm., II, 80. T. (sc. *for us to appeal to*.)

Shops were open, especially places which sold things *to eat* and *to drink*. WALT. BESANT, By Celia's Arbour, I, 17. T.

The lawyer would have no bowels of compassion *to speak of*. GRANT ALLEN, The Tents of Shem, Ch. XVII.

The following sentence can only be rightly understood when such a phrase is distinctly supplied:

They like a man *to follow*. HOPE, Phroso, Ch. VI, 132 (= They like a man for them to follow).

Varied practice is shown by:

The wayfarer sees with each returning sun some new obstacle *to surmount*, some new light *to be attained*. DICK., Nich. Nick., 656.[1])

---
[1]) JESPERSEN, Mod. Eng. Gram., 15.88.

Bohemians who have no position *to lose* and no career *to be closed*. Shaw, The Doctor's Dilemma, 110.[1]) (Observe the difference in logical relation between the two infinitives to the subject.)

76. Obs. I. When the context does not in any way suggest a (pro)noun which might figure as the subject of the infinitive, the passive voice is unavoidable.

   i. You philosophers must not forget that we poor worldlings have bones *to be broken*. Kingsley, Hyp., Ch. II, 9a.
   The provision made by the Government was so ample and complete that it left little or nothing *to be desired*. Morn. Leader. (Compare with this the following quotation in which the person/object indicates the logical subject of the infinitive It was sung in a provincial, amateur fashion, such as would have left a critical ear much *to desire*. G. Eliot, Mill, VI, Ch. III, 355.)
   ii. He stood listening for the summons *to be repeated*. Stevenson.

II. The active voice sometimes appears to be obligatory because the use of the passive would convert the sentence into an accusative with infinitive. Compare Obs. V.

   Both our boys still like one of our cakes *to take* to school or college with them. Thack., Virg., Ch. XXIII, 241.
   A human beast of prey; an African cannibal ... wanted a boatman *to eat*. Ill. Lond. News, No. 3698, 356c.

III. According to De Drie Talen, XXXI, No. 11, 149, we say indifferently *I have a house to let* and *I have a house to be let*.

IV. When the agent of the action denoted by the infinitive is mentioned in a phrase consisting of *for* + (pro)noun, the passive voice is, of course, out of the question. Compare 75, b.

   He wishes every man to be registered, and to be paid, £ 4 a week, whether there is work for him *to do* or not. Westm. Gaz., No. 8509, 4a.

V. The passive infinitive, on the other hand, cannot be replaced by the active, when it is a constituent of an accusative + infinitive. Compare Obs. II; and 89.

   He commanded the bridge *to be lowered*. Mason, Eng. Gram., § 397.

77. Also when the infinitive modifies the subject of a sentence containing weak *there*, the mind readily suggests a logical subject in the shape of a (pro)noun contained in a prepositional phrase with *for*. The active voice is, accordingly, quite common. The numerous quotations given below distinctly bring out the fact that the choice depends, to a certain extent, upon whether a weak form of necessity or capability is to be indicated. Some of them, however, bear either interpretation.

[1]) Jespersen, Mod. Eng. Gram., 15.88.

i. Oh! there's not much *to learn*. SHER., School for Scand., III, 1, (389).
Is there no debt *to pay*, no boon *to grant?* WORDSWORTH, To a distant
Friend, 4.
There were no fine riddles of the human heart *to read*, no theories *to propound*,
no hidden causes *to develop*, no remote consequences *to predict*. MAC., Es.,
Southey's Colloquies, (100a).
I think that I have seen now all that there is *to see*. CON. DOYLE, Sherl.
Holm., II, 215, 1.
Are there interesting things *to see?* HICHENS, The Garden of Allah, I, 147. T.
There were the plates *to wash* and the knives *to clean*, and when they were
done there was cabbage, potatoes, onions *to prepare*, saucepans *to fill* with
water, coal *to fetch* for the fire. GEORGE MOORE, Esth. Waters, Ch. II, 14
If there had been a door *to bang*, she would certainly have banged it. BEATR.
HARRADEN, Ships, I, Ch. XV, 81.
If only she were there! If only her bright brown eyes were looking at him,
what thousands of things there would be *to say!* TEMPLE THURSTON, The
City of Beautiful Nonsense, I, Ch. XVI, 128.
That first evening of his arrival, there was John's work *to talk of*, the success
of his last book *to discuss*, the opinions of his criticisms *to lay down*. ib.,
III, Ch. IV, 142.
There's little *to tell* about me. BAR. VON HUTTEN, What became of Pam.
Ch. III, 23
How could you take so long, Anna, if there was no answer *to bring*. DOR.
GERARD, Exotic Martha, Ch. XVII, 210.
Then there are the educational history and practice of other nations from which
there is generally much *to learn*. Times.
There are nine runs *to make* and two wickets to go down. ONIONS, Adv.
Eng. Synt., § 173.

ii. There was little work *to be done*. G. ELIOT, Sil. Marn., Ch. III, 19.
There was nothing else *to be done*. MCCARTHY, Short Hist., Ch. XIII, 186.
After such an accident there was nothing else *to be done*. MRS. WARD, The
Mating of Lydia, I, Ch. IV, 86.
There is no more *to be said*. ib., III, Ch. XVIII, 373.
There were even cuckoos' eggs *to be found* there. SWIFT, Old Chapel.
There was true loneliness, loneliness not *to be imagined*. MORLEY ROBERTS,
Time and Thomas Waring, Ch. XXXI, 309.
There were such astonishing things *to be talked over* at this moment and
nobody to talk to. DOR. GERARD, Exotic Martha, Ch. XVIII, 212. T.
There is no sign of life *to be detected*. Westm. Gaz., No. 8414, 5a.
The lawyers of the nineteenth century have decided for us that the word
"man" always includes "woman" where there is a penalty *to be incurred*, and
never includes "woman" when there is a privilege *to be conferred*. Rev. of
Rev., No. 213, 322b.

Note. The following groups of quotations show that the choice
between the active and the passive infinitive does not always depend
on a consideration of the secondary notion implied, but is, apparently,
a matter of individual predilection, or even of mere chance.

i. There was no woman *to compare* to her. CONWAY, Called Back, 69.
ii. Erasmus asserted that there was no town in all Christendom *to be compared*
to it (sc. Ghent) for size, power or the culture of its inhabitants. MOTLEY,
Rise, I, Ch. I, 32a.

i. There's not a moment *to lose*. Dick., Nich. Nick., Ch. II, 63.
There's no time *to lose*. id., Ol. Twist, Ch. XI.
Obviously there was no time *to lose*. Dor. Gerard, Exotic Martha, Ch. XVII, 207. T.

ii. There was no time *to be lost*. McCarthy, Short Hist., Ch. XIII, 183.
There's no time *to be lost*. G. Eliot, Fel. Holt, I, Ch. II, 57.
There is no time *to be lost*. Oscar Wilde, The Importance of being Earnest, I, 35.
There is not an instant *to be lost*. Con. Doyle, Sherl. Holm., I, 248, I.

i. There were new and admirable things *to see* there. Froude, Oceana, Ch. XX, 335.
You say there was nothing *to see!* Shaw, Widowers' Houses, I, (14).

ii. Do you think it sensible to take a long and expensive journey to see what there is *to be seen*, and then go away without seeing it. ib., I, (10).

The two constructions may even be found in one and the same sentence.

But always, with a shock, I was brought back to earth, where there were no heroic deeds *to do*, no lions *to face*, no judges *to defy*, but only some dull duty *to be performed*. Annie Besant, Autobiography, 43.
There was so much *to see* at Florence. No — pardon me! — there is nothing *to be seen* at Florence. Mrs. Ward, Eleanor, 20.[1])

78. Obs. I. After *to fall* as a quasi copula, and *to remain*, the passive voice seems to be the normal form. The available evidence is, however, far too scanty to draw any reliable conclusions from.

Having placed so much to its (sc. the motor omnibus's) credit, however, there falls *to be considered* a totally different aspect of the case. Il. Lond. News, No. 3896, 1068a.
Meanwhile there still remained forty chestnuts *to be eaten*. Compton Mackenzie, Sylvia Scarlett, Ch. II, 82.
After that there remained nothing *to be done*. A. and C. Askew, The Lurking Shadow, Ch. XXXI.[2])

The same practice probably obtains after *to be left* = *to remain*.

I don't see that there is anything left *to be said*. Gissing, A Life's Morn., Ch. IV, 55.

II. The active voice sometimes appears to be obligatory, because the passive would convey another meaning than the one intended. Thus in:

There was no general *to send*. Onions, Adv. Eng. Synt., § 175. (= There was no general that could be sent. Compare: There was no general *to be sent* = It was determined that no general should be sent.)
There's nothing on earth *to do* here. Keble Howard, One of the Family, I, Ch. IV, 79. (= There is no business, sport, amusement, etc. going on here. Compare: There is nothing on earth *to be done* here = There is nothing on earth that can (or should) be done here.)
There is nothing *to do* here in the evenings but play billiards. ib. 80.

---

[1]) Jespersen, Mod. Eng. Gram., 15.88.
[2]) De Drie Talen, XXXI, No. 11.

Easter Sunday, for all its traditions, is a gladless day in London. There is positively nothing *to do*. TEMPLE THURSTON, The City of Beaut[iful] Nons., I, Ch. XVI, 123.

III. In some cases idiom hardly tolerates the active voice to be replaced by the passive, although the change of voice would involve no change of meaning.

ι. She had known before she died practically all that there was *to know*. MRS. WARD, Cousin Phil., Ch. III, 47.
The three men ... by now had learnt what there was *to know* of each other. Daily News.[1])

Compare the following quotation in which the verb *to be* is not accompanied by weak *there*:

She seemed to know all that was *to be known*. GALSW., Beyond, I, Ch. III, 36.

ii. There was the devil *to pay* with the girl's relations. G. ELIOT, Fel. Holt, I, Ch. XXI, 323.

79. a) For the rest the use of the active infinitive in a passive meaning appears to be common only when the noun modified is preceded by an adjective, especially one expressing fitness or suitability. The noun modified mostly stands in the grammatical function of nominal part of the predicate or predicative adnominal adjunct. Observe the frequent *the proper (correct, etc.) thing to do*. See JESPERSEN, Mod. Eng. Gram., 15.841; De Drie Talen, XXXI, No. 12.

ι. The only thing *to do* was to carry him into the nearest shelter. MRS. WARD, The Mating of Lydia, I, Ch. IV, 87. (*Only — only proper*.)
It's the only thing *to do* now. OSC. WILDE, The Importance of being Earnest, III, 144.
Now the first thing *to settle* is what to take with us. JEROME, Three Men in a Boat, Ch. III, 24.

ii. The baking part was the next thing *to be consider'd*. DEFOE, Rob. Crus., 145.[2])

Thus also when an adjective is distinctly felt to be understood.

ι. This is a book *to read*. ABBOT, Shak. Gram.[3], § 405. (= This is a fit book to read.)
According to him the Old Chapel was not a place *to visit* by night. SWIFT, Old Chapel.
It is a work *to read, enjoy,* and *discuss*. Advertisement.[4])
Furog is the bread *to eat* today and every day. id.)

ii. Her father was in truth not a man *to be treated with*. CH. BRONTE, Browning, 80.[1])

[1]) De Drie Talen, XXXI, No. 11.
[2]) JESPERSEN, Mod. Eng. Gram., 15.871.
[3]) De Drie Talen, XXXI, No. 12.
[4]) JESPERSEN, Mod. Eng. Gram., 15.872.

She was a person *to be trusted* and *relied upon*. (?), The Cap of Youth, Ch. XVIII.[1]

The variability of the practice is distinctly shown by a comparison of the following two quotations:

He is not a man *to know*. Dick., Cop., 306,[2] (= a man which one ought to know, or a proper man to know.)
Dombey was a man *to be known*. id., Domb., 78.[3]

Sometimes even both the active and the passive infinitive in identical functions are met with in one and the same sentence.

One of the very first and most practical things *to do*, and *to be done* at once, is to turn the Prisons into Industrial Asylums. Carpenter, Prisons, Police and Punishment, 61.[?] (The passive voice seems to be due to *at once*.)

Note. It will be observed that the adjective felt to be understood may also be inserted after the noun modified: *This is a book fit to read*. It is then to be considered as the constituent of an undeveloped clause which may be expanded into an adnominal clause introduced by a relative pronoun: *This is a book which is fit to read*. For discussion of the voice of the infinitive in such a connexion see 83; and 85, Obs. III.

b) When no adjective precedes the noun modified, nor is suggested by the context, the ordinary practice is to place the infinitive in the passive voice. For illustration see also 73, a.

To slam doors was an offence only *to be wiped out* by twenty lines of Virgil. G. Eliot, Mill, II, Ch. IV.
The agitation ... suddenly showed itself a thing only *to be laughed at*. McCarthy, Short Hist., Ch. VIII, 91.
He was not a man *to be lightly played upon*. Mrs. Ward, Marc., I, 121.

But even in this case the active voice is sometimes met with.

Shipping is laid up for want of goods *to carry*. Westm. Gaz., No. 8615, 4a.

For explanation of the frequent use of *to compare* in a passive meaning see 72, a.

For never yet, in beauty's braided hair, | Or haughty monarch's costly diadem, | Shone pearl or ruby with it *to compare*. Bernard Barton, Sir Philip Sidney, VII.

c) The active voice appears to be regularly preserved in the adnominal infinitive whose head-word is preceded by the preposition *with* in the meaning of *having*. See Jespersen, Mod. Eng. Gram., 15.852.

---
[1] De Drie Talen, XXXI, No. 12.
[2] Jespersen, Mod. Eng. Gram., 15.842; [3] ib., 15.88.

He had been married ... to a lady with no heart *to give* him. Dick., Domb.¹ Ch. I, 6.
You have left me with nothing *to do*. Wells, The New Macchiavelli, 519.¹)

d) The passive voice is, of course, unavoidable, when the inverted subject, i. e. a wordgroup with the preposition *by* (Sweet, N. E. Gr., § 313) follows.
Scrooge was not a man *to be frightened* by echoes. Dick., Christm. Car., I.

e) Conversely the adnominal infinitive is naturally placed in the active voice when preceded by *for* + (pro)noun.
This is a matter for the trade unions *to consider* forthwith. Times, Educ. Sup., No. 356, 427 b.

f) Some adnominal infinitives regularly preserve the active voice in certain of their applications.
I have a long wooden house with room enough and *to spare*. Mrs. Gask., Mary Barton, Ch. XXXVIII, 371.
Mrs. Jennings very likely belonged to a family which had had no funerals *to speak of*. G. Eliot, Scenes, II, Ch. I, 72.

g) Such a construction as is illustrated by the following quotation seems to be unusual:
What idle man can withstand the temptation of a woman *to fascinate*, and another man *to eclipse*. G. Eliot, Scenes, II, Ch. IV, 110. (= of fascinating a woman and eclipsing another man.)

80. Infinitives modifying a predicative adjective (or adjective equivalent) adverbially are mostly kept in the active voice, although related to the (pro)noun they refer to as predicate to object. Thus in such a sentence as *This question is difficult to answer* the infinitive is an adverbial adjunct (of restriction) of the adjective *difficult*, the subject, *this question*, being in the objective relation to it. The reason why the infinitive is mostly placed in the active voice may be that the sentence is felt to be a condensed form of a complex sentence: *To answer this question is difficult*, or *It is difficult to answer this question*.
It will be observed that the logical subject of *is difficult* is *to answer this question*. Indeed the case here described is an instance of a wide-spread tendency of many predicates to change their subjects, which has already been dealt with in Ch. II, but will receive fuller treatment in a paper specially devoted to this subject.
In the condensed construction the predicate, of course, depends for person and number on the illogical subject. Thus *To manage you (these children,*

¹) Jespersen, Mod. Eng. Gram., 15.832.

etc.) *is difficult* becomes in its condensed form *You (these children, etc.) are difficult to manage.*

The adverbial relation of the infinitive becomes evident from a comparison of the construction with that instanced by the following quotation, in which *of* + noun of action is placed after a predicative adjective, the combination bearing the same relation to it as the infinitive:

Quitch-grass ... has long creeping roots, which make it extremely difficult *of extirpation*. G. C. MACAULAY, Note to Ten.'s Ger. and En., 902.

As is shown by the following numerous quotations, the condensed construction is a very common one.

i. Her courage was beautiful *to behold*. LYTTON, Pomp., V, Ch. IX, 150a.
His luggage... was not difficult *to carry*. DICK., Ol Twist, Ch. IV, 50.
The Gods are hard *to reconcile*. TEN., The Lotos-Eaters, 126.
Mr. Faversham's position is indeed difficult *to understand*. MRS. WARD, The Mating of Lydia, III, Ch. XVIII, 362.
Lady Mary had reported that 'Companions' were almost as difficult *to find* as kitchenmaids. id., Cous. Phil., Ch. II, 32.
Cynthia's expression was hard *to read*. ib., Ch. VII, 109.
He isn't easy *to know*. ib., Ch. II, 30.
People were hard *to love*, different from birds and beasts and flowers, to love which seemed natural and easy. GALSWORTHY, Beyond, II, 105.
The causes of this imperfect sympathy are easy *to understand*. WALT. RALEIGH, Sam. Johnson, 30.
This is important *to observe*. SWEET, Words, Logic and Gram., 3.
Her disappointment was pathetic *to witness*. TEMPLE THURSTON, The City of Beautiful Nonsense, III, Ch. X, 302.
This is impossible *to do*. Westm. Gaz., No. 8203, 3a.
The treaty must in these respects do nothing which justifies Count Rantzau in saying that its demands are impossible *to fulfil*. ib., No. 8080, 2a.

ii.° There is hardly a page in this book that is not a delight *to read*. Westm. Gaz.

°° William Smith is not an easy name *to render* famous. SIMS, My Two Wives, Ch. I, 1.
That, of course, would have been the reasonable, the gentlemanly thing *to do*. MRS. WARD, The Mating of Lydia, I, Ch. IV, 87.
This is an excellent thing *to do*. Times.
This was not a wise thing *to do*. Westm. Gaz., No. 8203, 4a.
That is not a proper observation *to make* in the House of Commons. Daily News.[1])

°°° He was not much *to look at*. ASCOTT R. HOPE, Old Pot.
°°°° What sort of man is he *to see*? STEVENSON, Dr. Jekyll, Ch. I, 18.

81. Obs. I. The predicative adjective, especially *worth*, may be attended by a non-prepositional object.

The church was one of those fine old English structures worth travelling *to see*. G. ELIOT, Fel. Holt, I, Ch. III, 64.
I have heard it said, a bridge is a good thing — worth helping *to make*, though half the men who worked at it were rogues. ib., Ch. XVI, 272.

---

[1]) De Drie Talen, XXXII, No. 2.

The salmon is a valuable fish worth some expenditure of public money to preserve. Westm. Gaz., No. 8086, 10b.

II. The infinitive may be an intransitive verb followed by a preposition forming a kind of unit with it.

Her neighbour was not difficult *to talk to*. Mrs. Ward, Cous. Phil., Ch. II, 29.

This world will be intolerable *to live in*. Wells, Mr. Britling, I, Ch. V, § 13, 174.

III. It will have been observed that in some of the above quotations the condensed construction hardly admits of being replaced by the expanded without detriment to idiom. This is distinctly the case in the following:

Is my apparel sumptuous *to behold?* Shak., Henry VI, B, IV, 7, 106.
It was sad *to listen to*. Ch. Bronte, Jane Eyre, Ch. XXV, 338.
"My horses were never in harness", added the lady. "Bullfinch would kick the carriage to pieces, if you put him in the traces." — "But he is quiet *to ride?*" asked the civilian. Thack., Van. Fair, I, Ch. XXXII, 346.
These agricultural gentlemen are delicate customers *to deal with*. Meredith, The Ordeal of Rich. Fev., Ch. X, 63.
She was fair *to look upon*. Onions, Adv. Eng. Synt., § 67.
Good men are so rare *to find*. Westm. Gaz., No. 8149, 4b.

Note. Especially the collocation *far to seek* (= difficult to find).

If you ask yourself what you mean by fame, riches or learning, the answer is *far to seek*. Stevenson, Walking Tours (Peacock, Sel. Es. 542).
Examples of phrases tabooed by the fashion of the moment among some classes, but commonly employed by others, are not *far to seek*. Wyld, Growth, Ch. V, 64.
The remedies are not *far to seek*. Westm. Gaz., No. 8503, 1b.

IV. When the necessity arises to indicate the logical subject of the infinitive, this is done by placing *for* + (pro)noun before it.

The old fool ... was trying to reach a point three inches beyond what was possible *for him to reach*. Jerome, Three Men in a Boat, Ch. III.

Thus also in the expanded construction.

What it is necessary *for the Commons to face* is that they must either adopt these drastic measures or appeal to the country. Rev. of Rev., No. 203, 452b.

V. The illogical infinitive is also met with.

a) after such a quasi-copula as *to sound*.

The man trampled calmly over the child's body and left her screaming on the ground. It *sounds* nothing to hear, but it was hellish to see. Stevenson, Dr. Jekyll, Ch. i, 15.

b) after an adjective or adjective equivalent in the function of predicative adnominal adjunct.

Poor Rebecca felt it hard *to bear*. G. Eliot, Scenes, III, Ch. III.
Emily found the smile hard *to bear*. Gissing, A Life's Morn., Ch. VII, 85.
You find her troublesome *to search*. ib., Ch. VIII, 123.
The Government of a Parliamentary party means that what a popular statesman thinks it wise and feasible *to do*, he induces his Ministry to accept. Fred. Harrison, On Society, Ch. III, 75.
His loyalty did his mother's heart good *to witness*. Thack., Pend., I, Ch. III, 36.

c) as a constituent of an undeveloped adnominal clause.

This wavering in her mistress's temper probably put something into the waiting-gentlewoman's head not necessary *to mention* to the sagacious reader. Field., Jos. And., I. Ch. VII, 15.

VI. When the subject is attended by a lengthy adjunct, it is sometimes followed by *it*, representing the infinitive with its logical object. The insertion of *it* re-establishes the logical relations between the different elements of the sentence. Thus in:

A form more rigid than Miss Starke's it was hard *to conceive*. Lytton, My Novel, I, VI, Ch. XXV, 433.
The amount of plunder he collected in this way it is impossible *to estimate*. Mac., Bacon, (375 b).

The insertion of *it*, entailing the re-establishment of the logical relations between the different elements of the sentence, is distinctly the rule when the subject of the sentence, i. e. the logical object of the infinitive, is a subordinate question. It appears to be unusual when the subject is a relative pronoun.

i° Where the Doctor had studied, how he had required his medical knowledge, and where he had received his diploma, *it* is hard at present *to say*. Wash. Irv., Dolf Heyl.
How the Vicar reconciled his answer with the strict notions he supposed himself to hold on these subjects *it* is beyond a layman's power *to tell*. Hardy, Tess, II, Ch. XIV, 122.
What constitutes marriage *it* would be difficult exactly *to define*. Nineteenth Cent., No. 396, 259.
What passed at this gathering *it* is not lawful for me *to tell*. Times No. 1823, 973 d.
What may be the ultimate outcome of the present situation ... *it* is impossible *to forecast* at the present moment. Westm. Gaz., No. 5249, 1c.
What amount of truth there is in this statement *it* is, of course, impossible *to say*. ib., No. 5190, 2 b.

2° How the Duke of Burgundy must resent this horrible cruelty on the person of his near relative and ally, is for your Majesty *to judge*. Scott, Quent. Durw., Ch. XXVIII, 361.
How far I have followed these instructions or whether they have availed me is not for me *to decide*. Byron, Pref. to Mar. Fal. (London Ed., 351 a.)
Why the Head should sway about and shout like that was impossible *to conjecture*. E. F. Benson, David Blaize, Ch. II, 30.

ii.° I shall mention only a few points, which it is very easy for each one *to find out* for himself with a little careful observation. Wyld, Growth of Eng., Ch. II, 19.
°° It is a subject which will be requisite *to consider* carefully. Huxley, Man's Place in Nature and other Es., V, 182.
The former terms (sc. voiced and voiceless) have a clear and precise meaning, which is quite easy *to grasp*. Wyld, Growth of Eng., Ch. II, 18.
It was a characteristic bargain of the old diplomacy, which is hard *to fit* to the subsequent course of events. Westm. Gaz., No. 8062, 1 a.
There is hardly a page in this book that is not a delight *to read*. ib.

82. Although the grammatical head-word of the adverbial illogical active infinitive is mostly a predicative adjective or adjectival equivalent, it may also be a substantive or substantival equivalent. Such a substantive mostly denotes some kind of measure.

It required an immoderate expense *to execute*. Field., Tom Jones, VIII.
The book has cost about £ 30000 *to produce*. Daily News and Leader.[1])

Note. Of particular interest is the following construction with the verb *to take*, wich admits of two logical expansions. Thus *The letter took him an hour to write* may be expanded into *It took him an hour to write the letter* and *He took an hour to write, the letter*.

i. The young stranger comprehending in one glance the result of the observation which has taken us some time *to express*. Scott, Quent. Durw., Ch. II, 42.
The letter took him long *to write*. Hall Caine, The Christian, I, 95. T.
Such works take at least ten years *to complete*. Times.
These questions will take a little time *to answer yet*. Ruskin, The Crown of Wild Olive, Work, 35.
ii. To pen one took the writer an entire morning. L. B. Walford, Stay-at-homes, Ch. X.
iii. As he was a short, fat man, he took some time to mount into the saddle. Wash. Irv. Dolf Heyl.

The discussion of further modifications of which the above combination admits must be held over for a subsequent treatise.

83. The illogical active infinitive may also represent a kind of prepositional object, *to* corresponding to final *for*. Thus especially after such adjectives as *fit*, *good*. Compare 85, Obs. III.

This apple is not fit *to eat*. This water is not good *to drink*. Mason, Eng. Gram.⁸⁴, § 372.
She is not fit *to mention* in the same breath as the darling girl I love and reverence. B. Eardley, Natalie's Secret.[2])
Shredded atora is in tiny particles like rice, prepared ready *to mix* with the flour. Daily News and Lead.[2])

---
[1]) De Drie Talen, XXXI, No. 12.
[2]) De Drie Talen, XXXII, No. 2.

Note. α) With *fit to eat*, as used in the above quotation, compare *fit to be helped* as in the next, in which *to be fit ... to deserve* which requires the infinitive to be placed in the passive voice.
You're not *fit to be helped*. Galsworthy, The Silver Box, I. 33, I. (Compare. The man who can break the laws of hospitality, and tempt the wife of his friend, *deserves to be branded* as the pest of society. Sher., School for Scand., IV, 3.)

β) Such an adjective as *fit* would in Present English be inserted before the illogical active infinitive in a construction like that instanced by:
This disturbed sky is not *to walk in*. Shsk., Jul. Cæs., I, 3, 40.

Compare Abbot (Shak. Gram.³, § 405), who observes "We might perhaps say, *This is not a sky (fit) to walk under*, but not *This sky is not (fit) to walk in*".

84. Already in Early Modern English we find occasional instances of the adverbial illogical active infinitive being replaced by the passive infinitive. Shakespeare uses the two constructions successively in:

If *to do* were as easy as *to know* what were good *to do*, chapels had been churches, and poor men's cottages princes' palaces. It is a good divine that follows his own instructions: I can easier teach twenty what were good *to be done* than be one of the twenty *to follow* mine own teaching. Merch. of Ven., I, 2, 13—19.

Also in later English, down to that of the present day, the passive construction is not uncommon. Although, in going through the quotations with either construction, one sometimes fancies that change into the alternative would not give good idiom, it is difficult to determine any principle by which writers have been guided in choosing either one or the other.

'Sblood, do you think I am easier *to be played* on than a pipe. Shsk., Haml., III, 3, 389.
She is harder *to be understood* than a piece of Egyptian antiquity. Congreve, Love for Love, IV, 3, (287).
The handwriting is very difficult *to be read*. Bosw., Life of Johns. 24b.
The fate of Fergus seemed hard *to be averted*. Scott, Wav., Ch. LXVII. 166a.
It now became necessary for the party to consider what was best *to be done*. Jane Austen, Pers., Ch. XII, 116.
Dolf, who was at the mercy of chance, was not hard *to be persuaded*. Wash. Irv., Dolf Heyl. (Stof., Handl., I, 138.)
This was not so easy *to be done*. Trol., The Warden, Ch. VIII, 97.
Is that a calamity hard *to be borne*? Ten., Maud, I, XIII, 1.
But Enid answer'd, harder *to be moved*, | Than hardest tyrants in their day of power. id., Ger. and En., 693.
It was what the mother wished, to be alone with this stranger, whose story must be a sorrowful one, yet was needful *to be told*. G. Eliot, Dan. Der., I, III, Ch. XX, 312.

It was plain *to be seen* that everybody loved him. EL. GLYN, The Reason
why, Ch. XXII, 203.
By the year 1912 the leading lines of the Pan-German advance were plain *to be
seen*. Ninet. Cent. and After, No. 496, 1104
Witnesses could not be got who were necessary *to be examined*. Daily Chronicle.

Note the curious construction in:
The rubric expressly states that ... it shall suffice that the bread be such as is
usual *to be eaten*. ib.

85. Obs. I. When followed by the inverted subject, i. e. a prepositional phrase
with *by* (SWEET, N. E. Gr., § 313), the passive voice is, of course,
unavoidable.
> Our own language affords many (sc. writers) of excellent use and instruc-
> tion, finely calculated *to sow* the seeds of virtue in youth, and very easy
> *to be comprehended* by persons of modest capacity. FIELD., Jos. And.,
> I, Ch. I, 1.

II. Also when the adjective is preceded by *too*, the passive voice
seems to be peculiarly apposite. Usage is, however, divided. It
will be observed that the adverbial relation of the infinitive becomes changed.
> i. The burden is too heavy *to be borne*. DICK., Pickw., Ch. XI, 183.
> The temptation ... was too great *to be resisted*. (?), The Cap of
> Youth, Ch. XXI.¹)
> ii. This contraction is too vague *to define* precisely. DAN. JONES, Eng.
> Phon., § 398, Footnote
> The whole thing is really too extraordinary *to believe*. LE QUEUX, An
> Eve for an Eve, Ch. I.¹)
> The amber gloom cast by fringed curtains too heavy *to pull back* from
> the windows. Daily News and Lead.¹)

III. After such adjectives as *fit*, *good*, etc., the passive construction
seems, on the whole, to be the one preferred. Thus in the following quotations it could hardly be exchanged for the active.
Compare 83.
> It is fit *to be placed* on the cylinder of the printing-press. Good Words.
> You're not fit *to be helped*. GALSWORTHY, The Silver Box, I, 3, (33). T.
> Asking to see books which are not ready *to be seen*. (?) The Cap
> of Youth, Ch. VI.¹)

86. It will have been observed that in such a sentence as *The difficulty is easy to avoid* (or *to be avoided*) the adjective logically
modifies the following infinitive adverbially. Accordingly we
sometimes find *easy* changed into *easily*, curiously enough, only
in connexion with the passive infinitive. Thus instead of the
above we sometimes find such a construction as *The difficulty*

¹) De Drie Talen, XXXII, No. 2.

is *easily to be avoided*. So far as the available evidence goes, it is practically only *easily* which is thus found before the passive infinitive, its opposite *difficultly* being a word of rare occurrence, and *hardly* being avoided on account of its ambiguity. One instance of *hardly* + passive infinitive has, however, come to hand.

i. The insolence and resentment of which he is accused were not *easily to be avoided* by a great mind. Johnson, Life of Rich. Savage (Wall. Fanton, Sam. Johnson, 19).
(He) is not so *easily to be shaken* from the lasting attachment founded on esteem. Ch. Lamb, Es. of El., A Bachelor's Complaint.
Situated as the insurgents were, the loss of a man of parts and energy was not *easily to be repaired*. Mac., Hist., II, Ch. V, 146.
The nature of her influence over James is not easily *to be explained*. ib. Ch. VI, 303.
Jack Rapley is not *easily to be knocked* off his feet. Miss Mitford, Our Village, Ch. II, 23.
She could see Keith's eyes, so *easily to be read*, showing out the impulses that crossed and possessed his mind. Frank Swinnerton, Nocturne, II, Ch. IX, V, 193.

ii. He (sc. Lord Beresford) was a product of an old school, a type which, as the old order changes, is more and more *hardly to be found*. Westm. Gaz., No. 8179, 4a.

87. After the phrase *it needs not* we find either the active or the passive voice, the choice, apparently, depending upon wether *it* represents the infinitive with its enlargements or a subordinate clause. Compare 7, b.

i. It needs not *to tell* what she said and promised on behalf of Nelly. Besant, All Sorts and Cond. of Men, Ch. XLVIII, 318.
ii. It needs not *to be said* that much which is true of our country at that time is true also of others. Mary Bateson, Mediæval England, Pref.

Note. The function of *it* in the above collocation is uncertain. It may be understood as the representative of the infinitive or subordinate clause, but also as an indefinite pronoun. This last view will appear plausible from a comparison with such sentences as:

It needs no witness to his deficiencies. The Nation, XX, 9, 309a.
It was a speech which it needed no small courage for a politician in Mr. Asquith's position to make. Times.

88. Such a sentence as *It was intended to issue a cheaper edition of the work*, in which a passive sentence with anticipating *it* is followed by an active infinitive-clause containing a non-prepositional object, may be converted into *A cheaper edition of the work is intended to be issued*. This construction, in which a

passive infinitive is made to depend on a passive verb in the head-sentence, and which may, therefore, be called a double passive, may be due to a general tendency, prevailing in English from quite early times, to replace a non-personal construction by a personal one.

Awkward as the construction is, it answers a useful purpose, since in not a few cases it would be difficult to find a more suitable one conveying the same meaning and falling in with the structure of the discourse. Thus for *The Court was ordered to be cleared* (Times) we could hardly substitute *It was ordered to clear the court*. Exchanging the passive for the active voice in the head-sentence would, indeed, make for better idiom, but this would defeat the ends of the passive voice, whose main purpose is to eliminate the necessity of mentioning the person or thing from which the action proceeds. Thus *The judge ordered the court to be cleared* is certainly better English than *the Court was ordered to be cleared*, but it may be taken exception to as bringing in an undesirable personal element. Also in some of the following quotations interference with the double passive would appear to give rise to difficulties. For discussion see also Stof., E. S., XXXI.

A satisfaction which was but feebly *attempted to be concealed* under a cold invitation to her to defer her departure. Jane Austen, Sense and Sens., 22.
Chartism was *left to be represented* by an open air meeting and a petition to Parliament. McCarthy, Short Hist., Ch. VIII, 89.
A distinction *is attempted to be drawn* between the indigent and those in comfortable circumstances. Rev. of Rev., 1899, Jan. 16, 40a.[1])
His perfect honesty and loyalty to the Church of England *are left to be called* in question only by fanatics. Lit. World, 1894, Nov. 9, 354a.
Newcastle takes its name from the castle which *was begun to be rebuilt* by Rufus. ib., 1899, Feb. 3, 94b.[1])
Mr Winston Churchill's appointment to the Colonial Office is not yet officially announced, but *is generally assumed to have been arranged*. Westm. Gaz., No. 8597, 5a.
No building *is allowed to be erected* without special permission, except it be constructed of brick. Times.
Of the brutal and frequent murders committed by the "Black and Tans" no mention *is allowed to be made* in the English Press. id., No. 2304, 159a.

Note. α) In not a few double passives the first passive expresses some form of necessity.

This *was obliged to be repeated* before it could be believed. Jane Austen, Emma, Ch. VIII, 58. I.

----

[1]) Stof., E. S., XXXI, 110.

One of 'em (sc. chairs), with long service and hard usage, positively lost his
senses — he got so crazy that he *was obliged to be burnt*. Dick. Pickw.,
Ch. XIV, 125.
The fuller form *is obliged to be retained*. Morris, Elem. Les of Eng Accid., 71
The Prince is prudent to refuse to enter into negotiations that *are bound to be
detected*. Mari. Bowen, I will maintain, I, Ch. V, 65
Things had been rather better of late, and no more belongings *had been forced
to be parted with*. El. Glyn, Halcyone, Ch. X, 83.
Notice *is required to be given* at least ten days previously, not only of the hour
and place of meeting, but of the business to be brought forward. Bryce, Amer
Commonw., I, 566 [1])
Ladies ... *are required to be proposed and seconded* by two members of the
club. Times, No. 2304, 1c1c.

β) Like any other passive, the double passive may, of course, be followed
by the inverted subject in the shape of a prepositional phrase consisting
of *by* — (pro)noun (Sweet, N. E. Gr., § 313).

An alley which ran parallel with the very high wall on that side the garden
was forbidden to be entered by the pupils. Ch. Bronte, Villette, Ch. XII, 131.

89. Also the desire of discarding the object of an action from the
discourse has, in the latest English, given rise to a peculiar
passive infinitive construction, of which there is no parallel in
either Dutch or German. Thus such a sentence as *This lens
will enable a man to take pictures in rainy weather* may be changed
into *This lens will enable pictures to be taken in rainy weather*,
the object of the infinitive phrase having become the subject
of the finite verb in the head-sentence.

This passive construction is, no doubt, an extension of a variety
of the accusative + infinitive, such as *He ordered the house to
be pulled down*, which goes back to *He ordered his men to pull
down the house*. Comparing two such sentences as *He ordered
his men to pull down the house* and *He enabled his men to pull
down the house*, we find that they differ materially as to the
grammatical relations existing between some of its constituent
elements. While in the former *his men* represents the indirect
(or person) object and *to pull down the house* the direct (or
thing) object of *ordered*, these elements stand in the latter for
the direct and the prepositional object of *enabled* respectively.
Owing to its novelty such a passive construction as *This lens
will enable pictures to be taken in rainy weather* strikes us as
illogical, but it is hardly more so than *He ordered the house
to be pulled down* and similar accusatives + passive infinitive,

[1]) Stof., E. S., XXXI, 110.

to which long usage has made us accustomed. For discussion see also Stof., E. S., XXXI, III.

This lens will enable pictures *to be taken* in rainy weather. Ill. Lond. News.
Railways will enable the fruit *to be sent* to market with the necessary expedition. Times.
The big table enables maps and documents *to be laid* out with ease. Strand Mag., No. 325, 16a.
As her knowledge of it (sc. English) was limited, a certain amount of imagination was necessary to enable her *to be understood*. Beatr. Har., Ships, I, Ch. XV, 85.

The new construction appears to be practically confined to the verb *to enable*, but will in time, perhaps, be extended to other verbs. The following quotation, although not admitting of being reduced to an active sentence of the above type, may be apprehended as another instance.

To meet the new conditions new arrangements will require *to be made*. Graphic, No. 2691, 772a.
(The meeting of the new conditions will require us (you or them, etc.) to make new arrangements. It will be observed that in this paraphrase *to meet the new conditions* is placed in another grammatical function.)

N o t e. α) *To be enabled* being practically equivalent to *to be able*, the latter phrase is sometimes substituted for the former, giving rise to such an utterly indefensible construction as instanced in:

The hypothesis that Shakespeare was joint-author with Fletcher (sc. of the Two Noble Kinsmen), which on internal evidence *is not able to be sustained*. Lit. World, 1897, April 23, 391c.
I fear that, owing to the New Budget arrangements, the legacy for a new church at Aldershot *will not be able to be paid*. Ill. Lond. News, No. 3671, 312b.

β) The use of *capable of* + passive gerund in place of *able to* + passive infinitive, although also yielding questionable idiom cannot, from a grammatical point of view, be reasonably objected to: *capable* being often predicated of non-personal subjects.

The amount of wealth which *is capable of being transferred* from any country to any other country is a strictly limited quantity. Westm. Gaz., No. 8603, 2a.

THE GERUND

ORDER OF DISCUSSION.

The Grammatical Nature of the Gerund	§§ 1–4
The Verbal and Substantival Features of the Gerund	§§ 5–24
The Verbal Features of the Gerund	§§ 6–9
The Substantival Features of the Gerund	§§ 10–16
The Gerund exhibiting at once Verbal and Substantival Features	§§ 17–24
Further Syntactical Observations about the Gerund	§§ 25–37
The Distinction of Voice neglected	§§ 25–29
The Distinction of Tense neglected	§§ 30–31
The Gerund followed by an Adnominal Adjunct with *of*	§§ 32–33
The Gerund preceded by the Common Case of a (Pro)noun or the objective of a Personal Pronoun	§§ 34–37
Compound Gerunds	§§ 38–42
The Gerund compared with the other Verbals	§§ 43–52
The Gerund compared with the Infinitive	§§ 43–45
The Gerund compared with the Noun of Action	§§ 46–48
The Gerund compared with the Present Participle	§§ 49–51
The Gerund compared with the Past Participle	§ 52
The Distinction between Gerund and Verbal Noun not justifiable	§§ 53–57
Historical Survey of the Rise of the Gerund	§§ 58–65

THE GRAMMATICAL NATURE OF THE GERUND.

1. a) The gerund is a substantival form of the verb which is intermediate between the infinitive and the noun of action; i. e. it is of a less distinctly verbal nature than the infinitive, and of a more distinctly verbal nature than the noun of action.

    b) All verbs have a gerund, only those which have no infinitive excepted.

2. Gerund forms which correspond to complex predicates (Ch. I, 15) may be called complex gerunds. They include:
    1. Such as contain some auxiliary of voice or tense, e. g.: *being punished, having punished.*
    2. Such as contain a verb denoting a form of compulsion, e. g.: *having to return.*

        The *having to fight* with that boisterous wind took off his attention. DICK., Chimes, I.
        He dreaded the *having to return* almost as much as going forward. SAM. BUTLER, Erewohn, Ch. III, 20.

3. a) Complex gerunds should be distinguished from compound gerunds, i. e. such as are made up of a noun, adverb or preposition + verb, e, g.: *horse-breeding, bringing-up* (or *upbringing), listening to.* For detailed discussion see 38—42.

    b) The same name may be given to the gerunds of word-groups forming a kind of unit and consisting of:
    1) a copula + nominal (or nominal equivalent), e. g.: *being poor, remaining poor, becoming poor.*

        The clerk went down a slide on Cornhill, at the end of a lane of boys, twenty times, in honour of its *being Christmas-eve.* DICK., Christm. Car., I.
        All the drains were choked, it appeared, from their *being so very narrow.* MARRYAT, Olla Podrida.
        I should prefer *being a lady's maid* to remaining at home. MRS. ALEX., A Life Int., Ch. XVI, 266.
        ii. Instead of *remaining silent,* he soon took up the word again.
        iii. To think of your *turning book-hunter.* LYTTON, Caxtons, XVII, Ch. 1, 450.
        It was difficult enough *getting acquainted* with her. JACK LONDON, Martin Eden, I, Ch. II, 22.

        Note. It is, of course, more or less objectionable, to call these combinations compound gerunds when they contain, as they not unfrequently do, an adverbial modifier, as in:
        I told him of the church's *being so very well worth seeing.* JANE AUSTEN, Pers., Ch. XIV, 133.

2) a verb + nominal (or nominal equivalent) in the function of predicative adnominal adjunct, e. g.: *making known, keeping bright.*

<small>Greek scholars who first taught Greek in Italy found that what was demanded at their hands was not so much the teaching of the language as the *making known* its thought. Edinb. Rev., Oct. 1905.[1])
She also took pride in *keeping bright* the silver skillet. (?), The Mischief-maker, Ch. I.</small>

3. a verb + noun in the function of non=prepositional object. e. g.: *paying heed, taking notice, catching hold, paying respect, doing honour,* etc.

<small>Journalists of the most violently opposed political creeds vied with each other in *doing honour* to their English guests. Rev. of Rev., No. 207, 239b
No line is any longer drawn between combatant and non=combatant in many of the modern methods of *waging war*. Manch. Guard., V, No. 16, 302d.</small>

Compound gerunds may be made complex, i. e. made to show the distinction of voice or tense.

<small>This, Sir Lucius, I call *being ill=used*. Shrk., Riv., III, 4, (252).
Tennyson disliked *being* lionised or *run after*. Horace enjoyed *being pointed out* as he walked along the street. Daily News, No. 19 782, 5g.
The first of these emotions ... is an instinctive and almost universal rebellion against *being* bullied, *trampled on* and *dictated to by* Western men. Westm. Gaz., No. 8603, 5a.</small>

4. Gerunds may also be formed direct from:

a) nouns, e. g.: *ballooning, black=berrying, fowling, gardening, nutting, shopping, soldiering,* etc.

<small>The past year has been a particularly eventful one in South African *banking*. Times, No. 2299, 60b.
He saw the dangers of *day=dreaming*. id., Lit. Sup., No. 993, 49d.
Upper Silesia ... is perhaps the wealthiest *mining* district in the whole of Europe. ib., No. 992, 35a.</small>

Note. These *ing=*forms are also frequent enough in the function of present participle, but the other verbal forms corresponding to them, if they are at all used, must be set down as back=formations.

<small>Southampton went *soldiering* in France. Times, Lit. Sup., No. 909, 9b.</small>

b) adverbs, e. g.: *homing* (= home=coming), *innings, offing, outing.*

<small>She professed her entire indifference as to the route of her *outing*. E. F. Benson, Mr. Teddy, Ch. I, 25.</small>

Note. Nonce=words in *ing* which have the same grammatical function as gerunds are formed freely on words or phrases of many kinds, e. g.:

---

[1]) Kruisinga, Handb.², § 255.

oh-ing, hear-hearing, pooh-poohing, how-d've-doing (= saying 'how do you do?'), (I do not believe in all this) pinting (= having pints of beer) MURRAY, s. v. ing, 1.

THE VERBAL AND SUBSTANTIVAL FEATURES OF THE GERUND.

5. The gerund is of a variable nature: i. e. sometimes it exhibits only such features as are peculiar to verbs, sometimes only such as are peculiar to substantives, sometimes at once such as are peculiar to verbs and such as are peculiar to substantives.
Again in many positions the gerund is practically equivalent to, and even interchangeable with the infinitive on the one hand, or the noun of action on the other.

a) The grammatical features of verbs are:
   1. that they may be accompanied by objects and adverbial adjuncts
   2. that either by inflection or by periphrasis they may show the distinctions of tense, voice, mood, person, and number.
   Those mentioned under 2) are the most typical.

b) The grammatical features of nouns are:
   1. that they may be used in a variety of functions in the sentence, i. e. as subject, nominal part of the predicate, non-prepositional object, adverbial adjunct (as in *He came home, He came yesterday*)
   2. that they may be preceded by a preposition and form with it a prepositional object, an adverbial adjunct or an adnominal adjunct;
   3. that in the above functions they may be modified by adjectives, articles, adnominal pronouns and numerals, nouns in the genitive or in the common case;
   4. that they may be used as adnominal modifiers, either in the genitive or in the common case.

   Note. The variable nature of the gerund has its parallel in that of the participles, which exhibit in various degrees of prominence the features characteristic of either verbs or adjectives.

The Verbal Features of the Gerund.

6. The verbal characteristics of the gerund are the same as those of the infinitive and the present participle.

7. Like these verbals, it may be attended by a non-prepositional or prepositional object, or by an adverbial adjunct, or by both an object and an adverbial adjunct. For illustration see also Ch. VIII, 77.

Hating one's neighbour is forbidden by the Gospel. Mason, Eng. Gram.,[84] § 568.
  Making Germany pay in coal is having a disastrous effect on our mining industry. Westm. Gaz., No. 8603, 2a.
  There is nothing as bad as *parting with one's friends*. Jane Austen, Pride and Prej., Ch. LII, 522.
  Talking of great occasions and the Muses reminds me of our good Rienzi's invitation to the Lateran. Lytton, Rienzi, II, Ch. II, 83.
 II Nature's chief masterpiece is *writing well*. Pope, Es. on Crit. III, 724.
  Lying late in the morning is a great shortener of life. Leigh Hunt, A Few Thoughts on Sleep.
  Staring about aimlessly will do no good. Onions, Adv. Eng. Synt., § 180.
  She finds *lying up so much* very irksome. Wells, Ann Veronica, Ch. I, § 5, 25.
 III *Pushing the work so rigorously* will soon produce results.
  This is *driving me into a corner*. Doyle, Gir., The Eternal Woman, Ch. XIV.

8. Like these verbals, it may show the distinctions of:
  a) voice, e. g.: active gerund *showing*, passive gerund *being shewn*. Only the passive gerund requires illustration. Compare 25—29.
    She begged the favour of *being shown* to her room. Dick., Cop., Ch. IV, 24a.
    I don't like *being asked* to make a speech. Swift, N. F. Gr., § 325.
    If we escaped *being noticed and punished*, it was only because Mr Webb was away at a wedding or funeral most of the time. id., Old Chapel.
    His great misfortune was *being ploughed* for the army. Pinero, Iris, I, (10).
    She objects to *being ordered*. Graph., No. 2310, 402a.
    There is nothing the House of Commons resents more bitterly than *being jockeyed*. Rev. of Rev., No. 199, 8b.
    One of the real dangers in Belgium was *being shot* by one's own sentries. Eng. Rev., No. 72, 495.
    There's nothing quite so awfully hard as *being forgiven*. Morley Roberts, Time and Thomas Waring, Ch. XXXI, 305.
    He seemed to dread the prospect of *being sent* to his native country. Gissing, Tatterdemalion, IV, I, 96.

  b) tense, but only to show that its time-sphere is thought of as anterior to that of the predication with which it is connected, e. g.: imperfect gerund *showing*, perfect gerund *having shown*. Only the perfect gerund needs illustration. Compare 30—31.
    I acknowledge *having been* at such a meeting. Scott, Wav., Ch. XXXI, 94b.
    My mother, who never loved Mrs. H., now said that she should repent all her life *having allowed* me to spend so much of my time with that odious, ungrateful, woman. Thack., Sam. Titm., Ch. XIII, 176. (Observe that in strict grammar *never loved* should have been *had never loved*.)
    I am glad of *having met* you. Bain, Comp., 170.
    He mentioned *having read* it in the paper. Mrs. Alexander, For his Sake, II, Ch. XVI, 283.
    My companion seemed to regret *having invited* me. G. Gissing, Christopherson.
    If they are proud of *having beaten* them, they are still prouder of *having made* them their political brethren. Graph.

c) voice and tense together, e. g. perfect passive gerund *having been shown*.

> I relieved you from the bondage of *having been born* a Jew. G. Eliot, Dan Der., III, VII, Ch. LI, 124.
> Several noblemen and gentlemen were there already mounted, displeased at *having been kept* waiting. "Sir Walter Scott" Readers for Young People, The Story of the Abbot.
> The fact that … Mrs. Andrew had seen only yesterday a stranger woman talking to the house-agent … constituted a strong case for the house *having been let*. E. F. Benson, Mr Teddy, Ch. II, 59.

9. Obs. I. Like the infinitive and the present participle, the gerund is incapable of indicating that its time-sphere is posterior to that of the predication with which it is connected, the imperfect gerund being used in this case in like manner as in sentences in which the two time-spheres are co-incident.

> I'm so afraid of mamma *hearing*. Aus. and Eg. Castle, Diamond cut Paste, II, Ch. I, 117.
> He is afraid of my *breaking* down. Dor. Gerard, The Eternal Woman, Ch. XX.
> It looks like *being* a very interesting autumn season. Manch Guard, V, No. 14, 273b.

Phrases expressing immediate futurity blended with some other notion are, of course, frequent enough, and may, in a manner, be regarded as substitutes for the auxiliaries of the future tense. Such are *to be about* (or *going*) *to*, *to be on the point of*, *to be in act to*, etc. See my Treatise on Tense, 68–71.

> The news of his *being about to return* home instead of *having been slain* by the enemy. Murray, s. v. *ing*, 2.
> He wished that before he called, he had realized more fully than he did the pleasure of *being about to call*. Hardy, Under the Greenwood Tree, I, Ch. IX, 82.

II. The tense of the gerund is not affected by a change of time-sphere in the predication with which it is connected. See also Tense, 12, c; and compare Infinitive 57, a; and Participles, 3, Note †

> In *coming come* { he always meets with some accident.
> he always met with some accident.
> he will meet with some accident.

III. As will be shown below (25–31), the distinctions of both voice and tense are often disregarded.

THE SUBSTANTIVAL FEATURES OF THE GERUND.

10. The substantival features which may be observed in the gerund are, in the main, the same as those of ordinary nouns. In some cases these features are shared by the infinitive, in some they are not.

11. Like the infinitive, the gerund may be used in the function of subject, nominal part of the predicate and non-prepositional object. For a comparison of the areas of incidence of the two verbals see Ch. XIX.

> i   *Talking* mends no holes — Prov.
> ii This is *anticipating*. Stead's Annual of 1906, 24b.
> iii The curate dropped *calling*. EM. BRONTË, Wuth Heights, Ch. VIII, 35a.
>   I have only just finished *dusting*. CH. BRONTË, Jane Eyre, Ch. IV, 31.
>   He succeeded in abolishing *flogging*. Rev. of Rev., No 195, 228a.
>
> Note the peculiar construction in:
> Whenever Diggory sees *eating* going forward, ecod! he's always wishing for a mouthful himself. GOLDSMITH, She stoops, II (178).

12. Unlike the infinitive, the gerund may be preceded by any preposition to form with it a prepositional object, an adverbial adjunct or an adnominal adjunct, the former tolerating no other preposition than *to* before it in Standard English. See Infinitive, 3, Obs. III.

> i   You must hear us talk, and not think *of talking*; you must see us drink, and not think *of drinking*; you must see us eat, and not think *of eating*. GOLDSMITH, She stoops, II. (178).
>   She was deaf *To blessing* or *to cursing* save from one. TEN., Ger and En., 578.
>   I shall begin *by reading* the earlier will. G. ELIOT, Mid., Ch. XXXV, 247.
>   Three hours she gave *to stitching*. CH. BRONTË, Jane Eyre, Ch. XXI, 286.
> ii She had laid her little bag of documents upon the table *on coming in*. DICK., Bleak House, Ch. V, 35.
>   *In passing* I may remark that this young lady has done a thing which is, in its way, little short of heroic. RID. HAG., Mees. Will, Ch. XXI, 224.
> iii No person ever had a better knack *at hoping* than I. GOLDSMITH, Vic., Ch. XX, (362).
>   If I had the money *for studying*, I should go in for medicine. DOY. GIR., The Etern Wom., Ch. XI.
>   You would like to decide your own hour *of getting up*. ib., Ch. XI.
>
> Note. The gerund of an intransitive verb may be preceded by weak *there*.
> I was willing to trust to *there being* no harm in her. JANE AUSTEN, Emma, Ch. VIII, 59.
> He spoke of *there being* a danger. ONIONS, Adv. Eng. Synt., § 180.

13. Unlike the infinitive, the gerund may be preceded by all the ordinary noun-modifiers, i. e. by:

a) an adjective or an adjective equivalent.

> He was greeted with *vociferous cheering*. DICK., Chuz., Ch. XXXV, 281a.
> Many people had, after *hard begging*, thrown her pence. EDNA LYALL, We Two, I, 21, 1.

Pioneers engaged in *hand-to-hand* fighting with the Mahsuds. Times No. 2298, 23a.

The following idioms are of some special interest:

i. It was easy *talking* till you came to that. G. Eliot, Mill. II, Ch. III, 146. It is fine *talking*. id., Scenes, I, Ch. VI, 47.
ii. That was bitter *hearing* to both parents. Ags. and Eg. Castl., Diamond cut Paste, III, Ch. VII, 290.
iii. All seems smooth *sailing* until the Opposition detect a chance of embarrassing the Government. Westm. Gaz., No. 5255, 4b.
iv. Easy *writing* makes hard *reading*. Times, Lit. Sup., No. 999, 149b.

b) the definite or the indefinite article. For illustration see also Ch. XXXI, 37.

i. I shall never forget *the waking* next morning, *the being cheerful and fresh* for the first moment, and then *the being weighed down* by the stale and dismal oppression of remembrance. Dick., Cop., Ch. IV, 30a.
The killing goes on; the search for arms, in spite of the fulmination of the death penalty, has had little or no result. Westm. Gaz., No. 5597, 2b.
You have to present a fairly accurate opinion upon the play and *the acting*. ib., 6a.
ii. It is rather *a hovering* and *nodding* on the borders of sleep than sleep itself. Leigh Hunt, A Few Thoughts on Sleep.
A knocking at the door was heard. Dick., Christm. Car., II.
It seemed doubtful whether we should escape *a wetting*. Times No. 1809, 701a.

The following idioms are of some special interest.

i. I might have had this prize for *the asking*. Thack., Pend., I, Ch. XXIV, 253.
The great rivers swarmed with fish for *the taking*. id., Virg., Ch. III, 27.
The story of Mulcahy always took an hour in *the telling*. id., Sam Titm., Ch. I, 8.
The story . . . has lost nothing in *the telling*. Mrs. Ward, Cousin Phil., Ch. X, 154.
The story is rather long, but must not be spoilt in *the telling*. Times No. 2297, 1b.
ii. I do not remember that he had so bad *a beating*. Times, No. 2301, 99c.
That's *a bad hearing*. Dick., Cop., Ch. IV, 22a.
Sulivan could scarcely obtain *a hearing*. Mac., Clive, (529a).

Note. *α)* Unusual is the use of either article before the gerund after *worth*, as in:

i. "How was it?" — "Well worth *the seeing*." Shak., Henry VIII, IV, I, 60.
It was worth *the getting-up-for*. Hor. Hutchinson, (Westm. Gaz. No. 6011, 2c).
The secret . . . was well *worth the giving*, though how the public may receive the gift, I do not know. Westm. Gaz., No. 5627, 6b.
ii. We had . . . nothing for our millions but newspapers not *worth a reading*. Farquhar, Recruit. Of., II, I, (266).

β) It may be observed that modification by an adjective placed before the gerund, and modification by an adverb placed *after* it, often has practically the same effect. Thus *I do not like early rising* and *I do not like rising early* only differ in so far as the latter emphasizes the earliness of the rising more emphatically than the former. For the rest the difference is chiefly one of style. Compare:

  i. Those matters belong rather to the subject of *early rising* than of sleep. LEIGH HUNT, A Few Thoughts on Sleep.
  ii. *Rising early* is a wholesome practice. MASON, Eng. Gram.⁸⁴, § 260, N.

Nor can it be maintained that placing the modifier before the gerund inexpugnably settles its grammatical function, inasmuch as adverbs of quality in *ly* may also be found be fore it. Compare Ch. VIII, 77.

I was so afraid of Mr. Jarndyce's *suddenly disappearing*. DICK., Bleak House, Ch. VI, 39. (Placing *suddenly after* the gerund would give it undue stress.)

Also the difference between *This vigorous pushing of the work will soon produce results* and *Pushing the work so vigorously will soon produce results* (CURME, E. S. XLV, 36a) is chiefly one of emphasis, the latter implying greater vigour than the former, even if the adjective receives more stress than the following noun.

c) adnominal pronouns and numerals, including phrases which have the value of numerals.

  i. *This giving back* of dignity for dignity seemed to open the sluices of feeling that Boldwood had as yet kept closed. HARDY, Far from the Madding Crowd, Ch. XIX, 145.
   Even amid *this wilful bottling* of all talk ... a mirthful hour has been provided by Lord Charles Beresford. Westm. Gaz., No. 5249, 4 b.
  ii. *What moving about* of lanterns in the courtyard and stables, though the moon was shining. THACK, Pend., I, Ch. III, 36.
  iii.⁹ She could read any English book without *much spelling*. GOLDSMITH, Vic., Ch. I.
   They (sc. the servants) want as *much training* as a company of recruits the first day's muster. id., She stoops, I, (171).
   The font, reappearing, | From the raindrops shall borrow, | But to us comes *no cheering*, | To Duncan *no morrow*. SCOTT, Lady III, Coronach, I
   There is hardly *any desiring* to refresh such a memory as that. JANE AUSTEN, Emma, Ch. V, 35. T.
   "The man's a great deal past the average, you know", cried Mr. Filer, breaking in as if his patience would bear *some trying*. DICK., Chimes,⁸ I, 35.
   There was undeniable truth in Beatrice Redwing's allusion to his *much talking*. GISSING, A Life's Morn., Ch. III, 36.
   He used to play croquet all August, when there was *no hunting* and *no shooting*. E. F. BENSON, Mr. Teddy, Ch. II, 47.
   The world has seen nothing like this grim settling down to the suffering of death, wounds and privations beyond *all imagining*. Westm. Gaz., No. 7577, 4 b.
   No one fancies that he can ... criticise Chinese poetry without *some little training* for the task. ib., No. 8597, 6 a.

I retired to the front (sc. of the premises) to do some thinking. Punch No. 3810, 66 a.

⁰⁰ For a term or two he stayed on in Oxford, acting as my private secretary and doing a certain amount of teaching and lecturing for the Workers Educational Association. BROWN, The French Revol. in Eng. Hist. Introd.

We should have seen a great deal of acting. Westm. Gaz., No. 8597, 6 a.

iv. Oliver, having had by this time as much of the outer coat of dirt which encrusted his face and hands removed, as could be scrubbed off in one washing, was led into the room by his benevolent protectress. DICK. Ol. Twist., Ch. II, 26.

v. It (sc. the bill) is then circulated, and a day is fixed for the second reading. Royal Readers (STOF., Leesb., I, 48).

d) a genitive or possessive pronoun, 1. standing by way of subject to the predication it expresses. For illustration see also Ch. XXIV, 19.

i. She played till Fanny's eyes, straying to the window on *the weather's being evidently fair*, spoke what she felt must be done. JANE AUSTEN, Mansf. Park, Ch. XXII, 213.

Paul was quite alarmed at *Mr. Feeder's yawning*. DICK., Domb., Ch. XII, 104.

ii. I heard of *his running away*. MASON, Eng. Gram.³⁴, § 494.

The following idioms deserve some special mention:

i. I promised to eat all *of his killing*. SHAK., Much ado, I, 1.

My daughters undertook to adorn the walls with pictures *of their own designing*. GOLDSMITH, Vic., Ch. IV, (255).

Will you take a husband *of your friends' choosing*? SHK., KIV, I, 2.

A chance and hope *of my procuring*. DICK., Christm. Car., I, 23.

Is it the natural end of your precepts and mine, that this should be the creature *of your rearing, training, teaching, hoarding, striving for*? id., Chuz. Ch. LI, 395 a.

The events of the last few months have not been *of the Government's making* or *of Mr. Redmond's making*. Westm. Gaz., No. 5347, 1 c.

ii. Her songs are *her own making*. LYTTON, Pomp., I, Ch. III, 19 a.

It was all *Cornelia's doing*. WALT. BESANT, The Bell of St. Paul's, II, 155, I.

He couldn't look me in the face and say it . . . But of course it's *aunt's doing* really. WELLS, Ann Veronica, Ch. I, § 2, 14.

Entirely *his own making*, too, is his personal popularity. Times, No. 2299, 55 c.

Note. α) Also the indefinite *its* is found in this function. Its comparative frequency, especially before *being*, nominal, shows that WILLERT (l. c., 35) is mistaken in considering this use of *its* in the following quotation from DICKENS's Christm. Carol as a bad joke. See also CURME, l. c.; MÄTZN., E. Gr.², III, 82; and compare Ch. XL, 63.

The clerk . . . went down a slide on Cornhill in honour of *its being Christmas-Eve*. DICK., Christm. Car.⁵, I, 18.

You were talking *of its being a girl*. id., Cop., Ch. I, 4 b.

The notion *of its being Sunday* was the strongest in young ladies like Miss Phipps. G. ELIOT, Scenes, III, Ch. V, 218.

Do not run away the first moment of *its holding up*. JANE AUSTEN, Mansfield Park, Ch. XXII, 213.
I won't hear of *its raining* on your birthday! OSC. WILDE, Lady Wind.'s Fan, I, 1, (19).
There is very little chance of *its clearing* for us to shoot to-day. EL. GLYN, Refl. of Ambros., II, Ch. X, 207.

β) Similarly instances of the anticipating (personal pronoun) *its* before a gerund appear to be common enough.

Mademoiselle doubts . . . *its being so easy* to forgive. DICK., Little Dorrit, Ch. II, 12 b.
After some talk about *its being hard* upon Nan to have to take leave so suddenly of her governess, Clara's wish was granted. DOR. GERARD, The Etern. Woman, Ch. XIII.
Such an inquiry ought in such a case to be a matter of course, and the mere idea of *its needing* to be demanded by the threat of a strike ought to be dismissed as gratuitous and unnecessary. Westm. Gaz., No. 8615, 2 a.

2. standing by way of non-prepositional object to the predication it expresses. Compare 27; also Ch. XXIV, 20; Ch. XXXIII, 7.

i. It (sc. the tormenting humour) was still held to be necessary to *my poor mother's training*. DICK., Cop., Ch. VIII, 58 b.
He began to give a half-humorous account of the troubles and storms of *Hester's bringing-up*. MRS. WARD, The Case of Rich. Meyn., II, Ch. X, 201.
On the day of *Hester's burying* Long Whindale lay glittering white under a fitful and frosty sunshine. ib., IV, Ch. XXIV, 499.
He was glad to receive early lights on the subject of *his daughter's up-bringing*. AGN. and EG. CASTLE, Diamond cut Paste, I, Ch. V, 67.

ii. I never meant this miscreant should escape, | But wish'd you to suppress such gusts of passion, | That we more surely might devise together *His taking-off*. BYRON, Mar. Fal., I, 2, (355 a).
His pore (= poor) mother . . . made a mistake at *his christening*. HARDY, Far from the Madding Crowd, Ch. X, 91.
They now put the finishing touch to *their training* and equipment. II. Lond. News, No. 3940, 569 a.

3. indicating the duration of the action or state it expresses.

After *eight years' suffering* she was quickly and entirely cured. Westm. Gaz., No. 5261, 7 c.
Yokohama is *fifteen days' steaming* from San Francisco. Rev. of Rev., No. 212, 113 b.

4. denoting the epoch of the action or state it expresses.

She has as many tricks as a hare in a thicket, or a colt *the first day's breaking*. GOLDSMITH, She stoops, II, (295).

e) the common case of nouns or such pronouns as have no genitive, or the objective of personal pronouns, the relation of these modifiers to the gerund corresponding to that of subject to predicate. Compare 34—37.

I don't approve of *young men getting engaged* until they have some prospect of being able to marry. Asser, Voces Populi, Christm. Kamp., 206
She listened to *the door slamming*. Edith Thomson, City of Beaut. Nons., II, Ch. II, 214.

ii. You seem to understand me by *each at once her choppy fingers laying upon her skinny lips*. Shak., Macb., I, 5, 34.
You will oblige me by *all leaving the room*. Mason, Eng. Gram.², § 414.
I have my doubts as to *this being true*. ib.

iii. Excuse me *putting* in a word. Dick., Domb., Ch. 1, 7.
Pardon *me saying it*. Tin., Princ., I, 154.

Note. The subject-indicating element may be a lengthy word-group.
On a sudden, many a voice along the street, *And heel against the pavement echoing*, burst. Their drowse. Tin., Ger. and En., 271 (= *the echoing of the heel against the pavement*)

14. Unlike the infinitive, the gerund may be followed and modified by a prepositional word-group with *of*, representing either a subjective or objective genitive. The relative frequency of the *of*-construction, as compared with the subjective or the objective genitive has already been discussed in Ch. XXIV, 19 and 21. Naturally the gerund, when followed by a word-group with *of*, is mostly preceded by an other adnominal modifier. Compare also 32.

i. He was suddenly startled from his slumbers by *the bustling-in of the housekeeper*. Wash. Irv., Dolf Heyl. (Ston., Handl., I, 113).
He would not stand *the bullying of the doctor* any more. Thack., Pend., I, Ch. II, 31.
We could never listen ... to *the speaking of Sir James* without feeling that there was a constant effort, a tug up hill. Mac., Rev., (311 b).
We had hoped ... *for a better pulling together of all parties* in dealing with a serious national problem. Westm. Gaz., No. 8591, 2 a.
They will not submit to be treated ... as children expected to accept blindly *the teaching of a benevolent parent*. ib., No. 8603, 5 a.

ii. There's no *pressing of women* surely! Farquhar, Recr. Of., III, 1, (285).
The milking of cows was a sight Mrs. Poyser loved. G. Eliot, Ad. Bede, VI, Ch. XLIX, 412.
Without question, *the use of oil fuel in place of coal* means a great saving of labour. Ill. Lond. News, No. 3698, 347.
Modern conditions do not lead to *the quick weeding out of the feeble and the diseased*. Westm. Gaz., No. 8603, 4 a.

Of some special interest are constructions in which the gerund is also modified by a subjective genitive or another prepositional word-group.

i. Leigh Hunt was undoubtedly both pained and puzzled by *Byron's misunderstanding of this attitude*. J. H. Lobban, Sel. in Prose and Verse from Leigh Hunt, Introd.
Another distinction of the French visit was *the King's opening of the Kingsway*. Rev. of Rev., No. 191, 460 a.

ii This will hinder the growth of better relations with Germany and *the granting to her of concessions* in the economic life. Westm. Gaz., No. 8579, 3 a.

Note. A gerund with an objective *of*-combination is equivalent to, and often interchangeable with a gerund with a non-prepositional object. Thus *The purchasing of needless things has ruined many a one* = Purchasing needless things has ruined many a one. For further discussion see 32.

15. Unlike the infinitive, the gerund may be used as an adnominal modifier. Compare, however, Infinitive, 73.

    Godolphin was not a *reading* man. Mac., Ad., (745 b). (= a man given to reading.)
    Mrs. Bretton was not generally a *caressing* woman. Ch. Brontë, Villette, Ch. I, 5.
    His wealth consists in land, factories, machinery, and a vast *selling* organisation. Westm. Gaz., No. 8603, 4 a.
    The Entente has been in thorough *working* efficiency. Times, No. 2299, 55 a.

    Note. In this function the gerund often forms established designations, graphically distinguished from occasional collocations by the use of the hyphen. Such are *carving-knife, dancing-master, dwelling-house, fowling-piece, laughing-stock, meeting-house, reaping-hook, stumbling-block, spinning-wheel, turning-lathe, turning-point, walking-stick*, and a great many others. In the same position and function we also find the present participle, likewise often forming with its head-word a kind of compound.

    The general is a *serving* officer. Westm. Gay., No. 8121, 3 a.
    The Bill has passed through *Standing* Committee. ib.
    Comforts for *fighting* men. ib. [i. e. men fighting in the field. But *fighting* is a gerund in *There's no justice for a fighting man* (Shaw, Cash. Byron's Prof. Ch XIII, 239), i. e. a man who makes his living by prize-fighting.]

    Many combinations leave room for a two-fold interpretation. Thus those in:

    I am not yet on friendly and intimate terms with the Coupon system, but I have a *nodding* acquaintance with it. Punch, No. 3998, 126 a.
    The new ministry ... appears as a good *working* combination. Westm. Gaz., No. 8597, 3 a.

    For further dicussion and illustration see Ch. XXIII, 13, Obs. VII.

16. Unlike the infinitive, the gerund may be inflected for number and for case. Inflection for number is quite common; not so that for case, which seems to be confined to collocations in which *sake* is the word modified.

    1. At length the tumult died away in low *gaspings* and *moanings*. Mac., Clive, (514 a).
    Good *beginnings* make good *endings*. Mrs. Craik, A. Hero, 68.
    It is difficult to conceive how *borrowings* and *lendings* could to any large extent be carried on without the medium of the Stock Exchange. Escott, England, Ch. IV, 42

He ignored the sayings and doings of the ladies of his family. Sykes, Guessed Our man, Nat. 32.
She hated hole-and-corner doings. Nos. and In. Cassels Dick's Cut Paste, Ch. V, 72.
I never saw such doings. Swift, N. L. Gr., No. 529.
There have been indiscriminate burnings, pillagings, and shootings, with what discernible results? Times, No. 2501, 99 a.

ii. Calm Temperance whose blessings those partake / Who hunger and who thirst for scribbling's sake. Pope, Dunciad, I, 50.
He (sc. the moor-hen) does not kill for eating's sake like those other enemies that have been named. Westm. Gaz., No. 5249, 12 b.
It is nobler to talk for talking's sake than to talk with a purpose. ib., No. 5607, 4 b.
The extinction of the great auk was ... the result of ... the love of killing for killing's sake. The New Statesman, No. 252, 423 b.
It was evident that he wanted to talk, if only for talking's sake. Bram Stoker, Dracula, Ch. II, 22.

The Gerund exhibiting at once Verbal and Substantival Features.

17. The gerund is often attended by both verb- and noun-modifiers. Not a few instances may be found in the preceding sections. Among the numerous possible combinations it is especially the following which deserve some attention.

18. Very frequently we meet with gerunds that are modified by a genitive or possessive pronoun and followed, or preceded, by one or more of the verb-modifiers, i. e. objects or adverbial adjuncts.

   a) all the verb-modifiers following the gerund:

   Perhaps my being here prevents her coming to you. Shs., School for Scandal, V, 3 (430).
   Sometimes I fancied that Peggotty objected to my mother's wearing all her pretty dresses. Dick., Cop., Ch. II, 11 b.
   It (sc. his trot) cost him a world of trouble; he could have walked with infinitely greater ease, but that was one reason for his clinging to it so tenaciously. id., Chimes³, I, 8.
   Mrs. Sedley had forgiven his breaking the punch-bowl. Thack., Van. Fair, I, Ch. V, 48.
   Will you consent to my putting an advertisement in the Times? Mrs. A., A Life Interest, II, Ch. I, 11.

   b) one of the verb-modifiers preceding the gerund:

   He excused his not waiting on me home. Fergusson, Rec. Of., IV, 2, (310).
   From the moment of his first speaking to me, his voice connected itself with an association in my mind that I could not define. Dick., Bleak House, Ch. VI, 94.

19. a) Also the definite or indefinite article is often found together with verb=modifiers of the gerund, especially prepositional objects or adverbial adjuncts. Compare 13, a) and b).

<small>i. The excitement of the events of the day, the quitting my home, *the meeting with captain Quin*, were enough to set my brains in a whirl. THACK., Barry Lyndon, Ch. III, 48
ii. In ancient times, no work of genius was thought to require so great parts and capacity as *the speaking in public*. HUME, Es. XIII, Of Eloquence, 99
iii. *The meeting with such formidable obstacles* at such an unseasonable time upset all his plans.</small>

b) Constructions in which the gerund is preceded by the definite article and followed by a non=prepositional object were, apparently, quite common in Early Modern English, but are now unusual, especially in the case of the object being a noun. In literary English, even of quite recent times, instances are not, however, so infrequent as is often believed. For discussion and illustration see also ONIONS, Adv. Eng. Synt., § 181—2; KONRAD MEIER, E.S., XXXI, 327; ELLINGER, Verm. Beitr., VII, No. 16; CURME, E.S., XLV, 361.

<small>Nothing in his life | Became him like *the leaving it*. SHAK., Macb., I, 4, 8. (The construction is revived in: Nothing perhaps in life became him like to *the leaving it*. MCCARTHY, Hist. of Our Own Times, 1, Ch. I, 3.)
Even grey hair itself is no objection to *the making new conquests*. MARY WORTLEY MONTAGUE, Let. 71.
When Mrs. Debora returned into the room, and was acquainted by her master with *the finding the little infant*, her consternation was rather greater than his had been. FIELDING, Tom Jones, 1, Ch. III, 3 b.
My attention was fixed on another subject, *the completing a tract* which I intended shortly to publish. GOLDSMITH, Vic., Ch. II, (243).
I confess I have since known no pleasure equal to *the reducing others* to the level of my own reputation. SHER,. School, I, 1, (364).
His present engagement might only end in his being exposed like a conquered enemy in a Roman triumph, a captive attendant on the car of a victor, who meditated only *the satiating his pride* at the expense of the vanquished. SCOTT, Bride of Lam., Ch. XIX, 194.
I have another reason for refraining to shoot besides *the fearing discomfiture and disgrace*. id., Ivanhoe, Ch. XIII, 134. T.
I regard it as a most happy thought, *the placing Miss Smith* out of doors. JANE AUSTEN, Emma, Ch. VI, 46.
Nothing he thought could bring a man to such wretchedness but *the having unkind daughters*. LAMB, Tales, Lear, 161. T.
He had certain inward misgivings that *the placing him* within the full glare of the judge's eye was only a formal prelude to his being immediately ordered away for instant execution. DICK., Pickw., Ch. XXXIV.
The excitement of the events of the day, *the quitting my home*, the meeting with captain Quin, were enough to set my brains in a whirl. THACK., Barry Lyndon, Ch. III, 48.</small>

The contemplating a father's death . . . it seems a kind of parricide. LYTTON, My Novel, II, VIII, Ch. IV, 30.
I am not sure if *the inhabiting this house* was not also believed to convey some unusual power of intellect. MRS. GASK., Cranf., Ch. VII, 129.
Next in importance was *the restoring peace and order to, and banishing misery and pauperism from the sister isle*. Lit. World.
I exhort you to take this as your aim — *the bringing into existence the peace of the world*. The Archbishop of York's Address to the Boy-Scouts (The Jamboree Book, 100a).

Note. α) In many cases idiomatic propriety can be easily re-established by replacing the non-prepositional object by an adnominal adjunct with *of*, or by simply removing the article.
i. Master Blifil objected to *the sending away the servant*. FIELDING, Tom Jones, IV, Ch. VIII, 53 b. (rewritten . . . *the sending away of the servant*, or, which seems even more usual . . . *the servant being sent away*.)
ii. I think it probable that she would be displeased on *the first hearing it*. TROL., Framl. Pars., Ch. XXXI, 303. (rewritten . . . *on first hearing it*.)
He suffered in *the saying it*. MRS. WARD, Rob. Elsm., I, 197. T.

β) Extremely awkward and harsh is the construction when the gerund is modified by an adverb of quality. Compare CURME, E. S., XLV, 361.

As certain dates are all important to *the well understanding my story*, I mention that it begins in the afternoon of March 28, 1823. Tales from Blackwood, II, 11 [1])

This is far less the case when the adverb is the negative *never* or *not*, as in:

It must be the unnatural way they're brought up — that and *the never hearing a single word of truth* from the hour they are born. FR. LAWLESS, A Col. of the Empire, Ch. IV.

γ) Sometimes the syntactical connections seem to justify the construction, any alternative construction being hardly available. Thus especially when the gerund is modified adverbially by a prepositional word-group standing after the object.
i That is a *turning English into French*, rather than a *tehning English by French*. DRYDEN, Defence of the Epilogue.
Then the shouting and the struggling, and the onslaught, that was made on the defenceless porter. The *scaling him with chairs for ladders* to dive into his pockets, despoil him of brown-paper parcels [etc.]. DICK, Christm. Car., II.
The *following them about*, and jesting with them, affords a cheap and innocent amusement for the boy population. id., Pickw., Ch. II, 10.
ii *The having originated a precaution* which was already in course of execution was a great relief to Miss Pross. id., Tale of Two Cities, III, Ch. XIV, 405.
In the last example (sc. He told them he had gone for a little walk, and saw a donkey) the pluperfect is justified by the fact that the going for a walk preceded seeing the donkey, and it is used here because *the seeing the donkey* is the really important event, to which the pluperfect makes it subordinate. SWEET, N. E. Gr., § 2247.

[1]) WILLERT, l. c., 380.

20. What has been said about the above construction with the definite article also applies, in the main, to that in which the gerund is preceded by a demonstrative pronoun and is followed by a non-prepositional object. CURME (l. c., 361) gives the following instances, observing, "It is most common with pronominal objects, but it is also often found with substantives":

I don't like *this javing one down* so.
This missing the mark so widely that everybody laughed discouraged him from shooting again.
I approve of *this holding the speakers* to the question
This pinning one's faith to a political party is very harmful to the country
I don't like *this scaring the very life* out of a fellow

The student will observe that unlike the two first, the three last examples in which the object is followed by a prepositional word-group fall pleasantly enough upon the ear.

And again, "Such a combination as *this missing fatally the train* or *this missing the train fatally*, instead of *this fatal missing of the train* is impossible."

21. The combination no + gerund + non-prepositional object is a peculiarly English idiom. For the rest the combination indefinite numeral + gerund + non-prepositional object appears to be unusual.

i. There is *no making you serious a moment*. SHER, School for Scand. IV, 2, (407)
There is *no trusting appearances*. ib., V, 2, (425).
There was *no mistaking the real nature* of the trial through which he had passed. RID. HAG., Mees. Will, Ch. XIV, 142.
ii. Emma thought she could so pack it as to ensure its safety without *much incommoding him*. JANE AUSTEN, Emma, Ch. VII, 47. (more usual English *incommoding him [very] much*.)

22. The gerund may be preceded by an adnominal modifier, and at the same time exhibit the distinction of either voice or tense, or of both together. According to CURME (l. c., 362) constructions of this description in which the adnominal element is represented by either an article or a demonstrative pronoun are clumsy and are mostly avoided. Conversely those in which the complex gerund is preceded by a genitive or possessive pronoun, or by *no*, appear to be quite common, at least in literary language.

i. He said that I should heartily repent *his being listed*. FARQUHAR, Rec. Off., V, 7, (345)

Bingley urged *Mr. Jones's being sent for immediately*. Jane Austen, Pride and Prej., Ch. VIII, 44.
You must excuse *my not being convinced* by assurances only. ib., Ch. XVIII, 49.
She was delighted with the idea of *her son's being brought up* to a profession worthy of his ancestors. Wash. Irv., Dolf Heyl. (Stof., Handl., I. 107).
The consequences of my incapacity was his driving my cattle that evening and *their being appraised and sold* next day. Hughes, Tom Brown.
My not being married is no reason why they should be disappointed. Shew, Getting Married, (231).

⁹⁹ There is no *being shot at* without a little risk. Sher., Riv., V, 3, (279).
*¹⁰⁰ The greatest pain I can suffer is *the being talked to* and *being stared at*. Addison, Spect., I.
I am not disposed to maintain that *the being born* in a workhouse is in itself the most fortunate and enviable circumstance that can possibly befall a human being. Dick., Ol. Twist, Ch. I, 19.
They enjoyed *the not being hurried*. Hughes, Tom Brown.
ii.⁰ Their greatness seems to consist in *their never having done* anything to distinguish themselves. Dick., Bleak House, Ch. IV, 54.
⁹⁹ Grandcourt ... was little else to her than a living sign of what she felt to be her failure as a wife — *the not having presented* Sir Hugo with a son. G. Eliot, Dan. Der., II, III, Ch. XXV, 4.
It is *the having been* so near claiming you for my own that makes the denial so hard to bear. Hardy, Far from the Madding Crowd, Ch. XXXI, 237.
iii He had been at great pains to atone for *the having been obliged* to make his toilet ... without the aid of dressing-case and tiring-equipage. Dick., Barn. Rudge, Ch. IV, 57 b.
This seemed a satire upon *his having been born* without that useful article of plate in his mouth. id., Nich. Nick., Ch. I, 2 a.
How he regretted, if not the giving away of his cake, at least *the having been caught* in such a strange act of charity. Ascott, R. Hope, Old Por.

23. Quite frequent are also those constructions in which a gerund preceded by a preposition exhibits the distinctions of either voice or tense, or of both together.

i Can't he be cured *by being taught* to be proud of his wife? Goldsmith, She stoops, I, (171).
An opulent city afraid *of being given up* to plunder. Mac., Clive, (538 a).
He is desirous *of being admired*. Mason, Eng. Gram.³⁴, § 197.
He preferred killing himself *to being killed* by a star. Westm. Gaz., No. 5255, 5 b.
ii. Are you ashamed *of having done* a right thing once in your life? Sher., School for Scand., V, 3.
He went crazy *through having lost* his fortune. Mason, Eng. Gram.³⁴, § 197.
I thank you very much *for having responded* to my summons. Miss Braddon, Lady Audley's Secret, II, Ch. XI, 210.
She blessed her *for having saved* the child. Rn. Hag., Mees. Will², Ch. XIV, 144.
All this time Bathsheba was conscious *of having broken* into that stronghold at last. Hardy, Far from the Malding Crowd, Ch. XVII, 135.
iii. He went crazy *through having been robbed* of all his money.

24. Of equal frequency are those constructions in which a gerund is preceded by a preposition and is attended by a verb-modifier.

i. He escaped by *crossing the river*. Mason, Eng. Gram.³⁴, § 197.
By spending *money* like water, by corrupting *the Press*, and by intimidating *their opponents*, they succeeded. Ninet. Cent., No. 396, 248.

ii. What with *mugging at that blasted constituency* and hanging *about this beastly lobby*, I'm all out of condition. Westm. Gaz., No. 5255, 4a.
Recently there came to this country Mr. Harris Weinstock, charged by the State of California to investigate the means adopted of dealing *with strikes and lock-outs*. ib., No. 5255, 4c.

iii. There is no use in even talking *of a reformed Second Chamber*. ib., No. 5255, 2a
It is difficult in these days to escape from the topic of politics even by deliberately talking *about something else*. Il. Lond. News, No. 3694, 184a

FURTHER SYNTACTICAL OBSERVATIONS ABOUT THE GERUND.

The Distinction of Voice neglected.

25. The distinction of voice which the gerund is capable of expressing is often neglected. The reason why, apart from its origin (58—65), the gerund often preserves the active voice instead of the passive, apparently required by the sense, is that its passiveness is often more or less vague or uncertain (27). Naturally this is most frequently the case when, through the absence of verb-modifiers, especially objects, the verbal element in it is dimmed. It is then felt to differ little from a noun of action, which, indeed, if there is one to express the meaning intended, is mostly preferred (47). It should be observed that adverbial adjuncts modifying the sentence generally do not affect the voice of the gerund.

The student is strongly recommended to compare the following quotations with those in 8, a, in which for various reasons the passive gerund could not be replaced by the active.

He has not, in fact, either murdered his parents, or committed any act worthy of transportation or hanging *up* to the present day. Thack., Pend., 1, Ch. II, 25.
He retired with him to talk over the necessary preliminaries of *hiring*. Hardy Far from the Madding Crowd, Ch. VII, 56.
The Russian people are certainly not incapable of *training*. Rev. of Rev., No. 331, 76a.
His last essay... will repay *reading* and re-*reading*. Westm. Gaz., No. 8591, 13a
I doubt whether any specimen of the book can be quite fairly judged without both *seeing* and *reading*. Westm. Gaz., No. 8633, 10a.

Note. *a*) Adnominal adjuncts naturally favour the use of the active voice. Compare the idioms in 13, b.

i. Mr Gumbo's account of his mistress's wealth and splendour was carried to my lord by his lordship's man, ... and, we may be sure, lost nothing in the telling. THACK., Virg., Ch. XVI, 166
ii. The Frenchman has plenty of valour–that there is no denying. LYTTON, My Novel, VII, Ch. I, 438

β) It stands to reason that when the gerund is followed by a prepositional phrase with by, representing the inverted subject (SWEET, N. E. Gr., § 313) the passive voice is used when required by the sense.
One of the real dangers in Belgium was being shot by one's own sentries. Eng Rev., No. 72, 495

26. Some cases in which the gerund, when attended by no object adverbial adjunct, or inverted subject, is kept in the active voice notwithstanding its passive meaning, deserve special mention. We find it in this form practically regularly,

a) when it is the subject of the sentence and, as such, is placed in front-position.
   Hanging and *wiving* goes by destiny. SHAK., Merch., II, 9, 83.
   Horsewhipping would be too good for such a scoundrel. EDNA LYALL, A Hardy Norseman, Ch. XXXIV, 300.
   Compare: It's as sudden as *being shot*. RUD. KIPL., The Light that failed, Ch. VIII, 104.

b) when it is the object of a verb expressing a requiring. See also Infinitive 15, d.
   i. Only two small incidents that befell the novice *need mentioning*. W. BESANT, The New Prince Fortunatus, Ch. VIII.
   The children of men need to love as much as they *need loving*. MORLEY ROBERTS, Time and Thomas Waring, Ch. XI, 107.
   ii. The Duke of Northumberland and Lord Salisbury declared boldly that the institution which *required reforming* was the House of Commons and not the House of Lords. Westm. Gaz., No. 5261, 1b.
   Charley Beresford will *require looking after* one of these days. Punch.
   iii. Come boys! the world *wants mending*. MACKAY, There's Work for all to do, I.
   We didn't *want seeing home*. DICK., Great Expect., Ch. XVII, 158.
   He *wanted comforting*. ib., Ch. XVIII, 175.
   They did any little odd jobs that he *wanted doing*. Eng Rev., No 61, 87

   Thus even when the gerund is modified by an adverbial adjunct
   I want to know exactly what you *want doing* to this house. MRS WARD, Delia Blanchflower, I, Ch. V, 132.

Similarly, by the analogy of *to require*, some other verbs have the illogical active gerund.
   i. Helena (held) a dancing class under the cedars ... for such young men as panted to conquer the mysteries of 'hesitation' or jazzing, and were ardently *courting instructing*, in the desperate hope of capturing their teacher for a dance that night. MRS. WARD, Cous Phil, Ch VIII, 127

a. I thought the whole story altogether *deserved commemorating*. FIELDING, Tom Jones, IV, Ch. X, 53.
He *deserves hanging* for that. DOUGLAS JERROLD, Black-Ey'd Susan, II, 1, (30).
If I were such a consummate ass as that, I should *deserve hanging*. PUNCH, Mrs Bouverie, 86.

Also *to bear* seems to preserve the active voice as a rule, the passive voice appearing only occasionally.

i. Alas the life of such boys does not *bear telling* altogether. THACK., Pend., I, Ch. XVIII, 182.
These houses won't *bear dancing in*. MARRYAT, Olla Podrida.
It won't *bear thinking about*. COX DOYLE, Trag. of the Korosko, Ch. II, 65.
ii. Those soft words do not bear *being written down*. THACK., Virg., Ch. LXVI, 699.

In the following quotation the passive voice is, of course, due to the gerund being attended by an adverbial modifier of agency.

He sometimes could not *bear being teased* with questions. BOSWELL, Johnson, 575 a.

c) when it modifies *worth*. See also Ch. III, 15, Obs. I, and compare the quotations with *worth* in 15, b.

Such petty anecdotes as these are scarcely *worth printing*. GOLDSMITH, Letter to the Printer of the "St. James's Chronicle".
The debate was well *worth living through*. Westm. Gaz., No. 5243, 4 b.
The whole world has smiled, or sighed over that extraordinary diary in which Louis XVI entered, day after day, what seemed to him best *worth recording and remembering*. ib., No. 5249, 4 b.

d) when it stands after *for* with a final meaning or a preposition denoting a quality or state.

i. There were in the book things that were not ripe *for telling*. Westm. Gaz., No. 8333, 5 a.
Every block ... was shipped from the home quarries ready *for placing* in position. Il. Lond. News, No. 3862, 586 a.
ii. This fellow's formal, modest impudence is *beyond bearing*. GOLDSMITH, She Stoops, V, (222).
He tried her patience *beyond bearing*. EDNA LYALL, A Hardy Norseman, Ch. XVII, 157.
The Turks are *beyond reasoning*. Westm. Gaz., No. 6288, 1 c.

Compare with the above the following quotations, in which the gerund is followed by the inverted subject or a prepositional object, or is suggestive of either.

You are *above being dazzled* by good looks. H. J. BYRON, Our Boys, II, 38.
Mary, however sage and serious, was not *above being pleased* with the admiration of her rustic companion. SCOTT, Mon., Ch. XIV, 159.
He was ... *above being pleased*. JANE AUSTEN, Pride and Prej., Ch. III, 14.

27. In the case of the active gerund with a passive meaning being modified by a genitive or a possessive pronoun, the latter may be understood as an objective genitive or its pronominal analogue respectively. Compare 13, d, 2.

I must present your friend with some little token, on the occasion of *Paul's christening*. Dick., Domb., Ch. V, 34.
Where are those 17,000 officers to come from? ... How can the nation pay for *their training*. The Nation (Westm. Gaz., No. 6095, 18 c).
To the ambitions man life ... is a game to be won, in the long run, by the quick eye and the steady hand, and yet having sufficient chance about *its working out* to give it all the glorious zest of uncertainty. Jerome, Idle Thoughts, IV, 65
What Lord Lansdowne asks is that, the Lords having created one disastrous precedent to the prejudice of the Commons, the Commons should now avert the consequences by making another precedent to *their own undoing*. Westm. Gaz., No 5255, 1 b.

Thus even, notwithstanding the inverted subject, in:

He got much sympathy in the constituency for *his rough handling* by a band of hooligans. Manch. Guard., IV, No. 10, 185 a.

28. In view of the origin of the gerund (58—65), there is nothing surprising in the fact that in Early Modern English gerunds are often placed in the active voice where present practice, owing to their markedly passive meaning, would have used the passive voice. See especially FRANZ, Shak. Gram.², § 665; A. SCHMIDT, Shak. Lex., Gram. Obs., 5.

But like the owner of a foul disease, | To keep it from *divulging*, (we) let it feed Even on the pith of life. SHAK, Haml., IV, 1, 22.
If he steal aught whilst this play is playing, And 'scape *detecting*, I will pay the theft. ib., III, 2, 94.
You have learn'd ... to watch, like one that fears *robbing*. id., Two Gent., II, 1, 26.
Excuse his *throwing* into the water. id., Merry Wives, III, 2, 206.

29. Obs. The frequent disregarding of voice is not confined to the gerund, but may also be observed in the infinitive and in the present participle. The cases in which the illogical construction is found with either of the two last verbals differ from those which concern the gerund. Compare Infinitive, 72; and Participles, 5. In this place it is of some interest to observe that in cases in which the gerund varies with the infinitive, the illogical active voice of the former always corresponds to the passive of the latter. We must confine ourselves to a few striking instances.

1. The man who can break the laws of hospitality, and tempt the wife of his friend, *deserves to be branded* as the pest of society. SHER., School for Scand., IV, 3, (413).
Gallows-bird. One who *deserves to be hanged*. MURRAY.

ii. Vice to be hated *needs* but *to be seen*. Pope, Es. on Man, II, 218
I am sitting here with some vanity in me, *needing to be scolded*. G. Eliot, Fel. Holt, II, Ch. LI, 353.
His citations sometimes *need to be checked*. Lit. World
The House of Lords *needs to be wakened up*. Rev. of Rev., No. 203, 451 b
This unique and momentous change evidently *requires to be accounted for*. Henry Bradley, The Making of Eng., Ch. II, 49.
In this respect every county presents its own problems, and many still *require to be recorded*. Rippmann, The Sounds of Spok. Eng., § 55.
Were Mexico situated in any part of the world except America, the question *would not require to be asked*. Westm. Gaz., No. 2309, 354 a
Hungry people, remarked the Premier, did not want political intervention only, but *wanted to be fed*. Manch. Guard., V, 17, 326 b.

The Distinction of Tense neglected.

30. a) As in the case of the finite verb (See my Treatise on Tense, 141), the neglecting of the tense-distinction in the gerund is mostly due to the fact that no necessity is felt to consider the time-spheres of two or more predications in mutual relation, the mind being satisfied with viewing both of them from the primary dividing-point. (See my Treatise on Tense, 3.) Thus there is nothing strange in the use of the imperfect instead of the perfect gerund in such a sentence as *He was hanged for killing a man* (Mason, Eng. Gram., § 200), seeing that the difference of the time-spheres of the two predications may also be left unexpressed, if the gerund-clause is replaced by a full clause introduced by *because: He was hanged because he killed a man* (See my Treatise on Tense, 144).

Further instances of the two predications being placed in the general past, in place of two different periods of the past, are afforded by the following quotations.

After *giving* a masterly summary of the whole case, his Lordship concluded as follows. Rid. Hag., Mees Will, Ch. XXI, 219.
He thanked him for *saving* his life. Sweet, N. E. Gr., § 1257.
I wasn't very likely to return without *speaking* to you. Watts Dunton, Aylwin, II, Ch. IV, 66.

Note. The imperfect gerund may be equally frequent when the predication it expresses belongs to the pre-anterior past (See my Treatise on Tense, 2, d).

After *getting* some work in London, he had returned to Birmingham. Rid. Hag., Mees Will, Ch. XXII, 238

b) Also a gerund which describes an action or state which is anterior to a predication of the present time-sphere is often kept in the imperfect tense.

<small>Pray make my excuses to Pratt for not *keeping* my engagement — Jane Austen, Pride and Prej., Ch. XLVII, 285.
I don't remember *seeing* more than one or two drunken men on weekdays — J. G. Wood, Good Words (Stof., Leesb.), I, 72).
I thank you for *assembling* here — Dick., Chuz., Ch. IV, 29 b.
Not that I blame them for *coming* — id., Bleak House, Ch. XXXIX, 339.
I hope you are not angry with me for *coming* — Mrs. Alexander, A Life Interest, I, Ch. IX, 146.</small>

c) Comparing the above quotations, in which the tense-distinction is neglected, with those mentioned in 8, b, in which it is observed, it seems futile to attempt finding any principle which underlies the different practice. Thus by the side of the quotations in which *after* is followed by the imperfect gerund we find:

<small>i. After *having seen* him publicly thus comport himself, but one course was open to me — to cut his acquaintance — Thack., Snobs, Ch. I, 14.
ii. After *having married* you, I should never pretend to taste again — Sher., School for Scand., II, 1, (377).</small>

Also a comparison of the two following quotations goes far to show that the choice of tense may be a matter of mere chance.

<small>I don't remember ever *having* a keener sense of remorse — Smith, Old Chapel.
I remember *having* seen him — id., N. E. Gr., § 325.</small>

31. Like the passive gerund (28), the perfect gerund is rare in Early Modern English (62, c). Franz, (Shak. Gram.², § 665) mentions but three instances from Shakespeare, viz.: Two Gentlemen, I, 3, *16*; Temp., III, 1, *19*; and Cymb., II, 3, *130*. The following is another:

<small>Go in Nerissa; | Give order to my servants that they take No note at all of our *being* absent hence — Merch., V, *120*.</small>

The Gerund followed by an Adnominal Adjunct with *of*.

32. Instead of gerund + non-prepositional object we often find *the* + gerund + adnominal adjunct with *of*, the adnominal adjunct representing an objective genitive (14).

a) Sometimes the two constructions would seem to be interchangeable, replacing one by the other, however, involving, of course, a substitution of an adverb of quality for an adjective, or vice versa. Thus frequently after a preposition,

i. He had little taste or genius for *the pursuing of the exact sciences*. THACK., Pend., I, Ch. XVIII, 182. (= *pursuing the exact sciences*.)
I confess that, on *the first reading of this letter*, I was in such a fury that I forgot almost the painful situation in which it plunged me. id., Sam. Titm., Ch. XI, 144. (= *first reading this letter*.)
The Government has secured the whole time of the House in which to carry the supply necessary for *the smooth running of the business of the country*. Westm. Gaz., No. 5249, 4 b. (= *running the business of the country smoothly*.)
The week which begins with Boxing-day is not one for *the publishing of many books*. ib., No. 8579, 24 a. (= *publishing many books*.)

ii. The first half-hour was spent in *piling up the fire*. JANE AUSTEN, Pride and Prej., Ch. XI, 57. (= *the piling up of the fire*.)
A bird-fancier is one who takes pleasure in *rearing or collecting birds*. WEBST., Dict., s. v. bird-fancier. (= *the rearing or collecting of birds*.)
Mrs. Boxer was employed in *trimming a cap*. LYTTON, Night and Morn., 291. T. (= *the trimming of a cap*.)

b) In many cases, however, the first construction is impossible or, at least, highly objectionable, because it implies association of the predication it expresses with the subject of the head-sentence, which may be at variance with the meaning intended. The second construction, which is free from this implication, then appears as a welcome alternative.

I'll be with you in *the squeezing of a lemon*. GOLDSMITH, She stoops, I, (174).
He sits patiently waiting for *the drawing up of the curtain*. LEIGH HUNT, The Old Gentleman.
We have no doubt he regrets *the closing of the door* upon his re-appearance in the House of Commons. Westm. Gaz., No. 5249, 2 b.
We do not take too tragically *the carrying of the resolution*. ib., No. 8941, 3 a.

Thus also in the following quotation in which the *of*-adjunct is understood:

Thus he read; | And ever in *the reading* lords and dames | Wept, looking often from his face who read | To hers which lay so silent. TEN., Lanc. and El., 1275. (i. e. *the reading of the letter*.)

With the above compare the following quotations in which the association referred to above would be destroyed by the insertion of *the* and *of*.

He troubled himself little about *decorating his abode*. MAC., Hist., I, Ch. III, 315.
I do care about *filling properly the place* to which I am born. L. B. WALFORD, Stay-at-homes, Ch. I.

Curiously enough, the first construction is sometimes the preferable one, because the second would impart to the predication expressed by the gerund, almost the same specializing meaning as that with the possessive pronoun, which may be contrary to the meaning intended.

Mrs. Hard. Come, Mr. Hardcastle, you must allow the boy a little humour. Hard. I'd sooner allow him a horse-pond. If *burning the footman's shoes, frightening the maids* and *worrying the kittens* be humour, he has it. Goldsmith, She stoops, I. (168)

c) Sometimes the two constructions, although structurally equally legitimate, convey different shades of meaning, and cannot, therefore, be used interchangeably.

In *the making of an anthology* he displays a skill that almost entitles him to a share of Hazlitt's greatest fame. J. H. Lobban, Sel. from Leigh Hunt Intr. (Compare In *making an anthology* he displays a skill etc., in which the gerund-clause has a distinctly temporal meaning, which is absent in the above quotation.)

d) The second construction hardly admits of the gerund or the noun in it being encumbered by lengthy adjuncts, and could not, therefore, be very well used in place of the first in:

This insinuation put me upon *observing the behaviour of my mistress* more narrowly for the future. Smoll., Rod. Rand., Ch. XIX, 125
Accordingly, he set seriously about *sheltering and refreshing our hero* for the night. Scott, Wav., Ch. LX, 149a
It was the very room to which he had been shown when he first called about *sending his son to the school*. Anstey, Vice Versa, Ch. XI, 218
The benefits of free emigration would result in *freeing the country of a great number of undesirable characters*. Daily Mail

e) Apart from the above considerations, substitution of the one for the other construction is sometimes objectionable for reasons of euphony or idiom. Thus in such a sentence as *The Abolition of the House of Lords* means the granting of *Home Rule* (Saturday Review) the second construction is, no doubt, preferred, because it makes a better balance, than the first, with the preceding *the Abolition of the House of Lords*. If the writer had started his statement with *Abolishing the House of Lords*, the latter part of it would, most probably, have run *granting Home Rule*.

The same consideration has, no doubt, caused the second construction to be preferred in:

The art of printing and *the training of eye and ear* had not yet brought the world under the rule of uniformity of sound representation. Westm. Gaz. No. 5255, 3a.

The inscrutable laws of idiom seem to be responsible for the preference of the construction used in:

i. *The buying of this brooch* took a long time. Galsworthy, Tatterdemalion I, I, 17.
Jones resumes *the lacing of his boots*. id., The Silver Box, II, I (35)

The main purpose is now stated to be *the exploring of the present unknown regions north of Franz Josef Land and Spitsbergen*. Westm. Gaz., No. 5249, 8c.
He then described *the taking of hostages* as a barbarian and an un-Christian method of war. ib., No. 8574, 5a.
Quack remedies for *the building up of trade* were unsparingly derided. Manch. Guard., V, No. 16, 305b.
n. *Hating one's neighbours* is forbidden by the Gospel. MASON, Eng. Gram.⁸¹, § 368.
I always delight in *overthrowing such kind schemes*. JANE AUSTEN, Pride and Prej., Ch. X, 55.
He amused himself with *embellishing his grounds*. MAC., War. Hast., (656a).
A tradesman ought to be attentive to the wishes of his customers, and careful in *keeping his accounts*. CRABB, Syn., s. v. attentive.
I shall begin by *reading the earlier will*. G. ELIOT, Mid., Ch. XXXV, 247.
I think people ought to be as particular over *choosing their daughter's governess* as their son's wife. MRS. CRAIK, John Hal., Ch. XXX, 321.

In the following quotation only the first construction would appear to be admissible as an alternative for that with the noun of action.

Oliver was frightened at *the sight of so many gentlemen*. DICK., Ol. Twist, Ch. II, 28. (= at seeing so many gentlemen, not: 'at the seeing of so many gentlemen.)

33. Constructions in which the gerund is followed by an adnominal adjunct with *of* representing an objective genitive, without being preceded by such a definitive adjunct as an article or a demonstrative pronoun, were common in Early Modern English, but survive now only as archaisms or vulgarisms. See STOF., Taalst., III, 326; FRANZ, E. S., XII; id. SHAK., Gram.², 667; EINENKEL, Hist. Synt., § 3, γ. See also the Treatise on the Participles, 6, Obs. IX.

What have you lost by *losing of this day*? SHAK., King John, III, 4, 116.
Leave *wringing of your hands*. id., Haml., III, 4, 34.
Asahel would not turn aside from *following of* him. Bible, Samuel, B, II, 21.
But they thought that he had spoken of *taking of rest* in sleep. ib., John, XI, 13.
He left *beating of Paul*. ib., Acts, XXI, 32.
They, who have lately written with most care, have, I believe, taken the rule of Horace for their guide; that is, not to be too hasty in *receiving of words*, but rather to stay till custom has made them familiar to us. DRYDEN, Defence of the Epilogue.
I hear of a fellow, too, committed just now for *stealing of horses*. FARQUHAR, Rec. Of., V, 4, (333).
Dick, after *reading of the verses* was fain to go off; insisting on kissing his two dear friends before his departure. THACK., Henry Esm , II, Ch. XI, 246.
Addison, blushing, began *reading of his verses*. ib. II, Ch. XI, 249.
I could only be happy by *forgetting of her*. DICK., Cop., Ch. LI, 367a.
It is the fashion in this clime for women | To go twelve months in *bearing of a child*. TEN., Queen Mary, III, 6, (623b).

The Gerund preceded by the Common Case of a (Pro)noun or the Objective of a Personal Pronoun.

34. *a)* As has already been shown in Ch. XXIII, 12 and Ch. XXIV, 52—56, the common case of nouns often takes the place of the genitive, if the relation for which the latter stands is vague. The result is that in certain combinations the two forms are used side by side with no, or hardly any appreciable difference in meaning. In this place the following sets of quotations must suffice to illustrate this variety of practice.

i. It was her *life's* task and duty to dedicate all her powers to the prosperity and interests of her Fatherland. Times.
ii. He made it his *life* work to determine those positions for each sound. Trevs., Mod. Lang. Quart.
i. She had an *angel's* face. Mrs. Wood, East Lynne, I, 121. I
ii. So sweet a face, such *angel* grace. In all that land had never been. Tes., The Beggar Maid.
i. The Duke of Omnium (saw) with his *eagle's* eye that the welfare of his countrymen at large required that some great step should be initiated. Trol., Fram. Pars., Ch. VII, 78.
ii. Thou hast an *eagle* eye. Lytton, Rienzi, I, Ch. I, 16.
i. One would almost imagine that the *Government's* policy in Ireland was to create Sinn Feiners as fast as it eliminated them. Westm. Gaz., No. 8579, 3a.
ii. The signs of victory are not apparent, but if the *Government* policy is successful in crushing the whole opposition to it in Ireland, what then? ib., 2a.

The student may here be reminded of the fact that in Northern Middle English the mark of the genitive was often absent, and is still frequently dispensed with in Northern English. Compare Curme, E. S. XLV, 363 f; Einenkel, Synt., § 16, 8.

I 1275: At the *apposteli* biding (= at the apostle's bidding) sone þai went Til (= to) þam ogain þat þam had sent. Horstmn, Alteng. Leg., Neue Folge, 140/187. (Compare: at the *dukes* praying. In Babiloine þe appostels dwelled. ib., 140 211.)

b) In like manner the word denoting the originator of the predication expressed by the gerund is often kept in the common case even when it denotes a person. The practice is, naturally, the rule, when it indicates a thing to which, strictly speaking, no personal activity can be ascribed, and is unavoidable when it has no genitive inflection, as is the case with certain pronouns and with numerals.

In an analogous way the objective of a personal pronoun sometimes takes the place of the corresponding possessive pronoun. For discussion and illustration see Ch. XIX, 5. Compare also 13, e.

Instead of the objective, the nominative of the personal pronoun appears to be occasionally used, e. g.: *Instead of he converting the Zulus, the Zulu chief converted him.*¹) In view of the distinctly subjective relation in which the pronoun stands to the following verbal this seems to be natural enough. Instances, however, appear to be very rare, at least in the printed language.

35. Apart from the causes which may be assigned for the substitution of the common case for the genitive generally, the following factors may be, mainly, responsible for the shaking of the case system concerning the (pro)nouns which stand by way of subject before the gerund.

a) the uncertainty of the interpretation to be put on some constructions in which a (pro)noun in the common case or the objective of a personal pronoun stands before the verbal in *ing*.

1) Thus *I cannot imagine anybody disliking Jack* (FLOR. MARRYAT, A Bankrupt Heart) may be understood to mean *I cannot imagine that anybody should dislike Jack*, or *I cannot imagine anybody who would dislike Jack*; i. e. the object of *imagine* may be regarded to be the whole word-group *anybody disliking Jack* or the pronoun *anybody* alone. According as either the first or the second interpretation is applied, *disliking* is to be regarded as a gerund or a participle. To a person who would favour the first view, which seems the least rational, *anybody* would appear as an alternative form for *anybody's*.

A similar twofold interpretation may be put upon:

I cannot conceive a woman in her senses *refusing* Dick. RUDY. KIPLING, The Light that failed, Ch. X, 151.

He speaks of a young married man *being seized* and shot, though his wife pleaded on her knees for his life. Westm. Gaz. No. 8615, 1 b.

If the verbal in *ing* in such an ambiguous sentence is understood as a participle, the clause of which it forms part may sometimes be expanded into an adverbial clause of time. Thus in:

Mr. Macklean had collected us in the drawing-room, in order to listen to *him reading the history of Joseph*. DOR. GERARD, The Eternal Woman, Ch. IX. (= in order to listen to *him* as he read the history of Joseph.)

Compare with the above the following sentence, which admits of but one interpretation:

She listened to *the door slamming*. TEMPL. THURSTON, The City of Beaut Nons, II, Ch. II, 214 (= *the slamming of the door*.)

2) Another analysis may be applied to such a sentence as *Pardon me saying it* (TEN., Princ., I, 154). In it *Pardon me* gives complete sense, *saying it* imparting to the utterance more point by stating the matter as to which pardon is requested. The logical relation between *me* and *saying it* might be expressed by the preposition *in*: *Pardon me in saying it*. But grammatically *saying it* modifies *me* adnominally, and *saying* is a participle.

But we may also apprehend the whole of the notions expressed by *me saying it* as the object of *pardon*. This interpretation, which appears to be the more logical, would render the use of the possessive pronoun *my* more appropriate than the personal pronoun *me*. We may add that it is also more usual in Standard English.

3) If in such a sentence as *She's a bit lonesome, poor thing, with her husband being so much away* (EDNA LYALL, A Hardy Norseman, Ch. XXI, 188) the preposition *with* is eliminated, the undeveloped clause is changed into what is called a nominative absolute, the verbal in it being an unmistakable participle. It will be observed that, although the meaning of the sentence is hardly affected by the elimination, the grammatical relations between the component elements of the latter part have undergone a change. While in the sentence as it originally stands *her husband* is felt to be the modifying element and *being so much away* the element modified, these functions are reversed in the altered sentence: *her husband* now being the element modified, *being so much away* the modifying element. In sentences with *with* of the above type, which are frequent enough, the verbal never appears with a genitive or possessive pronoun; at least no instances of this practice have come to hand. They may, however, have borne a part in shaking the system of indicating the originator of the predication indicated by the gerund by either of these forms.

4) CURME, (E. S., XLV, 372) cites *I do not like to think of mother sitting all alone in the old home*, and observes that he feels "the construction as participial on account of the presence of the progressive idea, the conception of the continuation of the verbal activity", contrasting it with *I am not in favour of mother selling the old home*, in which he regards the construction as gerundial. The observation seems right enough, but it may be asked whether the alternative interpretation of considering the complex of the ideas indicated by *mother sitting all alone in the old home* as the (prepositional) object of *think* is inadmissible.

5) MURRAY, s. v. *ing*, illustrates the probable influence of the participle constructions in furthering the use of the common case before gerunds by comparing the following sentences: *John was digging potatoes. Who saw John digging potatoes? Who ever heard of John (= John's) digging potatoes.*

c) It may here also be observed that in constructions with the common case of a (pro)noun, or the objective of a personal pronoun, before the verbal in *ing* of verbs which may also be construed with an accusative + infinitive, the verbal is best understood as a participle after such as express a perceiving. But the alternative interpretation of regarding this (pro)noun as a variant of a genitive or possessive pronoun, and, consequently, the verbal as a gerund is the more plausible one after other groups of this class of verbs. This view is borne out by the fact that an alternative construction with a genitive or a possessive pronoun is admissible only so far as the latter verbs are concerned.

i. The doctor now *felt all the dignity of a landholder rising* within him. WASH. IRV., Dolf Heyl. (STOF., Handl. I, 109).
You could *hear him eating*. TEMPLE THURSTON, The City of Beaut. Nons., II, Ch. I, 206.
They had *noticed the German sitting* far down the woodland path. BUCHANAN, That Winter Night, Ch. XI, 92.

ii. I can't *abide a woman whistling*. J. M. BARRIE, The Admirable Crichton, III, 107.
Compare: I cannot *bear your remaining* at Bell-thorpe like a jewel in a sty. MEREDITH, Ord. of Rich. Fev., Ch. XX, 137.
Mrs. Barthwick wouldn't *like him coming* about the place. GALSWORTHY, The Silver Box, I, 2, (20).
I don't *like my daughter playing* hockey. CHESTERTON, Il. Lond. News, No. 3841, 793a.
Compare: I don't at all *like your going* such a way off. JANE AUSTEN, Pride and Prej., Ch. LI, 310.
I don't *like your binding* yourself to work for so many years. EDNA LYALL, A Hardy Norseman, Ch. VII, 55.

To *permit the present muddle-headed anarchy prevailing* in such a serious problem is little short of a social indictment. Eng. Rev., No. 58, 255.
Compare: The charms of melody and beauty were too strongly impressed in Edward's breast to *permit his declining* an invitation so pleasing. SCOTT, Wav., Ch. XXIII, 74a.

I *remember my poor grandmother once incidentally observing* [etc.]. JEROME, Idle Thoughts, V, 69. T.
I *remember you telling* me. BLAIR. HAR., Ships, I, Ch. XIII.
Compare: I *recollect your saying* one night [etc.]. JANE AUSTEN, Pride and Prej., Ch. XLV, 265.
Since we have parted, I can never *remember Emma's omitting* to do anything I wished. id., Emma, Ch. V, 35. T.
I can quite *understand you saying* so. CON. DOYLE, Sherl. Holm., I, 104. T.
Compare: I can hardly *understand a young Frenchman's not entering* the army. MEREDITH, Lord Ormont, Ch. V, 79.
We *understand Portia to hesitate* for a word which shall describe her appropriately. Note to Merch. of Ven., III, 2, 159, in Clar. Press. Ed.

b) the absolute phonetic identity of the genitive and the common case in the plural of practically all nouns, and also of the possessive and the personal pronoun *her*.

When we had dined, to prevent *the ladies leaving us*, I generally ordered the table to be removed. GOLDSMITH, Vic., Ch. II, (242).
He insisted on *his sisters accepting* the invitation. PHILIPS, Mrs. BOUVERIE, 82.

c) the frequent uncertainty whether a given noun whose last sound is the blade-sibilant should be understood as a genitive singular or as a plural. Thus a person, hearing such a sentence as *He spoke of the girl's* (or *girls'*) *coming*, may, in many cases, be in doubt whether the reference is to a single girl or to a plurality of girls. And it is only natural that the unsophisticated mind should hit upon the simple expedient of using the noun without the sibilant when only one individual is in question.

36. Obs. I. Grammarians have been greatly puzzled to tell the exact nature of the verbal in *ing* when preceded by the common case of a (pro)noun, or the objective of a personal pronoun, in the connection described above, and have, consequently, felt a difficulty in giving it an appropriate name.

SWEET, in § 2328 of his N. E. Gr., commenting on two such sentences as *I do not like his coming here so often* and *I do not like him coming here so often* calls the verbal in *ing* in the last sentence a present participle, but being aware of the form differing, as to its relation to the other elements of the sentence, from an indisputable participle as in *I saw him coming*, styles it a half-gerund, thus tacitly admitting that he is unable, or considers it immaterial, to tell what the difference consists in.

The same hesitation is shown by KRÜGER, who in his Schul-grammatik, § 549, dubs the construction gerundial participle construction, which name in his paper, Die Partizipiale Gerundialfügung, ihr Wesen und ihr Ursprung (E. S., XXXVII, 385), he changed into participial gerund-construction, evidently considering this an improvement upon the first denomination.

It is difficult to see why two names should be needed for a verbal form which, although preceded by modifiers of a grammatically different description, remains unaltered in its relations to the other elements of the sentence. Comparing two such sentences as *Excuse the boy's saying so* and *Excuse the boy saying so*, we find that the logical relations between what is expressed by the different elements of the sentences are absolutely identical. And this appears to be the case with almost every pair of sentences which differ only as to the form of the noun preceding the verbal in *ing*. Compare Obs. III.

We have seen (34) that also before an ordinary noun the genitive is often enough replaced by the common-case form of an adnominal noun. But nobody will for a moment entertain the notion that in this case the relations between modifier and head-word are altered.

Also CURME (E. S., XLV, 364) sees no occasion for the verbal in *ing* being called by a different name when, instead of the genitive, the common case is used. Commenting on such a sentence as *I am not in favor of mother selling the old home*, he observes, "A number of distinguished grammarians regard *selling* in this sentence as a present participle. There is, however, not a single established fact upon which this theory is based." And again (l. c. 371), "It (sc. the common case of the noun indicating the originator of the action or state denoted by the gerund) is the natural extension of the endingless subjective form which we see extending itself to-day also to names of persons and to pronouns in the position after verbs and prepositions. The evident tendency is to make the subject of the gerund endingless. We have here to do with inner development within the powerful gerundial construction."

Similarly JESPERSEN holds to the view that the nature of the verbal in *ing* undergoes no change through the substitution of the common case for the gerund. See his Growth and Structure², § 204; De to Hovedarter av Grammatiske Forbindelser, 19.

An appropriate name for the construction illustrated by such sentences as *I do not like him coming here so often, Do you mind me smoking*, etc., is suggested by DEUTSCHBEIN (System, § 60, 4, c), who proposes to call it accusative + gerundium. The name implies the close resemblance to the accusative + infinitive, and suggests the fact that it provides for those cases in which the accusative + infinitive is not available or, at least, at variance with idiom. Compare Ch. XIX, 70. The denomination is, of course, only suitable for those cases in which the (pro)noun is the non-prepositional object of the preceding finite verb, as in the two examples given above, or depends on a preposition, as in:

I insist on Miss Sharp appearing. THACK., Van. Fair, I, Ch. XI, 108. She listened to the door slamming. TEMPLE THURSTON, The City of Beaut. Nons., II, Ch. II, 214.

Instances of what might be called a nominative + gerund, e. g.: *It's no good you hanging round* (Punch), *My daughter staying so late worried me* (CURME, l. c., 367) are not frequently met with.

11. Only in a few instances is the general meaning of the sentence materially modified by a change of construction. Compare *What do you think of my sister's singing* with *What do you think of my sister singing?* and *Paul was quite alarmed at Mr. Feeder's yawning* (DICK., Domb., Ch. XII, 104) with *Paul was quite alarmed at Mr. Feeder yawning*, and *What is the use of my speaking* with

What is the use of me speaking (= if I speak)[1], and *Papa did not care about their learning* with *Papa did not care about them learning* (Thack., Henry Esm., I, 242). See 37, b.

Omitting the mark of the genitive in *Another stirring passage describes Ney's crossing the Dnieper*, quoted by Kruisinga (Handb.², § 255) from the Athenæum, would be changing the meaning of the sentence entirely; i. e. it would be understood to have the value of *Another stirring passage describes Ney as he is crossing the Dnieper:* in other words, it would change the gerund into an indubitable participle. For detailed discussion of the subject see also Kruisinga, Handb.², § 279 ff; Dubislav, Beitr., § 14.

37. The different areas of the use of the construction with the genitive or a possessive pronoun and that with the common case of a (pro)noun or the objective of a personal pronoun, which in the following discussions will be, respectively, called construction A and construction B, have already been described, in broad outline, in Ch. XIX, 5—6. It seems advisable to revert in this connection to the subject and to supplement the observations there made.

a) Construction B is distinctly more colloquial than construction A. Naturally so. The propensity of the human mind, especially of the uneducated, is to use an analytical construction rather than a synthetical, the former admitting of the different elements of a complex of notions being thought of separately and in orderly succession and, consequently, preferred to the latter, which forces the mind to grasp these elements as a whole. Thus in *You must excuse the boy saying so* we are enabled to think of the notions expressed by *the boy* and *saying so* in succession, while in *You must excuse the boy's saying so* we are obliged to take in at once the ideas involved in *the boy's saying so*. For further illustration see Ch. XIX, 5, e.

We subjoin a quotation in which, notwithstanding the absence of all refinement of language, construction A is used.

An' when I see'd the book open upo' the stall, wi' the lady lookin' out of it wi' eyes a bit like your'n when you was frettin' — you'll excuse *my takin'* the liberty, Miss — I thought I'd make free to buy it for you. G. Eliot, Mill, IV, Ch. III, 258.

b) Construction B is in especial favour when the originator of the action or state has to be indicated with emphasis. This even causes the personal pronoun to be not unfrequently preferred to the possessive pronoun, although the practice of using the former is not, on the whole, in great favour in educated English. Murray, s. v. *ing*, observes, "Even a pronoun standing before the gerund is put in the

---
[1]) Murray, s. v. *ing*.

objective, in dialect speech; and when the pronoun is emphatic, this is common in ordinary colloquial English". He quotes:

> Papa did not care about *them learning.* THACK., Henry Esm.
> But who ever heard of *them eating* an owl. id., Newc.
> That is no excuse for *him beating* you. So what is the excuse of *me speaking?* READE, Hard Cash.

It will strike the observant student that MURRAY here overlooks the difference which substitution of construction A for construction B would involve in the first and third quotations. See 36, Obs. II.

As an instance of polite speakers preferring construction A, notwithstanding the emphasis, we quote:

> To think of *your turning book-hunter.* LYTTON, Caxtons, XVII, Ch. I, 450. (The author has *your* placed in italics.)

c) Construction B is preferable in the case of the verb being durative and durativeness being distinctly in the speaker's mind. Thus in *They insisted on my walking between them all the way to the station* the fact that the act of walking continued all the way to the station is less distinctly brought out than in the same sentence with *me* substituted for *my.* Compare CURME, E. S., XLV, 372.

d) Construction B is said to be more usual after a preposition than in other positions. WILLERT (E. S., XXXV, 381) even goes so far as to observe, "Heute kann man sagen, dass der Akkusativ mehr und mehr an Boden gewinnt und bei dem von einer Präposition abhängigen Gerundium fast ausschliesslich zur Anwendung gelangt". This is, however, an exaggerated statement. It would, at least, be easy to produce hosts of quotations, drawn from colloquial language, in which a preposition is followed by construction A. The following may be given as a striking instance:

> I may not have my objections to *a young man's keeping company* with me. DICK., Domb., Ch. XII, 111. (The speaker is Miss Susan Nipper, a servant in the house of Dombey, certainly not remarkable for refinement of language.)

For further illustration of the practice which MR. WILLERT pronounces in such sweeping terms to be unidiomatic, see Ch. XIX, 72 ff.

e) Construction B is distinctly the rule when the originator of the action or state is indicated by a compound indefinite pronoun with *body* or *one;* it is almost the only one in actual use when this originator is a thing. A few quotations showing the alternative practice may be deemed acceptable. See also Ch. XIX, 5, b. It is of some importance to observe that examples of the latter description are not so unusual as is commonly believed.

> i. We can put a great deal of copper into the gold without *any one's finding* it out. RUSKIN, The King of the Golden River, Ch. II.
> ii. The utmost that was in the power of a lawyer was to prevent *the law's taking effect.* FIELDING, Jos. Andrews, IV, Ch. III, 207.
>
> I told him of *the church's being* so very well worth seeing. JANE AUSTEN, Pers., Ch. XIV, 133.

She played till Fanny's eyes, straying to the window on *the weather's being evidently fair*, spoke what she felt must be done. id., Mansf. Park, Ch. XXII, 213.
The fact of *the pencil's falling* in the school-room the previous evening, occurred to him. Mrs. Wood, Orv. Col., Ch. VIII, 112.
There is a real danger of *our literature's being americanized*. H. W. and F. G. Fowler, The King's Eng., Ch. I, 24.
The case of *a bird's being run into* in flight, and killed, by a motor-car is comparatively rare. Westm. Gaz., No. 5613, 13a.

f) Construction B is the only one in actual use when the (pro)noun preceding the gerund is followed by an adnominal adjunct which is not an adjective.

Talk of *us girls being vain*, what are we to you? Thack., Henry Esm., III, Ch. ii, 323.
But it does signify about *the parishioners in Tipton being comfortable*. G. Eliot, Mid., Ch. XXXVII, 285.
We had never heard of *a man of his good sense refusing* such an offer. Curme, E. S., XLV, 365.

Also a word-group consisting of more nouns than one would hardly brook the alternative construction.

The father insisted on *John and Mary staying at home*.
On *the general and his staff appearing*. Curme, E. S., XLV, 365.
When we talk of *this man or that woman being no longer the same person*. Thackeray.[1])

g) Construction B is distinctly unusual when the combination is the subject of the sentence, unless, indeed, the modifying element is a word which has no genitive, or is rarely placed in the genitive, or contains a modifying adjunct following it. For illustration see also Ch. XIX, 6, Obs. I.

Your being Sir Anthony's son, captain, would itself be a sufficient recommendation. Sher., Riv., III, 2.
Harriet's staying away so long was beginning to make her uneasy. Jane Austen, Emma, Ch. VIII, 64, T.
Your being strangers is what makes me wish to accompany you. Onions, Adv. Eng. Synt., § 180.
John's sending so late a reply vexed me. Curme, E. S., XLV, 368.

The following are the only instances of the alternative practice that have come to hand:

And is *a wench having a bastard* all your news, Doctor? Fielding, Tom Jones, IV, Ch. X, 356.
I feel a bit unstrung, *that beast caterwauling* over yonder was just more than I could put up with. Con. Doyle, The Trag. of the Korosko, Ch. I, 27.
Young gentlemen calling at my apartments might cause remarks. M. E. Francis, The Manor Farm, Ch. XI. (For comment see below.)

But in such a sentence as *To-day being Saturday rather complicates matters*, the genitive could hardly take the place of the common-case,

---
[1]) Jespersen, Growth and Struct., § 204.

not, at least, in the English spoken in the British Isles. According to CURME (E. S., XLV, 371) American English prefers the genitive even here.

Construction B is, however, the usual one, also in the case of the subject=indicating word of the gerund being a **noun indicating a person**, when the gerund=clause stands **after** the head=sentence and is announced by the anticipating *it*.

It was no use *Virginie venting* her wrath upon Humphrey. FIOR. MONTGOM, Misunderstood.¹)
It was no use *men being angry* with them for damaging the links. Times.¹)

Instances with the **personal pronoun** in the same position are met with only in vulgar or very colloquial language.

Doesn't seem the least use *me speaking* to her. PETT RIDGE, Name of Garland, Ch. XIII, 219.¹)
Look here, Billy, it's no good *you hanging* round. Punch.
Compare: It's rather rich *your talking* of beating me at billiards, considering that I've devoted the last three years to billiards and nothing else. H. J. BYRON, Our Boys, II, 40.
It's rather amusing *your bragging* of rivalling me. ib., II, 41.

It should also be observed that construction B may sometimes be preferred on account of the conditional notion implied. Compare 36, Obs. II.

Young gentlemen calling at my apartments might cause remarks. M. E. FRANCIS, The Manor Farm, Ch. XI.

Thus also in the following quotation it would, most probably, have been used instead of construction A, if the predicate had been *would be unbearable*. The sentence would then, however, be unidiomatic.

My girl's singing, after that little governess's, I know is unbearable. THACK., Van. Fair, I, Ch. XIX, 196.

h) Construction B appears to be impossible when the combination is the nominal part of the predicate.

Emma, this is *your doing*. JANE AUSTEN, Emma, Ch. VIII, 50.
"It is *his doing* and his money!" said my father; "good actions have mended the bad." LYTTON, Caxt., I, Ch. IV, 21.

Similarly after verbs which express a modified *to be*.

Your making the match . . . means only *your planning* it. JANE AUSTEN, Emma, Ch. I, 13. T.

i) Construction A cannot be replaced by construction B when the gerund is felt as a mere equivalent of a noun of action. Naturally it then stands without a verb=modifier and the combination in which it occurs does not admit of being expanded into a full clause.

Ichabod prided himself upon *his dancing*. WASH. IRV., Sketch=Bk., XXXII, 363.
The day soon broke for *our going*. DICK., Cop., Ch. II, 14a. (= *departure*.)
My boy must not see me following him with a wistful face, and have *our parting* made more dismal by my weakness. THACK., Virg., Ch. IX, 90.

¹) KRUISINGA, Handb.², § 250.

Tom was migthy proud of *his running*. Hughes, Tom Brown.
He resumed *his listening*. Wells, Ann Veronica, Ch. 1, § 5, 26.
Substitution is also impossible in such a turn of expression as is illustrated by:
No sighs but of *my breathing*; no tears but of *my shedding*. Shak., Merch., III, 1, 82.
My daughters undertook to adorn them with pictures of *their own designing*. Goldsmith, Vic., (255).
Her songs are *her own composing*. Lytton, Pomp., I, Ch. III, 19 a.

j) Finally it may be observed that construction B appears to be less common in American English than in British English. Thus to MURRAY's comment on the much-quoted sentence *I insist upon Miss Sharp appearing* (THACK., Van. Fair, I, Ch. XI, 108) to the effect that *"Miss Sharp's* would now sound pedantic or archaic", CURME (E. S., XLV, 368) observes, "In America we still cling here to the older literary usage, and many still prefer the genitive, although the new usage is also well-known". It would be of some interest to ascertain whether, as CURME's words imply, construction A was more in favour in the older stages of the language than it is to-day. This much is, at least, certain that JANE AUSTEN appears to have been extremely partial to it, her works containing numerous instances which would hardly be tolerated in Present English.

COMPOUND GERUNDS.

38. A gerund often enters into combination with a noun, an adverb, or a preposition to form with it a kind of compound (3, a). In these combinations the constituent parts are welded together with various degrees of closeness, in the written or printed language marked by junction, hyphening or separation of the component parts.

39. The nouns used in these gerundial compounds are mostly in the objective, less frequently in the subjective or adverbial relation to the verb with which they are connected. Sometimes also the relation is uncertain, more than one interpretation being possible. What distinguishes these compounds from combinations of gerunds with nouns which form no compounds is that the noun always stands without any modifier and, so far as it stands in the objective or adverbial relation to the verb, is placed before the latter. The compound as a whole can, however, be modified by any adnominal adjunct, which shows that it is felt as a substantive. For convenience of reference the following quotations are arranged alphabetically.

i. They talk about him (sc. a man who has betaken himself to the calling of letters) much as they would, had he adopted another sort of *book-making* as a means of livelihood. Rid. Hag, Mees. Will, Ch. IV, 42
John's family connexion with *bookselling* is not seen to have been particularly intimate. Times, Lit. Sup., No. 990, 11 a.
He gave up *cigar-smoking*. Thack., Pend., I, Ch. XXI, 219.
What do you think I am best fit for after my bringing-up? *Crossing-sweeping*, perhaps? Shaw, Cashel Byron's Prof., Ch. XIV, 249.
I had a desire to see the old family seat of the Lucys ... and to ramble through the park where Shakespeare ... committed his youthful offence of *deer-stealing*. Wash. Irv., Sketch-Bk., XXVI, 264.
If you want to see the whole philosophy of the matter admirably set out, you have only to look to speeches reported in Hansard by one Lloyd George on the *farm-burning* and other exceptionable measures taken against rebels during the South African War. Westm. Gaz., No. 8597, 4 b.
Let me hasten to wear the garment of repentance, and to apologize to Mr. Bell for being, as it seems, as ignorant of astronomy as of *horse-racing*. Westm. Gaz., No. 8597, 23 a.
How delighted I should be to devote my time to agriculture, especially to *horse-breeding*. Times, 1921, 21. Jan., 45 b.
Low at *leave-taking* ... bow'd the all-amorous Earl. Tenn., Ger. and En., 359.
Her original was at that moment sound asleep and oblivious of all love and *letter-writing*. Hardy, Far from the Madding Crowd, Ch. XIV, 114.
His *love-making* struck us as unconvincing. Wells, Ann Veronica, Ch. I, § 5, 26.
This will guarantee no end to the competition of *navy-building*. Westm. Gaz., No. 8591, 4 a.
Note-taking in such a position wastes no little time. Bookman, No. 310, 125.
Mr. Joseph Keating ... has given up coal-mining for *novel-writing*. Times, 11 Sect., No. 2300, 2.
An expert in *paper-hanging*. Murray,
The progress of *peace-making* depended on the employment of traditional methods. Times, Rev. 1921, 1 a.
There was a time when *sermon-making* was not so palatable to you as it seems to be at present. Jane Austen, Pride and Prej., Ch. LII, 322.
For *shoe-making* or *house-building*, for the management of a ship or locomotive engine, a long apprenticeship is needful. Spencer, Educ., Ch. 1, 26 b.
Tuft-hunting and tuft-hunter were originally University terms, and then passed into common use as descriptive of those who toadied to wealth or rank. Westm. Gaz., No. 8597, 22 b.
Your *turnip-hoeing* were (vulgar for was) in the summer and your malting in the winter for the same years. Hardy, Far from the Madding Crowd, Ch VIII, 72.

ii. He felt as if ... there had been ... no secret *heart-burning*. Agn. and Eg. Castle, Diam. cut Paste, I, Ch. VI, 88.
Where he may be seen from *Sun-rising* to *Sun-setting*. Addison, Tatler, No. 20[1]).
All this drudgery from *cock-crowing* to starlight. Emerson, Young American (Wks, II, 301)[1]).

iii. He had the mother wit that is often quicker to detect a fallacy than *book-learning*. Times, No. 2303, 139 b.

---
[1]) Murray.

That I could have been at our old church in my old *church-going* clothes, on the very last Sunday that ever was, seemed a combination of impossibilities, geographical and social, solar and lunar. Dick., Great Expect., Ch XXII, 220.
Golf kills *church-going*. Westm. Gaz., No. 6147, 7 a.
This is a poor *home-coming*. Marj. Bowen, The Rake's Progress, Ch II, 24.
By refusing her husband the conventional welcome she had partly brought upon herself the punishment of this sordid *home-coming*. Acs. and E. Castle, Diam. cut Paste, I, Ch. V, 72.
In the coal country of Upper Silesia the Poles have done most of the farming and the Germans most of the mining and *metal-working*. Manch. Guard. V, No. 16, 302 b.
This principle will predominate in future reforms of *school-teaching*. ib., V, No. 23, 471 c.

40. It is only adverbs that are also used as prepositions, such as *down, in, up*, etc., which can form real compounds with gerunds. They are mostly placed after the latter, prepositiveness making for closer union. Sometimes the language has pairs of these compounds with the adverb in different positions, e. g.: *bringing-up* and *up-bringing*.

i. The master of the week came down in cap and gown to *calling-over*. Hughes, Tom Brown, I, Ch. V, 94.
This *falling-off* (sc. of output) cannot be ascribed to any slackness on the miners' part. Westm. Gaz., No. 8597, 1 a.
There is first to be a great *speeding-up* of shipbuilding. ib., No. 7401, 1 a.

ii. He stood watching the pageant of the sun's *down-going*. Hal. Sutcl., The Lone Adventure, Ch. I, 8.
To be a queen disthroned is not so hard as some other *down-stepping*. G. Eliot, Dan. Der., II, III, Ch. XXVI, 21.
All the changes in me have come about . . . by the *inbreathing* of a spirit not my own. Mrs. Ward, The Case of Rich. Meyn., I, Ch. V, 106.
Kossuth was a powerless exile, and looked with a jealous eye on the *ingathering* by others of the harvest. Times.
All the sounds hitherto described imply *out-breathing* or expiration. But they can also be formed with *in-breathing* or inspiration. Sweet, Sounds of Eng., § 139.
Please help to maintain the many activities of the Church Army for *uplifting* those who have fallen in Life's Struggle. Westm. Gaz., No. 8438, 24 b.
She understood something of the struggle provoked . . . by the *uprising* of the typical modern problems. Mrs. Ward, The Case of Rich. Meyn., I, Ch. IV, 68.

iii.° In him woke, | With his first babe's first cry the noble wish | To save all earnings to the uttermost. | And give his child a better *bringing-up* | Than his had been, or hers. Tennyson, En. Arden, 87.
He began to give a half-humorous account of the troubles and storms of Hester's *bringing-up*. Mrs. Ward, The Case of Rich. Meyn., II, Ch X, 201.
t° She divined his home and *upbringing*. ib., I, Ch. V, 106.

Her French biographers attribute her lack of maiden modesty in conducting her own matrimonial arrangements to her English *upbringing*. ETHEL COLQUHOUN, The Husband of Madame de Boigne (Ninet. Cent., No. 398, 700).
Dora has had a scallawag *upbringing*. Graph., No. 2264, 617.
There were many romantic stories as to the humble birth and *upbringing* of the late Lord Strathcona. Il. Lond. News, No. 3902, 161a.

Note. *α*) When the collocation is only an occasional one, i. e. does not form a fixed designation, the adverb regularly stands after the gerund, and makes no real compound with it.

They smoked out his singing=school by *stopping up* the chimney. WASH. IRV., Sketch=Bk., XXXII, 357.

β) Other adverbs than the above may form compounds with nouns of action, not with gerunds.

Mr. C. B. Cochran has been writing to the papers concerning their *ill=treatment* of "The League of Nations". Westm. Gaz., No. 8621, 10a.
I maintain that it was sheer disinterested concern on my part for the *welfare* of humanity. ib., 7a.

41. Verbs which govern fixed prepositions may form compound gerunds with these prepositions. The fact that the preposition is separated from the (pro)noun it refers to goes far to show that verb and preposition form a kind of unit. The union is naturally closest when the compound is preceded by an ad= nominal modifier.

i. You will never read anything that's worth *listening to*. SHER., Critic, I, 1, (445).
ii. That needs no *accounting for*. DICK., Chuz., Ch. I, 389a.
People occasionally called him a prig; now and then he received what the vernacular of youth terms 'a *sitting upon*'. GISSING, A Life's Morn., Ch. III, 36.
I wish you'd come round and give the gurl a *talkin to*. SHAW, Candida, 1, (130), T.
The poor fellow almost got the Georgian knock=out, for finally the Prime Minister went for him in a letter, and gave him a good *talking=to*. Eng. Rev., No. 106, 264.

42. Obs. I. Only one instance of a gerund compound whose first member is an adjective has come to hand, viz.: *well=being*.

The *well=being* of society is of more importance than the interest of the individual. Westm. Gaz., No. 8579, 4b.

Also in *merry=making* the first member is, indeed, an adjective, but in *to make merry*, from which the compound is formed, *merry* is felt rather as a noun than an adjective. As has already been observed in Ch. I, 5, *to make merry* stands for *to make oneself merry*. Compare also NESFIELD, Hist. Eng. and Deriv., § 218.

He came clattering up to the school=door with an invitation to Ichabod to attend a *merry=making* or "quilting frolic", to be held that evening at Mynheer Van Tassel's. WASH. IRV., Sketch=Bk., No. XXXII, 358.

II. Compounds in which a noun stands in an objective or adverbial relation to the verb, can in many cases be replaced by gerund phrases in which the noun is placed after the verb, no material change of meaning being involved. Thus there is no appreciable difference between *I do not like letter=writing*, *Note=taking in such a position is very difficult*, *Great festivities took place at his home=coming*, *He gave up cigar=smoking*, and, respectively, *I do not like writing letters*, *Taking notes in such a position is very difficult*, *Great festivities took place at his coming home*, *He gave up smoking cigars*.

Compare also the two following quotations:

The somewhat superfluous *heart=searchings* he has undergone. Аthin., 1885, 28. Nov. 697 1.

By the water=courses of the Lagan and the Foyle there must be *searchings of heart*. Westm. Gaz., No. 8603, 2 b.

Some of these compounds, however, hardly admit of being split up into their component parts. This applies, for example, to *coal=mining*, *horse=racing*, *tuft=hunting*.

Numerous as these compounds are, especially such as have the noun in the objective relation to the verb, they cannot be formed freely. Thus we could not substitute *call=paying* for *paying calls* in:

Chapters on dress, *paying calls*, letter=writing. Business Letter Writer.

III. When the connection between gerund and adverb is weak enough to admit of another verb=modifier separating them, they cannot be said to form a compound.

Mr. Bagg had a passion for *ordering people about*. Westm. Gaz., No. 8603, 12 a.

The connection is also considerably weakened when another verb= modifier follows the combination.

She finds *lying up so much* very irksome. Wеlls, Ann Veronica, Ch. I, § 5, 25.

IV. Compound gerunds containing an adverb may form a further compound with a preposition.

Both the peace and the rending of it were worth the *getting=up=for*. Hor. Hutchinson (Westm. Gaz., No. 6011, 2 c).

V. Like simple gerunds, compound gerunds of the first and the second kind are often used as adnominal modifiers, sometimes forming fresh compounds with their head=words.

He was a slow and *time=taking* speaker. Dick., Nich. Nick., Ch. I, 3 b.
The prosperity of our mercantile marine and of our *shipbuilding* yards, depends on our total trade, both coming in and going out. Westm. Gaz., No. 8591, 4 a.
December was a turning=point for the worse for the *shipbuilding industry*. ib.
We are ceasing to be a *game=playing nation* and becoming, instead, a nation that looks on at games. ib., 8603, 10 b.

ii. „The *lying-in* room, I suppose?" said Mr. Bumble. DICK., Ol. Twist, Ch. XXXVII, 340.
The *getting-on* races took place last week. Pall Mall Gaz.

VI. Finally it may be observed that these compounds have the mark of the plural attached to the verbal part. Of none of them the plural is, however, at all common; of those of the third kind it is non-existent.

It is only natural that she could not attach much importance to *home-comings*. AGN. and EC. CASTLE, Diam. cut Paste, I, Ch. VI, 75.
(That ball) is kicked about anyhow from one boy to another before *callings-over* and dinner. HUGHES, Tom Brown, I, Ch. V, 93.
She felt sure there must be *goings-on* when her back was turned. AMBER REEVES, The Reward of Virtue, Ch. II, 16.

THE GERUND COMPARED WITH THE OTHER VERBALS.

The gerund compared with the Infinitive.

43. It has already been observed (1) that the gerund bears a close resemblance to the infinitive on the one hand and to the noun of action on the other.

44. Most of the features which distinguish the infinitive from the gerund have already been referred to in the preceding pages, and it is, therefore, sufficient to pass them rapidly in review. Owing to its being more distinctly verbal in its functions than the gerund, the infinitive, unlike the latter,

a) does not suffer the distinction of tense to be disregarded, except so far as futurity is concerned. Compare Infinitive, 57. Thus, granted that idiom would tolerate the change, the imperfect gerund would take the place of the perfect infinitive in:

To have *taken* the field openly against his rival would have been madness. WASH. IRV., Sketch-Bk., XXXII, 355. (*Taking* the field etc.)

Conversely the imperfect gerund would correspond to the perfect infinitive in:

I don't remember *seeing* more than one or two drunken men on week-days. J. G. WOOD, Good Words (STOF., Leesb., I, 72.). (I don't remember *to have seen* etc.)

Note. Like the gerund, the infinitive is frequently enough placed in the active voice when it is passive in meaning, but the cases in which the two verbals exhibit this grammatical peculiarity differ entirely. See Infinitive, 72, ff; and compare 29.

b) can take no other preposition before it than *to*, save for archaic or dialectal English, which sometimes have *for* placed before *to* + Infinitive. Compare Infinitive, 3, Obs. III; and also Ch. XVIII, 24, Obs. III.

<small>It is not lawful *for to put* them (sc. the silver pieces) into the treasury. Bible, Matth., XXVII, 6.
Miss Arabella wondered why he always said he was going *for to do* a thing. G. Eliot, Scenes, I, Ch. II, 14.</small>

c) cannot be attended by adnominal modifiers (13—14). It may here be observed that the genitive or possessive pronoun (sometimes replaced by the common case or objective personal pronoun respectively) often placed before the gerund to denote the originator of the action or state it expresses (13, d), is sometimes represented by *for* + (pro)noun before the infinitive. Compare the following groups of quotations:

<small>i. I feel quite certain it is worth while *for you to be very industrious* with your painting. F. F. Benson, Mr. Teddy, Ch. II, 49.
ii. Anyhow, it's worth while *my having* a game of golf-croquet with you. ib., 50.
i. There is no use *for me to cry* about the matter. Kingsley, Westw. Ho!, Ch. XIV, 118b.
ii. There is no use *your telling* me that you are going to be good. Osc. Wilde, Dor. Gray, Ch. XIX, 268. T.</small>

For detailed discussion of *for* + (pro)noun + infinitive see Ch. XVIII, 45 ff. Compare also Ch. XIX, 7.

d) cannot be used as an adnominal modifier (15).

e) admits of no inflection for number or case (16). In Old English, as we have seen in Infinitive, 3, Obs. I, the infinitive had a dative, but no further inflection.

<small>He is *to cumenne* = He is about to come.
Thone calic the ic *to drincenne* hæbbe = The cup that I am about to drink.</small>

45. For the rest, when no subject-indicating word precedes, either the gerund or the infinitive can be used in numerous cases, sometimes with a marked difference in meaning, sometimes with no, or a hardly appreciable, distinction. In Ch. XIX an attempt has been made to delimit the cases in which the two verbals are, apparently, interchangeable, and in which either one or the other is obligatory or preferable. Although continued investigation has shown that the results set forth require some rectification and considerable supplementing, the student must, for the time being rest satisfied with the information there offered. For detailed discussion see also ELLINGER, gerund, infinitiv and that=satz als adverbiale oder adnominale ergänzung (Anglia, XXXIII, 480ff).

The Gerund compared with the Noun of Action.

46. a) The noun of action is distinguished from the gerund,
   1) by its utter incapability of showing the distinctions of voice and tense. In other words nouns of action are strictly neutral as to voice and tense.

   Thus *ill=usage* might take the place of *being ill=used* in: *This, Sir Lucius, I call being ill=used.* SHER., Riv., 4, (252).

   punishment might be substituted for *being punished* in: *If we es= caped being punished, it was only because Mr. Webb was away at a wedding most of the time.* SWEET, Old Chapel.

   admiration might replace *being admired* in: *He is desirous of being admired.* MASON, Eng. Gram.⁵⁴, § 397.

   Conversely *being uttered* might be substituted for *utterance* in: *She had started up with defiant words ready to burst from her lips, but they fell back again without utterance.* G. ELIOT, Romola, II, Ch. XL, 310.

   2) by its incapability of taking a non=prepositional object. The (pro)noun which in the case of a gerund may be used in this function, figures as part of an adnominal adjunct with *of* when the noun of action is used.

   Thus *Arranging flowers is a favourite pastime of mine.* (HABBERTON, Helen's Babies, 55) might be changed into *The arrangement of flowers* etc.
   Conversely in *To doubt his originality in the creation of poetic phrases would be to show the extreme of poetical incapacity.* (A. C. BRADLEY, Com. on Ten.'s In Memor., Ch. VII, 73) *the creation of poetic phrases* might be replaced by *creating poetic phrases.*

   When the non=prepositional object is represented by a subordinate clause, substitution of the noun of action for the gerund is impossible. Thus in:

   Upon Johnson's *inquiring* what injury he had suffered at the hands of those persons to justify so splenetic an outburst, Goldsmith showed him a copy of "The Elysian" [etc.]. Westm. Gaz., No. 8579, 6b.

   In like manner as in the case of gerunds (39), nouns in the objective relation to the verbal idea implied in nouns of action are often enough found before the latter, forming with them a kind of compound. Such a compound mostly admits of being expanded into a noun of action — adnominal adjunct with *of*.

> The much larger sum of £ 10.000.000 will go to the provision of relief works, such as *land reclamation* and afforestation. Manch. Guard., V, No. 16, 302 b. (= reclamation of land.)
> We have grave doubts whether the country can afford to foster the complacency of Mr. Austen Chamberlain any longer by setting aside large sums for *debt redemption*. Times, No. 2303, 138 a. (Compare: There are signs in the King's Speech that the pride of the Chancellor of the Exchequer in the heavy demands made upon the Country for *redemption of debt* is not now shared by his colleagues. ib.)

> Note. It may here be observed that the subjective genitive standing before a noun of action is never replaced by the common case, which, as we have seen, is often the case before a gerund (13, e; 34—37).

> The arguments for *Lady Clementine's rejection* of Christianity had been given with terrible power. E. F. Benson, Mr. Teddy, Ch. II, 29.
> There certainly was force in *Daisy's contention* that matter published in a serial is not to be judged in the same way when it appears in book form. ib.
> The higgling about status was ended by *Mr. Loyd George's invitation* and *Mr. de Valera's acceptance* to a conference. Manch. Guard., V, No. 14, 261 a.

b) The noun of action, however, is like the gerund in being, in a manner, capable of modification by a prepositional object or an adverbial adjunct containing a preposition. Prepositional word-groups, whether corresponding to prepositional objects or adverbial adjuncts, owing to the more markedly substantival nature of the noun of action, are, however, felt as adnominal modifiers. For illustration see also the next section.

> i. Haven't you made yourself the jest of all your acquaintance by your *interference in matters* where you have no business. Sher., Critic, I, 1.
> On his *persistence in the scheme* depended one of his precautions for his own safety. Dick., Chuz., Ch. II, 390 b.
> (The chimes were) incapable of *participation in any of the good things* that were constantly being handed through the street-doors and the area railings to prodigious cooks. id., Chimes³, I, 10.
> ii. She did not make this sacrifice without a motive, which may have sprung from a keen sense of justice, and of gratitude to the plaintiff for his *interference on her behalf*. Riv. Hvo., Mees. Will, Ch. XXI, 224.
> We shall all regret his *disappearance from the House of Commons*. Westm. Gaz., No. 5255, 2 a.

Note. Nouns of action are very rarely found attended by an adverb of quality, the markedly verbal notion, which is implied in the use of such a modifier, rendering the employment of the gerund practically obligatory.

Mark actually held him to prevent his *interference foolishly*. DICK., Chuz., Ch. XXXV, 281 a.

This applies also, although in a less degree, to modifiers which would figure as predicative adnominal adjuncts to the gerund that might be substituted for the noun of action, these modifiers partaking of the nature of adnominal and adverbial modifiers at once.

Life alone at twenty-six is lonely. HOPE, Instructions of Peggy, 44[1]).

47. a) When a verb has no noun of action, the gerund supplies the want as a very useful make-shift. For the rest there is a distinct tendency to use the former in preference to the latter when the grammatical function is mainly substantival. A few moments' attentive reading will bring this fact home to any student interested in the subject. Thus idiomatic propriety would appear to suffer in most of the following quotations, if the gerund were substituted for the noun of action.

Ah, Charles, if you associated more with your brother, one might, indeed, hope for your *reformation*. SHER., School for Scand., IV, 3, (428).

He gave up his *attendance* at that course, and announced to his fond parent that he proposed to devote himself exclusively to the *cultivation* of Greek and Roman Literature. THACK., Pend., I, Ch. XVIII, 185.

He was in debt nearly a hundred pounds to tradesmen, chiefly of Mrs. Hoggarty's *recommendation*. id., Sam. Titm., Ch. XI, 141.

And in due course there was bed, where, but for the *resumption* of the studies which took place in dreams, were rest and sweet forgetfulness. DICK., Domb., Ch. XII, 110.

Bathsheba looked up at the *completion* of the manœuvre. TH. HARDY, Far from the Madding Crowd, Ch. XVIII, 140.

A resolution to avoid an evil is seldom framed till the evil is so far advanced as to make *avoidance* impossible. ib., Ch. XVIII, 141.

They speak it (sc. the standard dialect) without effort and without *thought*. SWEET, Sounds of Eng., § 229.

The Reverend Charles forbade the further *mention* of her name by any member of his household. HUGH WALPOLE, The Captives, I, Ch. I, 13.

The Westminster Gazette Information Bureau has been established for the purpose of assisting readers who are house-hunting or contemplating *removal* to another neighbourhood. Westm. Gaz., No. 5249, 13 c.

The whole performance is a great joke, a merry *incursion* into more serious debate. ib., 4 b.

I overheard him telling Tony a rather amusing story about a nun and a mousetrap which won't bear *repetition*. ib., No. 5255, 3 a.

[1]) JESPERSEN, Mod. Eng. Gram., 12.09.

Her judgments, in the main, are formed upon a *perusal* and not a *vision* of the dramas in question. ib., No. 8633, 10a.

The following quotations, in which gerunds and nouns of action, corresponding to different verbs, are used alternately, will bring out this fact still more clearly.

For *pickling, preserving,* and *cookery,* none could excel her. Goldsmith, Vic., Ch. I.

Sleep is, perhaps, Nature's never-failing relief, as *swooning* is upon the rack. Leigh Hunt, A few Thoughts on Sleep.

Large sums have been expended in the *rebuilding* of dwelling-houses, in the *laying-down* of main roads, in the *reclamation* of land by *drainage, planting* and *enclosure*. Escott, England, Ch. III, 33.

The Irisch Royal Commissioners ... had recommended the *improvement* of agriculture by the *reclamation* of waste lands, the *draining* of bogs, the *provision* of labourers' cottages and allotments, the *bringing* of agricultural instruction to the doors of the peasant, the *improvement* of land tenure, etc., reforms which only now are being introduced. J. Ellis Barker, Parliament and the Irish Party (Nineteenth Cent., No. CCCXCVI, 246).

Warren — piece of ground appropriated to the *breeding* and *preservation* of game or rabbits. Ann., Conc. Dict.

The *discovery* and *training* of one genius may pay for the *education* of a whole town. Westm. Gaz., No. 8574, 4a.

b) Sometimes, however, the gerund and the noun appear to be equally appropriate, being used in practically identical connections. This is shown by the following groups of quotations, which by assiduous reading could, most probably, be considerably added to:

i. No difficulties but *of my own creating*. Shak., Riv., IV, 3.

ii. A legion of goblins all *of my own creation*. Dick., Christm. Car., I.

i. Peter de Groot did not think it *worth mentioning*. Wash. Irv., Dolf Heyl. (Stof., Handb., I, 105).

ii. His remark ... is *worth mention*. Athen., No 4535, 297b.

i. Parliament has itself thought well to provide in advance for a review of its results by a statutory commission ten years after *the passing of the Act.* Westm. Gaz., No. 8597, 12a.

ii. The great revolution which was always feared, however, never took place, but this fear was responsible for *the passage of laws* which made it difficult in many of the States for a master to emancipate his slaves. ib., No. 5266, 16c.

They could do nothing to prevent the *passage of the Home Rule Bill.* ib., No. 6535, 12a.

i. The sudden conviction that they (sc. the Lords) *need reforming* is a very curious 'non sequitor' after the prolonged chorus of self-approval, which has gone up from the Peers during the last six months. Westm. Gaz., No. 5266, 1c.

The Duke of Northumberland and Lord Salisbury declared boldly that the institution which *required reforming* was the House of Commons, and not the House of Lords. ib., No. 5261, 1b.

n. Some of the Peers in the debate on Lord Rosebery's motion have suggested that it is the House of Commons, and not the House of Lords, which needs *reform*. ib., No. 5261, 9.

c) In not a few cases the gerund and the corresponding noun of action stand for different notions. Thus in the above quotation from GOLDSMITH *cookery* and *preserving* differ considerably in meaning from respectively *cooking* and *preservation*.

The discussion of these differences belongs to the department of lexicography and is not, therefore, attempted in these pages.

48. Obs. I. In SHAKESPEARE not a few instances are met with of nouns of action for which Present English would have the gerund. See FRANZ, Shak. Gram.², § 670.

If chance will have me king, why, chance may crown me without my *stir*. Macb., I, 3, 144.

She... appear'd not: | And, to be short, for not *appearance* and | The king's late scruple, by the main assent | Of all these learned men she was divorced. HENRY VIII, IV, 1, 30.

II. Owing, apparently, to the influence of nouns of a kindred meaning, nouns of action which correspond to transitive verbs sometimes take another preposition than *of* in the adnominal adjunct containing the (pro)noun which is in the objective relation to the verbal idea implied in them. Thus regularly, or frequently, *attempt*, *(dis)like*, *hate (hatred)*, *love*, etc. Compare Ch. XIX, 49, Obs. II and III. The discussion of this subject belongs to the Chapter of the Government of Verbs, Adjectives and Nouns, which the present writer has been a long time engaged in preparing. One instance must here suffice.

This is best promoted by an incessant preaching of Liberal doctrine on great issues, on the saving of the world through the League of Nations, on *resistance to* Carsonism in Ireland [etc.]. Westm. Gaz., No. 8521, 6b.

The Gerund compared with the Present Participle.

49. Although the present participle, in its grammatical function, markedly differs from the gerund, the one being as distinctly adnominal as the other is substantival, it overlaps the area of incidence of the latter to a considerable extent.

As we have seen in sections 34—37, the verbal in *ing*, when preceded by the common case of a (pro)noun or the objective of a personal pronoun, is more or less of a doubtful nature, assuming as it does, in various degrees, a function which causes it to be considered, with some reason, as a present participle or, at least, as a verbal form which partakes considerably of the character of a present participle. As the following sections will show, this is not, however, the only connection in which the character of the verbal in *ing* is disputed.

50. a) Through the suppression of a preposition the verbal in *ing* has often come to be used in a way which causes its grammatical function to be changed, to the extent that it is no more to be distinguished from an ordinary present participle. Sweet (N. E. Gr., § 2333) commenting on two such sentences as *She caught cold sitting on the grass, He tears his clothes climbing trees*, observes that they have arisen through the dropping of a preposition. On the strength of this suppression of a preposition he calls the verbals used in them half-gerunds. Although this view may be inexpugnable when the genesis of the construction used in sentences like the above is taken as the determining factor, it cannot be denied that the verbals they contain, considered in their present function, are pure participles used as predicative adnominal adjuncts.

b) In Sweet's sentences it appears to be the preposition *by* which might be supplied. Thus also in:

He had half ruined himself *buying* new music. Mrs. Wood, Orv. Col., Ch. VIII, 116.
He made a fool of himself, *marrying* a child like Leo. Shaw, Getting Married, I, (206).
What do you all mean, *interfering* with my work *and disturbing* the peace of my garden? Birn. Capes, The Pot of Basil, Ch. III, 31.
He gets to feeling very low *walking about* all day after work, and *being refused* so often. Galsworthy, The Silver Box, I, 2, (20).

c) More frequently insertion of the preposition *in* would seem to be more in harmony with the meaning of the sentence. Thus in:

The stream, in struggling onward, turns the mill-wheel; the coral insect, *fashioning* its tiny cell, joins continents to one another. Jerome, Idle Thoughts, IV, 62. (Note the remarkable variation of construction.)
I broke my looking-glass, *dressing* to go out. Hall Caine, Christ., II, 32.
I was detained *playing* bridge with your father. Fl. Guys, The Reason why, Ch. XXVI, 237.
The most masculine woman looks graceful, *playing* tennis, and the most graceful woman looks ugly, *playing* hockey. Chesterton (Il. Lond. News, No. 3841 a, 793 b.)

I have spent many hours in the last few days, *reading* the Treaty. Westm.
Gaz., No. 8121, 4b.
Part of the year he spends, *visiting* Museums. ib., No. 6135, 1b.

Of particular interest are the participle-constructions after:

1) such verbs as *to catch, to surprise* and *to take*, the participle modifying the object. Compare Ch. XX, 21.

> Old Momus caught me *construing* off the leaf of a crib. Hughes, Tom Brown, II, Ch. VII, 309.
> She caught a glimpse of him *walking* up and down between the roses. Agn. and Eg. Castle, Diamond cut Paste, II, Ch. VII, 192.
> Actæon. A huntsman, who, having surprised Diana *bathing*, was turned by her into a stag and torn by his own dogs. Annandale, Conc. Dict., s. v. *Actæon*.

The participle, of course, modifies the subject when the sentence is thrown into the passive voice.

> I suppose these fellows have been taken *robbing* your house. Smollett, Rod. Rand., Ch. XVII, 115.

2) *to be long, to be a long time* and similar phrases. Compare Ch. II, 37 f.

> People thought he would not be long *getting* through his property. Thack., Pend., II, Ch. XX, 218.
> We were a long time *delivering* a bedstead at a public-house and calling at other houses. Dick., Cop., Ch. III, 14b.
> He had been an unconscionable time *dying*. Mac., Hist., II, Ch. IV, 12.
> I have been some time *answering* your question. W. Morris, News from Nowhere, Ch. X, 69.

d) Sometimes there does not seem to be any particular preposition expressing the exact adverbial relation.

> What should such fellows as I do *crawling* between heaven and earth? Shak., Haml., III, 1, 130.
> I shall be contented *waiting* here for the year to come round to bring you both to see me. Temple Thurston, The City of Beaut. Nons., III, Ch. XIV, 337.
> We are little likely to be afraid of him *fighting* on. Westm. Gaz., No. 6122, 2a.

51. Obs. I. In generalizing sentences there is sometimes no particular (pro)-noun to which the participle can be said to refer.

> Is not a bouquet rather in the way *dancing*? El. Glyn, Reflect. of Ambros., Ch. III.

II. The suppression of the preposition, although leading to vagueness, has this advantage that it enables the speaker to express a wider range of relations than the use of the preposition would involve. Thus in Sweet's sentences, cited above, the relation between what is expressed by the head-sentence and the participle-clause appears to be a blending of cause and time, so that it would not have been adequately expressed by *by*.

Thus also the participle-construction in the second group of the above quotations, although, apparently, implying a distinctly temporal relation, may be replaced by a gerund-construction with different prepositions. Compare the following quotations:

i. The first half-hour was spent *in piling* up the fire. JANE AUSTEN, Pride and Prej., Ch. XI, 57.

ii. Katharina spent more time than necessary *over dressing* for dinner MAR. CRAWF., Kath. Laud., II, Ch. XIV, 247.

III. It should also be observed that, in explaining a given construction, it is often exceptionable to assume the suppression of a word. This assumption seems to be proper only if it can be proved that such a word is sometimes met with in parallel cases, or was employed in an earlier stage of the language. Thus, although it seems probable that the construction in the above quotations has arisen through the dropping of a preposition, it would certainly not do assume the suppression of a preposition in a large number of sentences in which also the participle forms part of a clause in the function of predicative adnominal adjunct. This will soon be brought home to the student if he takes the trouble of glancing through the numerous quotations given in Ch. XX, 12 ff. We copy a few, in which suppression of a preposition is out of the question. Also CURME (E. S., XLV, 372) warns against hastily assuming the suppression of a preposition.

The doctor, *having felt* his pulse, and examined his wounds, declared him much better. FIELDING, Jos. Andrews, I, Ch. XVI, 47.
Having had no facilities for learning, he was forced to teach. MAC., War. Hast., (635b).
Seeing a crowd, I stopped. SWEET, N. E. Gr., § 2344.
Lady Holmhurst presently left the room, *leaving* them to settle it as they liked. RID. HAG., Mees. Will, Ch. XVII, 169.
We fled to the hills, *seeking* shelter and *walking* all night. Manch. Guard., V, No. 18, 346d.

IV. For a full discussion of those cases in which a verbal in *ing*, through the loss of the preposition *on* (or *an*) or *in*, has changed its grammatical character, the student is referred to Participle, § 6, Obs. VII and VIII.

The Gerund compared with the Past Participle.

52. Although the past participle has, grammatically, nothing in common with the gerund, this seems a suitable place to discuss a case in which a construction with the one is equivalent to a construction with the other

a) In such sentences as

> He heard the chain and bolts *withdrawn*. Dick., Pickw., Ch. XVI, 146.
> He had never seen a human being *killed*. Reade, The Cloister and the Hearth, Ch. X, 57.

the logical object of the predication in the head=sentence is represented by the grammatical object and the following participle together with their modifiers. Indeed, this word=group would, in many cases, bear being replaced by another consisting of *the* + gerund + adnominal adjunct with *of* (14, 32). Thus the first of the above quotations might be turned into *He heard the withdrawing of the chain and bolts*.

b) Also in other connexions (pro)noun + past participle has the value of a gerund=combination

1) In literary language we find constructions which bear some resemblance to the well=known Latin idioms post urbem conditam, ante Christum natum, post hoc factum, in which noun + past participle stands after a preposition governing an accusative.

> Bacchus, that first from out the purple grape | Crush't the sweet poison of misused wine, | *After the Tuscan mariners transform'd*, | Coasting the Tyrrhene shore, as the winds listed, | On Circe's iland fell. Milton, Comus, 48. (= *after the transforming or transformation of the Tuscan mariners*.)
> 'Twas at the royal feast, *for Persia won* | By Philip's warlike son. Dryden, Alexander's Feast, I.
> Not tho' he built *upon the babe restored;* | Nor tho' she liked him, yielded she, but fear'd | To incense the Head once more. Ten., Princ., VII, 60.
> By this the lazy gossips of the port, | Abhorrent *of a calculation crost,* Began to chafe as at a personal wrong. id., En. Ard., 470.
> Lo! ever thus thou growest beautiful | In silence, then *before thine answer given* | Departest, and thy tears are on my cheek. id., Tithonus, 44.

2) More common, but also, to all appearance, purely literary is a construction in which the same combination, noun + past participle, stands as the subject, or, more rarely, as the non=prepositional object. Also this construction may be an imitation of a Latin original. Thus Tennyson's *things seen are mightier than things heard* (En. Ard., 762) appears to have been suggested by Horace's Segnius inritant animos demissa per aurem | Quam quæ sunt oculis subjecta. Ars. Poet., 180—181. (= things communicated through the ear stir men's feelings less

powerfully than things that are set before the eyes. For
discussion of the constructions under 1) and 2) see also
BIRGER PALM, The Place of the Adjective Attribute
in English, § 21; JESPERSEN, De to Hovedarter av
Grammatiske Forbindelser, B 8 and B 10.

i. Freeze, freeze, thou bitter sky, | That dost not bite so nigh | As benefits
forgot. SHAK., As you like it, II, 7, 186. (the forgetting of benefits.)
Since the day When foolish Stena's ribaldry detected Untis'd your
quiet, you are greatly changed. BYRON, Mar. Fal., II, 1, (561 a).
The guilty saved has damn'd his hundred judges. ib., II, 1, (561 b)
New shores descried make every bosom gay, id., Ch. Har., I, XIV.
It has often been observed that one truth concealed gives rise to a dozen
current lies. WASH. IRV., Dolf Heyl. (Stor., Handl., I, (120).
Cruel massacres followed by cruel retribution, provinces wasted, convents
plundered and cities raised to the ground make up the greater part of the
history of those days. MAC., Hist., I, Ch. I, 10.
Here her hand Grasp'd made her vail her eyes. TEN., Guin., 657.
ii. Nor is it Wiser to weep a true occasion lost. id., Princ., IV, 50.

THE DISTINCTION BETWEEN GERUND AND VERBAL NOUN NOT JUSTIFIABLE.

53. Most grammarians hold that we ought to distinguish two substantival verbal forms in ing, viz.: the gerund and the verbal
noun, the former mainly verbal, the latter mainly substantival
in character. It is, of course, easy to see that in some cases
the verbal features, in others the substantival features of the
verbal come to the fore. But, as has been shown in the above
discussions (17—24), there are a great many cases in which the
gerund exhibits at once verbal and substantival features. Though
it cannot be said that in all of them these several features appear
with equal prominence, any line of demarcation which should
divide gerunds from so-called verbal nouns seems to be drawn
more or less arbitrarily.

a) 1) Thus when a preposition precedes a gerund which is followed by either an object or an adverbial adjunct, or by
both, we have no hesitation in saying that the substantival
nature is subservient to the verbal. This is, for example,
the case in *making a speech, the expediency of getting
up early, the necessity of writing the letter at once*.

2) Also when a genitive or possessive pronoun precedes a
gerund which is accompanied by the above verb-modifiers,

the verbal features seem to be more marked than the substantival, as in *his breaking his arm, her staying in the town.*

b) Conversely one is inclined to ascribe rather a substantival than a verbal character to the gerund when it stands without any verb-modifier and is only attended by some adnominal adjunct, an adjective making it practically purely substantival. Thus in *The story took an hour in the telling, I heard a knocking, There was some dancing, I admire his singing, I don't like this shouting, I don't believe in early rising.*

c) But it seems, among other cases, difficult to decide whether the verbal or substantival character preponderates,
 1) when another adnominal modifier than a genitive or a possessive pronoun precedes a complex gerund (2), as in *this being kept in suspense, the not being hurried, the being born in a workhouse, the having been caught in such a strange act of charity, there is no being shot at without a little risk.*
 2) when a definite or indefinite article precedes a gerund with an object or an adverbial adjunct, as in *the quitting my home, the scaling him, a turning English into French, the running away in such haste.*
 3) when the gerund stands entirely by itself, and is not preceded by a preposition, as in *swimming is healthy, saving is having, I like skating,* both infinitives and nouns of action being, found in the same positions.
 Thus the gerund looks like a verbal form by comparison with the infinitive in:
 Travelling was recommended to her. MAC., Mad. d'Arblay, (723a) But: *To travel* in such severe weather was out of the question.

 It appears as a substantival form by comparison with the noun of action in:
 Powwow. A ceremony of the North American Indians especially one where *magic* was practised and *feasting* and *dancing* indulged in. MURRAY.

54. Nor can differentiation between a gerund and a so-called verbal noun be defended on historical grounds, the substantival verbal in *ing* in its present applications being, by common consent, the lineal descendant of practically only one form, the Old English noun of action in *ing* (earlier *ung*). See below 58—64.

From these considerations it does not seem advisable or even justifiable to distinguish two verbal forms in *ing*, and as no useful purpose is served by any differentiation it seems needless to insist on it.

55. Also JESPERSEN appears to lean to the view that any attempt to distinguish between the two verbals in *ing* is rather futile. His bestowing on them the common denomination of *ings* (Growth and Structure, § 200 ff.) hardly bears another interpretation.

Similarly CURME's statement (E. S., XLV, 359), "There is but one gerund and it is always a noun even where it has a strong verbal force" implies that in his view the variety of grammatical potentialities in the verbal in *ing* affords no sufficient ground for differentiation.

KRÜGER (Verm. Beitr., 20), while admitting that the verbal in *ing* can often be replaced by a noun of action, especially one in *ion* or *tion*, yet contends that we have to deal with a gerund, not a verbal noun, in such sentences as *He takes (a) pleasure in contradicting* (= contradiction), *Living is combating* (= Life is a combat, a struggle, a strife). The same grammarian (Verm. Beitr., 22) holds that the only adnominal adjuncts by which the gerund can be preceded are a possessive pronoun, a demonstrative pronoun and the indefinite *no*. As the same adjuncts may, of course, be found before a verbal noun, we are, if we endorse his reasoning, confronted with the difficulty to decide when the form in *ing* is a gerund, when it is a verbal noun, in the case of any of these adjuncts preceding. The writer's reasoning seems to lead to the conclusion that in such a sentence as *A letter announced his coming* the form of *ing* has to be looked on as a verbal noun, whereas in *A letter announced his coming in great haste* (or some such adverbial adjunct of quality), it has to be regarded as a gerund. But it is difficult to see any difference either in meaning or in grammatical function between *coming* in the first and in the second sentence. Similarly it would require subtle reasoning to define the difference between the forms in *ing* in two such sentences as *No whispering there!* and *No whispering there in such an offensive way!* Nor, indeed, is there any essential difference in meaning and grammatical function between the forms in *ing* as used in *My friend's singing disturbed me*, in which *singing* would be set down as a gerund, and *My friend's loud singing disturbed me*, in which it would be pronounced a verbal noun.

56. From what has been said above, it must not, of course, be inferred that all substantival forms in *ing* which have been derived from verbs, should be regarded as gerunds. Many such do not express any action or state at all and are, therefore, to be apprehended as pure nouns. This is the case with:

  a) a large number of nouns which have a distinctly material meaning, denoting things which may be understood to be in a subjective or objective, or also in a local or instrumental, relation to the action indicated by the verb from which they have been derived. Of these a great many appear exclusively or preferentially in the plural.

Thus *covering* = that which covers, or with which a thing is covered; *dripping* = melted fat which drips from roasting meat; *holding* = land which is held by legal right, especially of a superior; *sewing* = work sewn; *digging(s)* = a place where digging is carried on, especially in gold=fields; *lan= ding* = a place for disembarking passengers or unlading goods, also a platform in which a flight of stairs terminates; etc. Similar interpretations may be put upon *bearings, binding, blacking, clipping(s), cutting(s), drainings, drawing, earnings, engraving, hanging(s), incomings, leavings, lightning, losings, outgoings, parings, savings, scrapings, shavings, stitching, sur= roundings, sweepings, winding, winnings, workings, writing,* etc.

b) many nouns of a collective meaning denoting the substance or material employed in the action or process indicated by the verb from which they have been derived.

Thus *clothing* = things employed in clothing; *roofing* = things used in roofing, etc.

A similar collective meaning can be traced in *bedding, car= peting, ceiling, edging, flooring, gearing, gilding, housing, lining, rigging, shipping, tackling, tiling,* etc.

Note. The *ing*=nouns here referred to have, for the greater part, been formed from verbs that have been derived from nouns, and it is with the latter that they are most closely associated. Some have been formed direct from nouns, there being no corresponding verb. Such are *coping, piping, scaffolding, tubing; bagging, quilting, sacking, sheeting, shirting, trousering,* etc. These latter formations are especially frequent in industrial and commercial language.

The following quotations, arranged according to the alpha= betical succession of the *ing*=nouns in question may be accept= able to the student:

If Russia intervenes she (sc. Turkey) may find that the question of Asia Minor has been thrown into the *boiling* with that of her European territory. Westm. Gaz., No. 6294, 1 b.

Pig with pruin sauce is very good *eating*. GOLDSMITH, She stoops, II.
I'm for plain *eating*. ib.
I wonder when it (sc. the nation) will begin to see the folly of spending so much on *eating*. Westm. Gaz., No. 5555, 4 b.

And Enid heard the clashing of his fall. Suddenly came, and at his side all pale : Dismounting, loosed the *fastenings* of his arms. Tixs., Ger. and En., 511.

No small part of these speeches consisted of the merest personalities, and of attempts to represent the Coalition Liberals as injured innocents, who are the constant butt of plots on the part of Mr Asquith's *following*. Westm. Gaz., No. 8615, 2 b.

A sum of £ 200.000 is needed to put it (sc. the Scout movement) on a sound *footing*. Times, No. 2209, 55 a.

There is now a very heavy fall in the demand for *shipping*. Westm. Gaz., No. 8591, 4 a.

Shipping is being laid up for want of goods to carry. ib., 8615, 4 a.

There's some *writing* on it (sc. the card). Pinero, Mid-Channel, IV, (220).

This agreement has not been put into *writing*. Westm. Gaz., No. 6205, 1 b.

Grace was preeminent in all his *writing* which was at once easy and pointed. Athen., No. 4422, 93 a.

57. Some words in *ing*, although having no material sense, are only remotely associated with an action or state, denoting as they do,

  a) an event, a state, or ceremony characterized by or resulting from an action. Thus *meeting*, in the sense of an assembly of a number of people for purposes of discussion, legislation, etc. Thus also *gathering* in a similar meaning. Further instances are *wedding* (i. e. nuptial ceremonies), *christening* (in an analogous meaning), and a great many others, such as *merry-making, outing, sitting*, etc. in certain of their meanings, which need no definition in these pages.

  b) an art or ability acquired by assiduous or constant practice of an action. Thus *reading* and *writing* in such a sentence as *Reading and writing are now common acquirements.* Of a similar meaning are *drawing, engraving, fencing, swimming*, etc.

  Note. It is difficult to find an appropriate name for these words in *ing*. Noun of action is not quite suitable. Nor is abstract noun more serviceable, on account of its vagueness and its varied application by different grammarians. The term half-gerund might, perhaps, be used to good purpose, if it were not for the fact that it has been employed by Sweet and his followers for an entirely different function of the word in *ing*.

  Under these circumstances there seems no alternative but to stretch the denomination gerund sufficiently for it to include these words in *ing* of an immaterial meaning, which, although associated with an action or state, do not denote an action or state in the strict sense of the word.

Here follow some quotations with gerunds more or less of the nature described above, not a few of them being admittedly examples of a doubtful nature, and included after some hesitation.

Then came... orchards of fruit-trees in full *bearing*. Sam. Butler, Erewhon, Ch. IX, 90.

He began from very low *beginnings*, and odd stories are told about the origin of his fortune. Thack., Newc., I, Ch. VIII, 90.

He has betaken himself to the high and honourable *calling* of letters. Rud. Hag., Mees. Will, Ch. IV, 42.

He isn't to take any notice of the *crossings-out* in red ink. Arn. Bennett, The Card, I, Ch. III, 7.

And ever in her mind she cast about ; For that unnoticed *failing* in herself. Ten., Ger. and En., 46.

It may be doubted whether even now a number of petitions ought not to be brought without regard to the recent *findings* of judges. Westm. Gaz., No. 5231, 4b.

The Government definitely refuse to publish the *findings* of the Strickland Report. Times, No. 2303, 138d.

The party conference... will produce its own schemes to be brought before a special *gathering* on January 27. Westm. Gaz., No. 8591, 2a.

She felt sure there must be *goings-on* when her back was turned. Amber Reeves, The Reward of Virtue, Ch. II, 16.

Some unforeseen *happening* may change their minds. Times, No. 2298, 25d.

Another cause which makes candidates unwilling to attempt prosecutions or to bring petitions is the remembrance of judgments in certain recent *hearings* of election petitions. Westm. Gaz., No. 5231, 4b.

A little *learning* is a dangerous thing. Pope, Es. on Crit., II, 215.

He seemed to have the *makings* of a very nice fellow about him. Dicks., Pickw., Ch. XXXVII, 343.

You've not the *makings* of a Person in you, or a Leibnitz either. G. Eliot, Fel. Holt, II, Ch. XVI, 258.

Serious people, who know how vital to this country and to the world is a friendly relationship between Britain and America, will be quick to realise its *meaning*. Westm. Gaz., No. 8597, 2a.

Larger political questions were referred to *meetings* of the Prime Ministers. Times, Rev. of the Year 1920, 1c.

After payment of necessary *outgoings*, he has a larger proportion of his income remaining for luxuries and saving. Westm. Gaz., No. 8574, 23a.

He was a man of great *reading*. Thack., Newc., I, Ch. VIII, 97.

The German Government made strong representations that in view of the disturbed state of the country and the communist *risings*, they could not carry out the clauses of the Treaty. Times, Rev. of the Year 1920, 1d.

He is, according to *his showing*, guilty of a twenty-thousand-fold act of treason. Rev. of Rev., No. CC, 161b.

The corn duty, on *their own showing*, could not possibly injure anybody. Times.

On *this showing* all Governments would be open to the same reproach. Westm. Gaz., No. 6465, 1a.

Had it not been for that factor, South Bucks would have made a better *showing*. ib., No. 6465, 3a.

The Government ... insist on keeping the investigation of the Mallow *shootings* in military hands. Times, No. 2303, 138d.
Poor aunt J., she was in a regular *taking*. AGS. AND E. CASTI, Diamcut Paste, II, Ch. II, 133.
He's a man of an excellent *understanding*. GOLDSMITH, She Stoops, I, (170).
The complete fulfilment of British *undertakings* is not likely to be delayed when the people of India have fully proved their capacity in the art of government. Times, 2301, 98d.

HISTORICAL SURVEY OF THE RISE OF THE GERUND.

58. The origin of the gerund has been the subject of much speculation, and the rise of some of the syntactical applications of which it is capable has not yet been satisfactorily cleared up. The following exposition is not based upon any independent investigation, but rather intended as a summary of the views ventilated by various scholars.

Many of the following quotations I owe to the courteous assistance of my friend Dr. W. v. d. Gaaf, to whose extensive reading and sound knowledge of Old and Middle English I have great pleasure in paying a grateful tribute.

59. The main source of the gerund, as we know it in Present English, is the noun in *ung* or *ing*, or its inflected form in *unge* or *inge*.

According to EINENKEL (Die Entwicklung des englischen Gerundiums, Anglia, XXXVIII, 5), *ung* was the ordinary ending in Old English, *ing* appearing but occasionally. See, however, DEUTSCHBEIN, System, § 60, 1.

Nouns in *ung* (or *ing*) seem to have been formed originally from nouns in a way which has its analogue in the formation of such words as *schooling, shirting, stabling*, etc. in Modern English. As some of the nouns from which such words in *ung* or *ing* were derived, were also used as weak verbs, the latter came to be regarded as the stems of these derivatives. This led to the formation of similar words from other weak verbs, even including such as were of French origin. Gradually the practice was extended to strong verbs, and towards the beginning of the sixteenth century words in *ing*, which had become the usual termination, or *yng*, which towards the end of this period was used as a frequent variant, could be formed from practically any verb.

It may be interesting to the Dutch student to observe that the *ing*-nouns were, originally, as limited in number as similar formations in Dutch, which has verkooping, verspreiding, wandeling, ontroering, etc., but not *kooping, *spreiding, *looping, *roering, etc.

60. The process described above may have been accelerated by the present participle becoming uniform with the *ing*-noun. It may be assumed that this levelling commenced in those dialects in which the suffix of the former was *inde;* i. e. in those spoken in the south and some of the adjacent Midlands. With persons speaking any of these dialects it may have become a habit to drop the oral dental *d* after the nasal dental *n*, i. e. to change *inde* into *inne*. The latter suffix could not fail to be frequently confounded with that of the verbal nouns in *inge*, the point nasal being often replaced by the back nasal, and vice versa, in unstressed syllables after high-front or mid-front vowels. These substitutions may still be observed in the language of many illiterate speakers of the present day, who may be constantly heard to say *capting, kitching,* etc. instead of *captain, kitchen,* etc., and conversely *puddin, nothin, readin,* etc. instead of *pudding, nothing, reading,* etc.

The stressless positions of the suffixes must, moreover, have occasioned a frequent dropping of the final *e*, which in course of time became regular.

The confusion was, no doubt, aggravated by the futile attempts at accuracy of some precisians, who, objecting to the back nasal being replaced by the point nasal, made a point of re-establishing the former, and, being often ill-informed, effected this so-called correction in the wrong place.

Some further comment on the endings of the present participle in Middle English may be acceptable.

a) In the Southern dialects the normal ending was *inde*.

± 1280. Idul nolde he neuere beo: ake euere *doinde* he was. South Eng. Legendary, 116, 337. (= Idle he would never be, also he was always active.)

al *fastinde* he lay | At þio holi mannes toumbe. ib., 173, 2343. (= Fasting he lay at the tomb of that holy man.)

Swete lorde ... Ich am *cominde* to þine feste. ib., 416, 469. (= Sweet lord, I am coming to thy feast.)

1272—1307. Selde comeþ lone *lahynde* hom. HENDYNG, Prov., XXV (SKEAT, Spec.) (= Seldom cometh loan *langhing* home.)

1340. Vader oure þet art ine heuenes | y-halʒed by þi name. cominde þi riche. Dan Michel of Northgate, Sermon (Skeat, Spec., 105).

The same form of the present participle is to be found in the Kentish Ayenbite of Inwit (1340) (or Remorse of Conscience) and many other texts.

b) In the early texts of most Midland dialects the normal ending is *ende* but the later texts, through Southern influence, mostly have *inde*.

± 1150. Gif twá men ǫþer ðrǐ coman *ridend* tó an tún, al þe túnscipe flugen for heom. The Peterborough Chronicle (Emerson, Mid. Eng. Read., 4). (= If two or three men came *riding* to a town, all the inhabitants flew to meet them.)

The following quotation is of some interest:

11th cent. Forþe þenne munecas þære æran andan *awyrpende*, þysene oþerne mid hatan wyline soðre lufe ʒeornlice beʒan. Bibl. des angels. Prosa, Vol. II, 67 | 1 (ed. Schröer). (= Therefore then, monks *rejecting* the first (kind of) zeal (should) practise this other eagerly with the hot passion of true love.) N. B. Three Mss. read *awyrpenne*.

In the romance Havelock the Dane (author unknown), written about 1300, the ending is usually *ind(e)*, but *ende* occurs in line *2702: driuende* (= driving); while the Northern ending *ande* is found in line *2283: gangande* (= going). In the same work the gerund ends in *ing(e)*, but in one case it has *ende*, viz. in line *1386: he hauede his offrende* (= offering) on the auter leyd.

c) In the Northern dialects the ending was *and*.

before 1300. Vpstegh reke in his ire, | And of face of him brent þe fire; | Koles þat ware *dounfalland* Kindled ere of him *glouand*. Northumbrian Psalter, XVII, 23—26 (Skeat, Spec.). (= Smoke rose (from his nostrils) in his ire, And from out of his face burnt the fire; | Coals that were falling down | Are kindled glowing by him. Compare Auth. Vers., Psalm XVIII, 8.)

1303. Echone seyd to oþer *jangland*, | þey toke neuer gode at Pers hand. Rob. of Brunne, Handlyng Synne, 5593 (Skeat, Spec.). (= Each said *chattering* to the other | They never took alms from Peter's hand.)

1350--1360. þe herd sat þan ... | *Clouʒtand* kyndely his schon. William of Palerne 14 (Skeat, Spec.). (= The cowherd sat then ... | *Patching* in his usual manner his shoes.)

1375. His man said, 'schir, that may nocht be; | Abyde ʒe heir, ʒe sal soyn se | V hundreth ʒ*arnand* ʒou to sla. John Barbour, The Bruce, Book VII, 11 (Skeat, Spec.). (= His man said,' Sir, that must not be; | Abide you here, you shall soon see | Five hundred *yearning* to slay you'.)

d) In the Southern and Midland dialects *inge*, or *ynge*, as a participial ending began to appear ± 1200, and gradually ousted the original endings *inde* or *ende*. In the Northern dialects the participle ending *and* maintained itself longer; in some, indeed, the participle and the gerund ending are still distinguished, being respectively, and or an', and *ing* or *in'*. See Murray, s. v. *and* and *ing*[2].

± 1250. Nū bōþe twō þes swēte þinge | Crīe hire merci al wēpinge. Floris and Blauncheflur. (EMERSON, Mid. Eng. Read., 38/14.) (= Now both these sweet things (or creatures) weeping cry to her to have mercy upon them.) 1356. the holy lond, that men callen the lond of promyssioun, or of beheste, passynge all othere londes, is the most worthi lond. MANDEVILLE, Prologue, 3 (SKEAT, Spec.).

1362. A feir feld ful of folk, fond I þer bi-twene, | Of alle maner of men. þe mene and þe riche, | Worchinge and wondringe, as þe world asketh. LANGLAND, Vision, Prol., 19 (SKEAT, Spec.).

± 1380. Jhon was in desert baptisynge, and prechinge the baptym of penaunce. WYCLIF, Mark, 1 (SKEAT, Spec.).

± 1420. I gave them my playnt Vppon my knee; | They lyked it well, when they had it reade: | But, lackyng mony, I could not be sped. LYDGATE, London Lyckpeny, V (SKEAT, Spec.).

± 1420. his (sc. Chaucer's) hye vertu astertesh | Vnslayn from the, which ay vs lyfly herteth | With bookes of his ornat endityng, | That is to alle this land enlumynyng. THOMAS OCCLEVE, Lament for Chaucer, II (SKEAT, Spec.). (= his high virtue escapes | Unslain by thee, which will for ever give encouragement | With books of his ornate enditing | That is illumining to all this country.)

61. Nouns in *ing* having thus to the ear become indistinguishable from the participle in *ing*, the way was paved for extending the constructions of the latter to the former, in other words for the noun in *ing* to become capable of practically all the constructions which are peculiar to verbs. In course of time we, accordingly, find it, like the present participle, capable of being modified by any variety of adverbial adjuncts, taking a non=prepositional object, and showing the distinction of voice and, to a certain extent, that of tense.

The development of the verbal character in the nouns in *ing* was most probably furthered by the influence of the French en + gérondif. This appears from the frequency of constructions with *in*, instead of the older *on*, in Middle English.

± 1250. þu sittest in longynge. O. E. Misc., 201 (ed. RICH. MORRIS). þe sorouful soulus in hel þat were þer in turmentyng. ib., 262.

± 1280. Heo was a gast (= aghast) and in feringue (= in fearing). Childh. Jesus, 75 (ed. HORSTMANN). (Compare in grete fering. ib., 467; in mourninge. ib., 749.)

1303. Pers lay yn hys slepyng. BRUNNE, Handl. Synne, 5723.

± 1350. And thei seye, that we synne dedly in schavynge oure Berdes. MAUNDEVILLE.[1])

± 1387. I slow Sampsoun in shaking the piler. CHAUC., Cant. Tales, A, 2466.

---

[1]) KELLNER, Hist. Outl., § 417.

Interesting is the following quotation with *on* + gerund, for which one manuscript has *in* + gerund:

And, as he lay on *deying* in a traunce. Chauc., Cant. Tales, 13, 3906.

Also the uncertainty which attaches to the interpretation of certain constructions may have been of some influence in this direction. Thus, as has already been pointed out (35, a), in such a sentence as *Pardon the boys saying so* the object of *pardon* is *the boys saying so*, in which *saying* is the head-word, *the boys* the modifying element. But there is another, although less rational interpretation, according to which *the boys* is the object of *pardon*, *saying so* modifying *the boys*. The latter interpretation, which to an unschooled mind would, most probably, appear more plausible than the former, would lead to the view of considering *saying* as a present participle.

62. a) The first traces of the noun in *ing* assuming a verbal regimen consist in its taking such adverbial modifiers as *down, in,* etc. This came about by such compounds as *downcoming, downfalling, ingoing,* etc. being resolved into their component parts and the adverb being placed after the verb, which resulted in such forms as *coming down, falling down, going in,* etc. The earliest instances of this altered practice appear about the middle of the fourteenth century.

± 1444. We pray you hertily, that ye wil yeve (= give) attendaunce at such day and place as ye ... shal mow (= may, be able) attende to the *making up* of the seide evidencez. Paston Let., No. 43.

± 1464. the same Prentys toke of Wylliam Dallynge at Norwyche V mark for *smytynge of* of hese feteris when he was there in preson. No. 144.

± 1440. *Rysynge vp* from set (= seat) or restynge place. Promptorium, Parvulorum col. 375 (ed. Mayhew).

The following is, however, a much earlier instance of the gerund being modified by an adverb standing after it:

± 1275. þe appostels thurgh *precheing lele* (= loyally) | Gederd (= gathered) þam (dative) desciples fele (= many). 140 223. Alteng. Legenden, Neue Folge (ed. Horstmann).

b) The construction in which the noun in *ing* governs a non-prepositional object may also have arisen from a transposition of the component parts of such compounds as *peace-making, book-selling,* etc. mentioned in 39. Of such compounds instances may be found in the earliest English. Kellner,

11*

(Hist. Outl., § 416) quotes some which would not be tolerated in Present English.

± 700. Biscopas mid folcum buton ǣnigre are sceáwunge fornumene wǣron. Bede, Eccles. Hist., I, 5 (ed. Schipper). (= Bishops and people without any *mercy=showing* were destroyed. Probably an imitation of the Latin sine ullo respectu honoris.)

± 1175. bi his *cloðes wrixlunge*. Old Eng. Hom., I, 207. (= by his *clothes=changing*.)

± 1377. late usage be ȝowre solace of *seyntes lyues redynge*. Piers Plowman, Text B, VIII, 87. (= let the custom of *the lives of the saints reading* be your solace.)

Further instances are found in:

± 1300. for *oure lord ennoyntynge*. Cursor Mundi, Cotton M. S., Insertion after 93.

± 1300. of *truage askyng* he had wonder. Brunne, Chron., 4263. (truage = tax, tribute.)

Heigh labour, and ful greet apparaillinge | Was at the service and the *fyr= makinge*. Chauc., Cant. Tales, A, 2914.

Redeth the Bible, and finde it expresly | Of *wyn=yeving* to hem that han justyse. ib., C, 587.

± 1464. Master Constantyn sewyd (= sued) hym for *feith and trowth brekyng*. Paston Let., No. 490.

The following are early instances of the new practice, which appears to have come in about the last quarter of the fourteenth century.

1455. He be meke to God in not amyss *tempting God aȝens reson*. Pecock, Repressor, I, 13.

Here upon y durste leie a waiour (= lay a wager) of *lesing* (= losing) myn arme. ib., I, 82.

± 1470. I suppose that he hath slayn her in *fulfyllynge his fowle lust of lecherye*. Malory, Morte Darthur, 166 19 (ed. Sommer).

c) When the verbal regimen of the noun in *ing* had been fully established, we find the construction with the definite article and a prepositional phrase with *of* varying with that in which this form is followed by a non=prepositional object. Both are found in:

Concerning the means of *procuring unity*, men must beware that, in *the procuring or muniting of religious unity*, they do not dissolve and deface the laws of charity and of human society. Bacon, Es., Of Unity in Religion, 8. (to munite = to fortify, to strengthen.)

d) By the side of these constructions we sometimes meet with that in which the *ing=word* is not preceded by any adnominal modifier, beyond a potential adjective, and followed by *of*. The verbal may, or may not, stand after a preposition.

Sometimes two different constructions are found in one and the same sentence. Thus in some of the following quotations, which seem to show that the construction with *of* is rarely used when the object of the action is represented by a pronoun.

i. Afterward, *in getting of your richesses* and *in usinge hem*, ye shul alwey have three thinges in your herte. Chauc., Cant. T., B, *2813*.
I am *in bildyng of a pore house*. Paston Let., No. 348.
Thou art so fat witted *with drinking of old sack* and *unbuttoning thee* after supper and sleeping upon benches after noon that thou hast forgotten to demand that truly which thou wouldst truly know. Shak., Henry IV, A, 1, 2, 2.
I had the misfortune to displease him *by unveiling of the future* and *revealing all the dangers*. Lytton.[1])

ii. ± 1420. Vnto the Roll[e]s I gat me from thence, | Before the Clarkes of the Chaunceryve, | Where many I found *carnyng of pence*, | But none at all once regarded mee. John Lydgate London Lyckpeny, V (Skeat, Spec.).
1545. and lykewise as *burnyng of thistles* and diligent *weding them* oute of the corne doth not halfe so moche ryd them as when ye ground is falloed. Roger Ascham.[2])

e) According to Curme (E. S. XLV, 362), it was not until the close of the sixteenth century that the gerund began to adopt formations showing distinctions of voice and tense. In Roger Ascham's works there are no instances of complex gerunds. Thus:

1545. A shootynge Gloue is chieflye for to save a mannes fyngers from *hurtynge*. Toxophilus. (Present English: *being hurt*.)

Similarly the following quotations show that at one time the gerund was neutral as to voice.

1330—1340. þe toþer (sc. thyng þat clenses vs) es: schryft of mouth. again þe syn of mouth: | And þat selle be hasty withouten *delaying*. | Naked with outen *excusyng*. | Hale with outen *partyng*. Rich. Rolle of Hampole, Works, I, 25, Cambr. M. S., ed., Horstmann. (= the other is shrift of mouth against the sin of mouth. And that shall be hasty (i. e. must be done at once) without *being put off*. Naked without anything *being excused*. Entire without *being divided* (i. e. the whole sin must be confessed without *part of it being kept back*).

1455. Poul wrote his bothe Epistles to Corintheis eer he was bounden by *prisoning* in Rome. Pecock, Repressor, I, 57. (= *being imprisoned*.)
Whanne money or other temporal good . . . is to be paied . . . it may iustli be restreyned and aȝen holde (= withheld) from *paiying*. ib., II, 384. (= *being paid*.)

---

[1]) Deutschbein, System, § 60.
[2]) Curme, E. S., XLV, 352.

1458. It please you to remembre (= remind) my maister at your best leiser, wheder his old promise shall stande as touchyng my *preferryng* to the Boreshed. Paston Let., No. 318. (= my *being preferred*.)

The following are the earliest instances of the gerund showing the distinction of voice that have come to hand:

1585–1591. by *being* unto God *united*. HOOKER, Eccl. Pol., I, XI, § 2.[1]) Thou wert dignified enough, | Even to the point of envy, if 'twere made | Comparative for your virtues, to be styled | The under-hangman of his kingdom, and hated | For *being preferr'd* so well. SHAK., Cymb., II, 3, 136.

Complex gerunds showing tense are yet very rare in SHAKESPEARE. See 31.

MURRAY, s. v. *ing* cites:

1580. Want of consideration in not *having demanded* thus much. SIDNEY, Arcadia, I, 68.

Even for a considerable time after SHAKESPEARE'S days the simple gerund was mostly used for the complex, in other words continued neutral as to voice and tense, which, as we have seen (25—27) it is, to a considerable extent, even in Present English.

63. The construction in which the common case of a noun or the objective of a personal pronoun stands before the word *in ing* has been traced to quite early times. KELLNER (Hist. Outl., § 418) quotes:

1330—1340. Alle waters als þai sall rynne | And þat sal last fra þe son *rysyng* | Till þe tyme of þe son *doungangyng*. HAMPOLE, Pricke of Conscience, 4777 f. ± 1400. After the sunne *goyng* down. WYCLIFF, Gen., XXVIII, 11.

The construction may have been used in direct imitation of Latin originals with participles.

± 700. se he *Diocletiane lyfgendum* Gallia rice rehte. BEDE, Ec. Hist., I, 8. (= qui vivente Diocletiano Galliam regebat.) Wæs he ðæm breðer *lifigendum* wræcca in Gallia. ib., II, 15. (= qui *vivente* adhuc *fratre* cum exularet in Galliam.)

Thus also the participle form is used in:

To-janes þo sunne *risindde*. Old Eng. Miscellany, 26.[2]) (= towards the time of the sun *rising*.)

± 1275. Tiþings come to þe Emperoure, | þat . . . A fer cuntre bud him wend to | For *chargeand* thinges þat war to do. Alteng. Leg., Neue Folge (ed. HORSTMANN.) (= Tidings came to the Emperor, that . . . commanded him (to) go to a far country, for *ordering* things that were to be done.)

---

[1]) MURRAY.
[2]) KELLNER, Hist. Outl., § 418.

64. A secondary source of the gerund is, perhaps, to be traced to the inflected infinitive, which, so far as it ended in *ende* or *inde*, must have had a tendency of taking the suffix *enge* or *inge*. This may have given rise to the notion of there being two infinitives, e. g.: *(to)binden* and *(to)bindenge* or *bindinge*. This notion would appear all the more rational, because also in Latin and French there were also two forms, viz.: the infinitive proper and, respectively, the gerundium and the gerondif, differing only in grammatical function.

The second form *(to)bindenge* or *bindinge* gave way to the first *(to)binden* when purely verbal functions had to be expressed, but maintained itself when distinctly substantival functions made themselves felt. In the latter case it coalesced with the verbal noun in *ing*.

The use of *ende* instead of *en(n)e* as the ending of the inflected infinitive is characteristic of the South and South-East Midlands. The ending *ende* occurs in three Mss. of WULFSTAN's Homilies (B, D and N) viz.: *to halgiende* (34/15), *to smeagende* (185/6), *to cweðende* (185/7), *to swerigende* (253/7), *to fyligende* (253/9). There are a few in the interpolations in Ms. A (PARKER) of the Old Eng. Chron. and 11 instances in Ms. F.

The ending *ende* for *enne* is also frequent in the Early Mid. Eng. Rule of St. Benet (ed. SCHRÖER), in the Trinity Homilies and the B text of LAȝAMON.

± 1010. þæt is ofer eal gemet *to smeagende* ... and on mycelre care *to cweðende*. WULFSTAN, 185 5—7. (= that is beyond all measure (i. e. exceedingly) to be considered ... and with great care to be said.)

± 1200. Ne com ic *to donde* mine aȝenum willan. Rule of St. Benet, 29 3 = 35 23. (= Non ueni facere voluntatem meam.)

þe nyȝeðe eadmodnysse stæpe is, ȝef þeo mynecena hyre tunga forwyrnoð *to specende*. ib., 39 27. (= Nonus humilitatis gradus est, si linguam ad loquendum prohibeat.)

1298. As þe hende he dude verst. and messagers him sende, þat he vnderstode him bet. is dede vor *to amende*. ROBERT OF GLOUCESTER, Chronicle (SKEAT, Spec., 14). (= Like a courteous man he did first and sent messengers to him That he should consider to amend his deeds better.)

± 1275. þe resone whi þat he hight swa, Es þis þat *to vndirstandige* is "A doufe sonne" in propir ynglikzsse. Alteng. Legenden, Neue Folge, 77 45 (ed. HORSTMANN). (= The reason why he was called so is this that it is to be understood "A dove's son" in proper English.)

± 1275. he þouȝt nouȝt: on noþing *to comyng* (rimes with þing). Barlaam and Josaphat, 94 (HORSTMANN, Alteng. Legenden). (= He thought not of nothing to come.)

A generacioun *to comyng* schal be teld to the Lord. WYCLIF, Psalm XXI, 32. (= Vulgate: Annuntiabitur Domino generatio ventura.)
Nyle ʒe gesse that I am *to accusinge* ʒou anemptis (= anent) the fadir. id., John, V, 45. (= Vulgate: Nolite putare quia ego accusaturus sim uos apud patrem.)

The following quotations are remarkable as showing different readings in two different Mss.:

± 1200. sæie me of þan þinge: þe me *to cumen* sonden. LAȜAMON, A, 1643 = sai me of þan þinge: þat me beoþ *to comende*. LAȜAMON, B. (= tell me about the things that are *to come* (i. e. to happen) to me.)
þis isæh Childric: and gon him *to charren*. ib., A, 21266 = þis i-seh Childric: and gan him *to flende*. ib. B. (= this saw Childric and began *to turn himself* = *to flee*.)
fiftene þusend anan: þrafte *to blawen*. ib., A, 27815. = fiften þousende: þrafte *to blowend*. ib. B. (= fifteen thousand anon thronged *to blow*.)

Confusion of final infinitives with final gerunds will appear natural enough on comparing the above with the fóllowing quotations given by CURME, E. S., XLV, 379.

þa steorran sint mannum to nihtlicere *lihtunge* gesceapene. SWEET'S Sel. Hom. of Ælfric, 28. (= the stars are created to give light to men at night.)
summe nolden his lare underfon heom sylfe to rihtunge. Twelfth Cent. Hom., 8. (= Some did not desire to receive His teaching for the purpose of reforming themselves.)
þe Hælend to heom spæc swiðe ilome on moniʒe biʒspellum, heoræ mod to trymynge. ib., 18. (= the Lord had spoken to them very often in many parables in order to strengthen their minds.) CURME observes that *mod* is here an accusative, for the dative would be *mode*. The distinction between the dative and accustive of nouns is well preserved throughout this book.

Similar final gerunds are found in:

± 1000. Swa swa we awriton seror on oðrum larspellum to geleafan *trimminge* ÆLFR. De Vet. Test., 4.15. (= as we have written before in other homilies for the *strengthening* of the faith. Cf. Dutch ... ter versterking des geloofs.)
Se cyning ðet mære hus Gode betæhte him and his folce to *trymminge*. THORPE, Hom., II, 578, 22. (= The King dedicated the glorious edifice to God for the *edification* of himself and his people.)

Observe also that the gerund is sometimes used in SHAKESPEARE where Present English would have a passive infinitive. Thus in:

Behold what honest clothes you send forth to *bleaching!* Merry Wives, IV, 2, 126. (= *to be bleached*).
Throw foul linen upon him, as if it were going to *bucking*. ib., III, 3, 140. (= *to be washed*.)

The gerunds in the following quotations have a similar function:

Put the liveries to *making*. Merch., II, 2, 124.
Happy are they that hear their detractions and can put them to *mending*. Much ado, II, 3, 238.

65. The change of the infinitive in *en* into one in *ing* may have come about through the same cause as that which affected the Old English participle in *ende* or *inde*, i. e. one with which every Englishman of the present day is familiar, who at any moment may hear *chicken, children, garden, luncheon*, etc. pronounced *chicking, childring, garding, lunching*, etc. Compare also the archaic *beholding* for *beholden*.

THE PARTICIPLES

ORDER OF DISCUSSION.

Name, Tense and Voice................................... §§ 1–6
Syntax .... §§ 7–44
    The Verbal and Adjectival Character of the Participles §§ 7–18
    The Present Participle in Detail .... §§ 19–27
    The Past Participle in Detail .... §§ 28–40
    The Participles compared with allied Verbal Forms ... §§ 41–44

NAME, TENSE AND VOICE.

1. Participles are those forms of the verb which partake of the nature of both verbs and adjectives.
For a comparison of the verbal and adjectival features in participles see 7.

2. There are two participles: the **present** and the **past** participle, e. g.: *speaking, spoken*.

    The terms p r e s e n t and p a s t, as applied to the participles are objectionable, seeing that neither is capable of expressing the time-sphere (Ze i t s t u f e) of an action or state. This is done by other elements of the sentence, mostly by the (finite verb of the) predicate, sometimes by an adverbial adjunct. Thus the time-sphere of the action denoted by *walking* is, respectively, expressed by *meet, met, shall meet* in *Walking home I meet (met, shall meet) my friend*. The adverbial adjunct *some time ago* indicates the time-sphere of the action expressed by *erected* in *A column, erected some time ago, stands in front of the building*.

    Also the terms a c t i v e, instead of present, and p a s s i v e, instead of past, which are used by some grammarians, are equally open to objection. The term p a s s i v e cannot possibly be applied to the participle used in the perfect tenses of an intransitive verb as in *I have walked a long way*.

    The terms i m p e r f e c t and p e r f e c t would be quite suitable as far as the simple forms *(walking, walked)* are concerned, seeing that they are descriptive of the two characters or aspects implied by these verbals; but, as they are currently applied to express tense-distinctions in the finite verb, their employment gives rise to uncertainty in nomenclature, besides entailing difficulties in naming such complex forms as *having walked, having been seen*. It seems, therefore, advisable to retain the time-honoured terms *present* and *past*. Compare Den Hertog, Ned. Spraakk., III, § 97, Opm.

3. In virtue of its verbal character the present participle is capable of exhibiting the distinction of:

    a) tense, but, as in the case of the infinitive and the gerund, only to show that its time-sphere is anterior to that of the predication with which it is connected, e. g.: **imperfect present participle** *walking*, **perfect present participle**, *having walked*. Only the perfect present participle requires illustration.

    > Society *having ordained* certain customs, men are bound to obey the laws of society. Thack., Snobs, Ch. I, 16.
    > The clock *having struck*, we had to go. Meiklejohn, The Eng. Lang., 91.
    > Not *having received* an answer, I wrote again. Sweet, N. E. Gr., § 2344.
    > *Having seen* all that was to be seen at Rome, we went on to Naples. ib., § 333.

b) voice, e. g.: active present participle *hearing*, passive present participle *being heard*. Only the passive present participle requires illustration.

<small>The water-plug *being left* in solitude, its over-flowings suddenly congealed. Dick., Christm. Car., I.
Not *being seen* by any one, he escaped. Sweet, N. E. Gr., § 333.</small>

c) tense and voice combined, e. g.: perfect passive present participle *having been observed*.

<small>These injuries *having been comforted* externally, with patches of pickled brown paper, and Mr. Pecksniff *having been comforted* internally, with some stiff brandy-and-water, the eldest Miss Pecksniff sat down to make the tea. Dick., Chuz., Ch. II, 6 b.
Sir Walter Besant was in his 65th year, *having been born* at Portsmouth on August 14, 1836. Times.</small>

Note *α*) Like the infinitive and the gerund, the present participle is incapable of indicating that its time-sphere is posterior to that of the predication with which it is connected. It differs, however, from these two verbals in never or, at least, very rarely implying such posteriority. For some further comment see the Addenda and Corrigenda. Compare Infinitive, 57, b; Gerund, 9, Obs. I.
As in the case of the infinitive and the gerund, certain phrases such as *to be about*, *to be going*, etc., are sometimes resorted to to supply the want.

<small>The train *being about to start*, he took a hurried leave of his friends.</small>

β) The present participle also resembles the infinitive and the gerund in that it is not affected by a change of time-sphere in the predication with which it is connected. Compare Infinitive, 57, a; Gerund, 9, Obs. II. See also Tense, 12, c.

Being well-to-do, { he is a liberal protector of all charities.
{ he was a liberal protector of all charities.
{ he will be a liberal protector of all charities.

γ) Neither tense nor voice can be expressed by the present participle when used attributively, or when forming part of an undeveloped clause that has the value of a relative clause (i. e. an attributive adnominal clause introduced by a relative pronoun). Compare Ch. XX, 3.

4. The distinction of tense is not always expressed; i. e. the imperfect present participle sometimes has to do duty for the perfect. Apparently this applies chiefly to complex sentences in which the relation of the participle clause to its head-sentence is one of pure time.

<small>*Passing* through the wall of mud and stone, they found a cheerful company assembled. Dick., Christm. Car.⁵, II, 65. (= *having passed*.)
So spake the kindly-hearted Earl, and she | With frequent smile and nod *departing* found, | Half disarrayed as to her rest, the girl. Ten., Mar. of Ger., 515. (= *having departed*.)</small>

Now this was very warm advocacy on the part of Mr. Tombey, who, *being called in* to console and bless, cursed with such extraordinary vigour. RID. HAG., Mees. Will, Ch. VI, 59. (= *having been called in.*)

The emperor Diocletian had thirty-three infamous daughters, who murdered their husbands, and *being set adrift* in a ship reached Albion, where they fell in with a number of dragons. COBHAM BREWER, Dict. of Phrase and Fable, s. v. Gog and Magog. (= *having been set adrift.*)

5. The active present participle is often used in a passive meaning, especially:

   a) when modifying the subject of a sentence or clause with *(there) is* or its variations.

      i. I guessed there was some mischief *contriving*. SWIFT, Gul., II, Ch. II., 143a.
      There is nothing *doing*. DICK., Domb., Ch. IV, 29.
      Sheets of ham were there, *cooking* on the gridiron; half-a-dozen eggs were there *poaching* in the frying-pan. id., Chuz., Ch. XLIII. 333a.
      Whenever Kew and Charles Belsize are together, I know there is some wickedness *planning*. THACK., Newc., I, Ch. X, 123.
      There is an answer *waiting*. SWEET, N. E. Gr., § 332.
      There is a glorious dish of eggs and bacon *making ready*. EDNA LYALL, In the Golden Days.

      ii. In the ashpit was a heap of potatoes *roasting*. HARDY, Far from the Madding Crowd, Ch. XV, 117.
      Similarly in: All round the present town the ruins of Kilkenny's former greatness testify to the decay. Nothing *doing*. Eng. Rev., No. 106, 273.
      There can hardly be much *doing*. EDNA LYALL, A Hardy Norseman, Ch. XVI, 145.

   b) when used in the function of nominal part of the predicate.

      Well, my lord: | If he steal aught the whilst this play *is playing*, | And 'scape detecting, I will pay the theft. SHAK., Haml., III, 2, 93.
      If they do so much labour after and spend so many tears for the things of this present life, how am I to be bemoaned, pitied and prayed for! My soul is dying, my soul is *damning!* BUNYAN, Grace Abounding, 320.[1])
      While this ballad was *reading*. GOLDSMITH, Vic., Ch. VIII, (281).
      The horses are *putting to*. id., She Stoops, IV, (218).
      A part of the game was *cooking* for the evening's repast. WASH. IRV., Dolf Heyl. (STOF., Handl., I, 130).
      Preparations were *making* to receive Mr. Creakle and the boys. DICK., Cop., Ch. VI, 40b.
      Let them look abroad, and contemplate the scenes which were *enacting* around them. Stage-coaches were *upsetting* in all directions; horses were bolting, boats were overturning and boilers were bursting. id., Pickw., Ch. I, 3.
      We asked him if he knew what was *doing* in it. id., Bleak House, Ch. LXV, 531.
      "Have you seen any numbers of The Pickwick Papers?" said he (they were then *publishing* in parts). "Capital thing!" MRS. GASK., Cranf, Ch. I, 21.
      While these preparations were *making* in Scotland, James called into his closet Arnold Van Citters, who had long resided in England as Ambassador from the United Provinces. MAC., Hist., II, Ch. V, 116.

---

[1]) FRANZ, Shak. Gram.

The King said that he had received from unquestionable sources intelligence of designs which were *forming* against his throne by his banished subjects in Holland. ib., 117.

While dinner was *preparing*, he sat in the arbour to read a book. STEVENSON.)
Similarly in: How little the things actually *doing* around us affect the springs of our sorrow or joy. LYTTON, My Novel, II, XII, Ch. X, 412.

She looked a trifle gauche, it struck me; more like a country girl with the hoyden *taming* in her than the well-bred creature she is. MERID., The Egoist, II, 280.²)

c) when modifying the object of verbs of perceiving and occasionally other verbs that may take an accusative with infinitive.

  i. I hear some fiddles *tuning*. FARQUHAR, Const. Couple, V, 3, (127)
  I can't say how I knew it was my dear, dear mother's coffin that they went to look at. I had never heard one *making*. DICK., Cop., Ch. IX, 63
  When Joe and I got home, we found the table laid, and Mrs. Joe dressed, and the dinner *dressing*. id., Great Expect., Ch. IV, 30.
  Annie seem'd to hear | Her own death-scaffold *raising*. TENNYSON, Enoch Arden, 175.
  "Simon, is supper ready?" — "Ay, my liege, I saw the covers *laying*". id., Queen Mary, III, 6, (625a).
  I have read of such things in books of the ancients, and I have watched them *making* continually. KINGSLEY, Hereward, Ch. XXV, 106a.
  To-morrow I shall expect to hear your mother's goods *unloading*. TH. HARDY, Tess, VI, Ch. LI, 461.
  I saw the thing *shaping*. Westm. Gaz., No. 5277, 4b.

  ii. And any man, wherever placed, however far from other sources of interest or beauty, has this *doing* for him constantly. RUSKIN, Mod. Paint, II, III, Ch. I.²)

  iii. I want a button *sewing on*. MASON, Eng. Gram.⁸¹, § 200, N.
  I want these (sc. rabbits) *sending off* by the first train. Punch, No. 3995, 66b.

d) in constructions instanced by the following quotations, the active form of the present participle appearing to be archaic and rare. Compare Ch. II, 38, Obs. I.

  Women are angels, *wooing*. SHAK., Troil. & Cres., I, 2, 312.
  That piano of ours is a jolly long time *mending*. ZANGWILL, The Next Religion, II, 91.

6. Obs. I. It will have been observed that among the above quotations there are none in which the active present participle in a passive meaning is connected with a word denoting a person. The following are the only instances that have come to hand:

---

¹) GENTH., Man., § 619.
²) PH. ARONSTEIN, Die Periphr. Form im Eng., Anglia XIII, 17.

Coming home to-night, a drunken boy was *carrying* by our constable to our new pair of stocks. PEPYS, Diary. ¹² 4, 66¹).

Being a boy of fourteen, cheaply *educating* at Brussels when his sister's expulsion befell, it was some little time before he heard of it. DICK., Our Mut. Friend, I, Ch. II, 21.

The rareness of the above construction in connection with a person= indicating word will create small wonder if it is borne in mind that in the majority of cases its use would involve ambiguity or awaken incongruous notions. In Late Modern English the passive voice has taken the place of the active (Obs. III), while in those days in which this passive construction had not yet established its footing in the language, the exceptionable active construction would be avoided by the use of some other form of expression.

II. As to the construction mentioned under a) it may be observed that substitution of the passive present participle would hardly be tolerated by idiom. Save for the forms with *doing*, the con= struction, however, seems to be unfrequent.

III. As nominal part of the predicate the active present participle with passive meaning is now getting more and more unusual, modern practice mostly substituting the passive present participle.

We are always *being complained of* and guarded against. DICK., Chimes, I, 11.

Whenever fights were *being talked of*, the small boys shook their heads wisely, saying, "Ah! but you should just have seen the fight between Slogger Williams and Brown". HUGHES, Tom Brown, II, Ch. V, 286.

His temper only failed him when he was *being nursed*. SWEET, N. E. Gr., § 2222.

The festivities at Cagliari, where the King and Queen of Italy are *being received* with great enthusiasm by the people of Sardinia ... are attract= ing a good deal of notice in Italy and throughout the continent. Times, 1899, 249a.

The work which is *being carried on* appeals by its practical side to a colonial statesman of eminently practical capacity. Times, 1899, 265b.

Despite many adverse criticisms, the affairs of England in Ghina are not *being neglected*. Il. Lond. News, 1899, 421 C.

Twelve months ago the effects of the coal strike were still *being felt*. Westm. Gaz. No. 6223, 2b.

The public will be shocked to learn that three men holding first=class certificates are *being employed* as managers for not more than £ 200 a year. Twelve are *being paid* not more than £ 200 a year. ib., No. 8086, 3a.

Substitution of the passive for the active present participle is, however, impracticable after *to be* in the perfect and pluperfect tenses. See especially STORM, Eng. Phil.², 793.

The birds were in blissful ignorance of the preparations which *had been making* to astonish them. DICK., Pickw., Ch. XIX, 162.

---

¹) PH. ARONSTEIN, Die Periphr. Form im Eng., Anglia, XLII, 16.

At length some supper, which *had been warming up*, was placed on the table. ib., Ch. XVII, 153.
He sat down to the dinner that *had been hoarding* for him by the fire. id., Christm. Car., IV, 97.

Nor would the passive present participle be possible after the future tense and the periphrastic conditional of *to be*. It should, however, be added that also the active present participle with passive meaning in like positions seems to be non-existent, no instances having come to hand of such sentences as *°The book will (would) soon be printing*.

The active voice is regularly retained in the present participle of *to owe*, is still quite usual in that of *to do*, and, apparently, frequent enough in that of *to build*.

i. A man's property and the sums *owing* to him are called his Assets; the sums *owing* by him, his Liabilities. HAMILTON and HALL, Bookkeeping, 5.
(He) paid all that was *owing*. Conc. Oxf. Dict.
Similarly: When Martha's wages and the rent are paid, I have not a farthing *owing*. MRS. GASK., Cranf., Ch. XIII, 250.

ii. We asked him if he knew what was *doing* in it. DICK., Bleak House, Ch. LXV, 531.
The good people knew all that was *doing* at London. LYTTON, My Novel, I, V, Ch. VIII, 317.
The peal and flash of gun after gun gave notice, from three different parts of the valley at once, that murder was *doing*. MAC., Hist., VII, Ch. XVIII, 24. T.
He took for granted that nothing had been done in Glencoe beyond what was *doing* in many other glens. ib., 28.
In this part of the world we are all so close together that everybody knows what is *doing* in the territory of everybody else. Times.

iii. At the end of March 1919, 4,183,523 tons were actually *building*. Times, No. 2298, 25 b.
Similarly: The tonnage *building* in the United Kingdom at the end of last year was 3,708,906 tons.
The destruction of vessels now *building* would require a fairly large amount of money. Manch. Guard., V, No. 21, 408 c.

Passiveness is more or less dimmed, passing into mere intransitiveness, in certain present participles when they assume the character of adjectives or have the value of a preposition, either by themselves or in connexion with another preposition. Thus

missing, as in: There is a page *missing*. A page is *missing*. Conc. Oxf. Dict.
He was *missing* during the whole day. DICK., Pickw., Ch. XI, 59.
owing, as in: All this was *owing* merely to ill-luck. Conc. Oxf. Dict.
Owing to the drought, crops are short. ib.
wanting, as in: One of the twelve is *wanting*. We have the means, but the application is *wanting*. WEBST. Dict.
Wanting common honesty, nothing can be done. He made a century *wanting* one run. Conc. Oxf. Dict.

IV. After the verbs that may take an accusative — infinitive the active present participle with passive meaning varies with the passive present participle, the passive infinitive and the bare past participle. There is, accordingly, a fourfold variety of construction, illustrated, respectively, by (α) *I want a button sewing on*, (β) *I want a button being sewn on*, (γ) *I want a button to be sewn on*, and (δ) *I want a button sewn on*. To these we may add a fifth construction, consisting of a head-sentence and a subordinate statement introduced by *that: I want that a button shall* (more frequently *should*) *be sewn on*. This last construction is common enough after most verbs of wishing, (dis)liking or commanding (Mood, 21, Obs. I), but is distinctly unfrequent after *to want*. The following are the only instances which have come to hand:

She did not want that Harry should quarrel with his aunt for her sake, Thack., Virg., Ch. XVIII, 187.

He seems to want that his wife should suspect the new crime he has in hand. Hudson, Note to Macb., III, 3, 52.

Here follow some quotations for illustration, a few of construction α) already given higher up being repeated for comparison

Verbs of perceiving.

Construction (α): I hear some fiddles *tuning*. Farquhar, Const Couple, V, 3, (127).

Construction (β): As to his title, he said that he felt himself *being called names* in his old age. Hor. Walpole, Castle of Otranto, Introd., 4.

Marjory watched the breakfast *being removed* with a sort of dumb anger. Mrs. Alexander, A Life Interest, I, Ch. VII, 117.

The incidents which we see *being debated* at the end of this affair seem trivial and petty. Westm. Gaz., No. 6199, 1 b.

At last Mr. Ismay saw the boats *being launched*. T. P.'s Weekly No. 499, 674 c.

He was to watch us *being drilled* by the sergeant. Don. Hankey, The Beloved Captain, IV, 7.

Construction (γ): instances non-existent.

Construction (δ): They had never seen a human being *killed*. Reade, The Cloister and the Hearth, Ch. X, 57.

I saw him *thrown* out of his trap. Sweet, N. E. Gr., § 331.

Constructions (α) and (β) are both fairly common, although not nearly so usual as construction (δ). They always imply a distinctly durative character (or aspect), whereas the last construction may be either momentaneous (or perfective), as in the two above quotations, or durative (or imperfective), as in:

I perceived him *led* through the outward hall as a prisoner. Smol., Rod. Rand., Ch. XVII, 111.

Sometimes also the character is far from clear. Thus in:

What was his discomfiture when he heard the chain and bolts *withdrawn* and saw the door slowly opening, wider and wider! Dick., Pickw., Ch. XVI, 146.

Verbs of wishing, (dis)liking or commanding:

Construction (α). I want these (sc. rabbits) *sending off* by the first train. Punch, No. 3995, 66 b.
Construction (β): Our people don't like things *being ordered and left*. Dick., Cop., Ch. V, 35 a.
You and I don't like our pictures and statues *being found fault with*. G. Eliot, Mid., IV, Ch. XXXIX, 288.
Construction (γ): Christ desired his mysteries *to be spread abroad* as openly as was possible. Green.
He commanded the bridge *to be lowered*. Mason, Eng. Gram.³¹, § 397.
Construction (δ): i. He wanted a Bill *passed* for forbidding the sale of alcohol in any form. Birmingham, The Advent. of Dr. Whitty, Ch. III, 66.
He wants these two letters *posted*. Dor. Gerard, Exotic Martha, Ch. XVII, 207.
He went on to ask whether she had any relatives to whom she wished the news of her plight *communicated*. ib., Ch. XX, 233.
Monkley told the Baron that he did not wish anything *said* about Sylvester's father. Compt. Mackenzie, Sylv. Scarlett, Ch. II, 68.
ii. You can tell me what you would like *done* in the rooms. G. Eliot, Dan. Der., II, IV, Ch. XXIX, 73.
You must tell us exactly what you would like *done*. Con. Doyle, Mem. of Sherl. Holmes, II, D, 191.
iii. He stood to it that Mr. Carlyle had ordered the work *done* in another way. Mrs. Wood, East Lynne, I, 257.
I ordered my bill *made out*. Savage, My Official Wife, 185.

Construction (α) is confined to some dialects of the Northern Midlands. Earle (Phil.⁵, § 580 h) observes, "While we are on this flexional infinitive (by which he means what is called a gerund in these pages), I must call attention to a well-marked provincialism, which might be thought to belong here. In all classes of society in Yorkshire it is common to hear *Do you want the tea making? I want my coat brushing. Father wants the door shutting.* I think this is not an infinitive, but a strong participle in *en* disguised to *ing*." Construction (β) seems to be distinctly uncommon, only a few instances having turned up. Construction (γ) is the ordinary one, while construction (δ), although not unfrequent after *to want, to wish, to like* and *to order*, is, apparently, rarely, if ever, used after most of the synonymous verbs. From the available evidence no conclusions can be drawn as to different shades of meaning implied by the various constructions.

Finally it may be observed that the verbal in *ing*, whether active or passive, on the strength of its logical relation to the preceding (pro)noun, may, with some justice, be regarded as a gerund. This applies especially to such as stand after verbs of wishing, (dis)liking and ordering. For detailed discussion see Gerund 35, a.

V. The active present participle with passive meaning should be distinguished from present participles in like grammatical functions, which are apparently passive, but are really intransitive, their original transitive application having through various processes been changed into an intransitive one.

i. This, madame, ... is *selling* very well. WILLS, The Wheels of Chance, Ch. I, 7.
Seed-potatoes are now *selling* at from £ 12 to £ 15 a ton. Eng. Rev., No. 99, 155.

ii. The door was open, and a number of carriages full of ladies were *drawing up* and setting down. THACK., Sam. Titm., Ch. II, 22.
There were no soldiers *drilling*. Westm. Gaz., No. 8098, 4b.

Comparing such sentences as *This is selling very well* (α), and *Her eyes were filling with tears* (β) with such a sentence as *The house is building* (γ) it is easy to see that in (α) and (β) the passive meaning which attaches to the participle is independent of its grammatical function, whereas in (γ) it extends no further than the participle in the particular function in which it is used. Thus we could very well say *This article sells well, has sold well*, etc., with the verb *to sell* in precisely the same, apparently, passive meaning, but **The house builds, has built*, etc. are impossible.

VI. The passive present participle as a variant of the active present participle with passive meaning is of comparatively recent date. KRÜGER (Synt.², 4 Abteil., § 2362) mentions an instance from the Calendar of Spanish State Papers, Elizabeth, 1558–67; MURRAY's earliest instance (s. v. *be*, 15, c) is dated 1596; FITZEDWARD HALL (Ralph Olmsted Williams, Some Questions of Good English examined in Controversies with Dr. Fitzedward Hall, New York, 1897, page 56) has unearthed a goodly number of instances from pre-nineteenth century English, the earliest instance being dated 1667. But, although sporadic instances have been brought to light from sources of an earlier date than the first quarter of the nineteenth century, the construction did not gain general currency until the middle of the last century. It has been obliged to fight its way against considerable opposition from purists and hide-bound grammarians, but is now generally recognized as an established and useful idiom. See HENRY ALFORD, 'The Queen's English ⁸, § 312.

VII. About the rise of the active present participle in a passive meaning quite an extensive literature has sprung up in the last few years. See STOFFEL, Taalstudie, III, 321 ff; BRADLEY, The Making of Eng., Ch. II, 70; STORM, Eng. Phil. ⁵, 787 ff; ALFRED ÅKERLUND, A Word on the Passive Definite Tenses, E. S., XLVII, 334 ff; CURME, History of the English Gerund, E. S., XLV, 371; JESPERSEN, Tid og tempus, IX; K. F. SUNDEN, A Categ. of Predic. Change in Eng., Es. II, 104; FRANZ, Shak. Gram.², § 665; EINENKEL, Hist. Synt.³, § 3.

The theory which has received the most general recognition and has been shown by JESPERSEN (Tid og Tempus, 416 ff) to be practically unanswerable is that the verbal in *ing* in such sentences as *The house is building* was originally a gerund, preceded by the preposition *in*, earlier *on* often weakened into *an*. The preposition *an*, owing to its unstressed nature was often reduced to a mere prefix *a*, which, as it did not express any distinct meaning, naturally enough, disappeared. According to K. F. SUNDEN (A Categ. of Predic. Change in Eng., Es. II, 104) the construction without a preposition or its reduced representative did not obtain any considerable currency until the 17th or the 18th century, it being improbable that it can be traced further back than the 16th century.

The use of *in* before gerunds in the function here described is common enough in Early Modern English, and has not yet become quite extinct. The parallel use of *on* (or *an*) + gerund does not seem to extend into Modern English. Conversely the placing of the prefix *a* before gerunds is still vigorously alive in most of the southern dialects, and the vulgar speech both in England and America. The prefix *o* in like position seems to be very rare.

It may, however, be assumed that in some cases the construction illustrated by *the house is building*, etc., has arisen independently of an earlier construction with *an* (*in* or *a*) — gerund, and is due to the influence of verbs which in all their forms admit of being used in a pseudo-passive meaning as illustrated by *the book is selling well, the book sold well; this fruit is spoiling rapidly, the fruit soon spoiled* etc.

Here follow some instances of the constructions of *on, in* or *a* — gerund. To those with *in* are added a few in which the gerund, mostly *making*, is preceded by the definite article.

i. Your wits are gone *on wool-gathering*. SCOTT, Abbot, Ch. XIX, 202.
   (Compare: The thoughts of the hare-brained boy went *a wool-gathering* after more agreeable topics. ib., Ch. XX, 217.)

ii.° A piece many years *in doing*. SHAK., Wint. Tale, V, 2.
   Forty and six years was this temple *in building*. Auth. Vers., John, II, 20.
   While these sentences are *in reading*. Book of Com. Pray., 156.
   My hair has been *in training*. SHAK., Riv. II, 1, (231).
   These here ones as is below, though, ain't reglar thorough-bred Sawbones; they're only *in trainin'*. DICK., Pickw., Ch. XXX, 266.
   °° The man was still *in the making*, as much as the Middlemarch doctor and immortal discoverer. G. ELIOT, Mid., II, Ch. XV, 108.
   She went on pinning and adjusting a serge skirt *in the making*. MRS. WARD, The Case of Rich. Meyn., II, Ch. VII, 133.
   Not action, but character, and not character formed but *in the forming*, there is the style of Browning's art. Athen., 1889, 855b.
   We are bound to assume that all possible suasion was used by the Imperial Government while the Constitution was *in the making*. Westm. Gaz., No. 5085, 1c.

iii.° The feast is sold That is not often vouch'd, while 'tis *a-making*. 'T is given with welcome. SHAK., Macb., III, 4, 34.

When once the long-suffering of God waited in the days of Noah, while the ark was a=preparing. Auth. Vers., Peter, A, III, 20.
While my mittimus was a=making, the justice was withdrawn. BUNYAN, A Relation of the Imprisonment, (108).
Their gallows must even now be o' building. CARL., Sart. Res., Ch. III, 15.

JESPERSEN'S theory receives vigorous support from the fact that the construction is identical, and often interchangeable, with one in which the preposition *in* stands before a noun of action, and is often an exact rendering of the Dutch *in* — noun of action, which may end in *ing*. See also 27, a, 2.

i. The plot was evidently *in execution*. DICK., Pick., Ch. XVI, 144. (= executing or being executed.)
The opera is *in rehearsal*. Punch 1889, 183c. (= rehearsing or being rehearsed.)
It (sc. this prescription) may take a little time *in preparation*. THACK., Pend., II, Ch. XV, 156.
ii. The house is *building* = Het huis is in aanbouw.
The measure is *preparing* = De maatregel is in voorbereiding.

VIII. The prefix *a* is also frequently found before active participles that are not passive in meaning. Thus:
(α) after *to go, to run, to be off, to come* and verbs of a similar meaning, the participle denoting the purpose of the action expressed by the preceding verb.
(β) after *to set* in the meaning of *to start* or *to cause*.
(γ) after *to fall* in the meaning of *to begin*.
(δ) after the copula *to be* or in positions where *to be* may be supplied, and also after verbs which approximate to the copula *to be* through weakening of their sense; similarly after verbs governing an accusative with infinitive.
(ε) after *to burst out*.

In the majority of these connexions this *a* also represents an earlier *an* (for *on*), although in some it may be a mere rhythmic insertion. The prefix has become extinct in Standard Modern English, but is still vigorously alive in the language of illiterates and in dialects where, no doubt, it has, at least in part, kept its ground for rhythmical reasons. In some combinations it may frequently be heard in good colloquial language. Such are *to go a=begging, a=courting, a=wooing; to set the clock a=going, the bells a=ringing, folk a=thinking*. See MURRAY, s.v. *a*, prep., 13b; FRANZ, Shak. Gram.², § 665; STORM, Eng. Phil.², 788; FIJN VAN DRAAT, Rhythm in Eng. Prose, Anglia, XXIV, 507.

For *to go a=hunting* and similar collocations modern Standard English mostly substitutes *to go out hunting*, etc. Further variants are *to go out a=hunting*, etc., which is found but rarely, and *to go hunting*, etc., which is not unfrequent. Such a turn of expression as *to go to hunt* seems to be rare, although the use of *to go — to — —*

infinitive in other connexions is common enough. Constructions
in which the verb *to go* is followed by an infinitive without *to*
occur now only archaically. Compare Infinitive 34, b.
To set may be followed by a bare participle and also, in a somewhat different shade of meaning, by an infinitive with *to*. The
construction with *on* — gerund is, apparently, still in common use,
although obsolete with reference to physical movement as in *to set
on going, packing*, etc., See MURRAY, s.v. *set*, 114 b.
Compare also: There's something in his soul O'er which his melancholy
sits *on brood*. SHAK., Haml., III, 1, *173*.
After *to fall* we also find a bare participle, a gerund preceded by
in (this but rarely), a gerund preceded by *to*, and an infinitive
with *to*.
For further discussion of these constructions, especially of the use
of the prefix *a* and the prepositions *in, on* (or *an*) before gerunds,
see also STORM, Eng. Phil.², 783 ff; MURRAY, s.v. *a* prep.¹; id.,
s.v. *burst*, 6; id., s.v. *go*, 32; FIJN VAN DRAAT, Rhythm in Eng.
Prose, Anglia, XXIV; my Grammar of Late Mod. Eng.,
Ch. XIX, § 44, s.v. *fall* and § 63, Obs. I–IV; my article on Hendiadys in Eng., Neophil., II, 202 ff and 284 ff.

Constructions after *to go, to come* and similar verbs.

i. So it befell in the month of May, Queen Guenever called unto her
knights of the Table Round; and she gave them warning that early
upon the morrow she would ride *on Maying* into the woods and
fields beside Westminster. SIR THOM. MALORY, Le Morte d'Arthur,
XIX, Ch. I, 315.

ii. A duke's income — a duke's — and *going a-begging*, as I may say.
LYTTON, CAXT., I, Ch. III, 43.
Have you any remembrance of what used to happen when Mr. Grundy
came *a-wooing*. THACK., Virg., Ch. LXIX, 725.
I should not like *to go a-begging*. CH. BRONTË, Jane Eyre, Ch. III, 23.
Qualities such as those could never *go a-begging* for long. JOHN
OXENHAM, The Simple Beguiler.
Politicians cannot have it both ways, and if they are all *going a-gunning*
for the moneyed man, the moneyed men naturally refuse to supply
them with ammunition. Rev. of Rev., CCXXVI, 5(26.

iii. How heavenly it would be *to go out boating* such a night as this!
MRS. ALEXANDER, For his Sake, I, Ch. V, 85.
He went out walking. RID. HAG., Mr. Meeson's Will, Ch. IV, 55.

iv. The man *went out a-shooting*. FIELDING, Tom Jones, II, 98.¹)
You don't want *to go out a-walking*, eh Fagin? DICK., Ol. Twist, 234.¹)
He *went out today a-wooing*. id., Barn. Rudge, Ch. III, 15 b.

v. The valet, wondering whether his master was *going masquerading*,
went in search of the article. THACK., Pend., II, Ch. II, 24.
I am *going travelling* upon a round of visits. id., Virg.,
Ch. XXXVI, 374.
He meant *to go hunting*. G. ELIOT, Mill, II, Ch. I, 119.

---

¹) FIJN VAN DRAAT, Rhythm in Eng. Prose, Anglia, XXIV, 512.

When my uncle says he'll give a gold watch, why, he will give it; there's no sham; so if any of you fellows do know about this, just go in and earn it. It ll be a shame to let a watch go-*begging*. Mrs. Wood, Orv. Col., Ch. V, 67. T.
If Isabel Vane were not the lady Isabel, they would think you *went* there *courting*. Mrs. Wood, East Lynne, I, 121. T.
I *am off shooting*. Rid. Hag., Jess, Ch. IV, 34.
Robert and I *go fishing*. Mrs. Ward, Rob. Elsm.
I am not *going shooting* to-morrow. Besn., The New Prince Fortunatus, Ch. VII.
You'll *go riding*, won't you? Galsworthy, Beyond, II, Ch X, 145.
Southampton *went soldiering* in France. Times, Lit. Sup., No. 990, 9 b.
You won't have to pay for your cabin on the Mauretania. It's *going begging*. Williamson, Lord Loveland, Ch. III, 21.

vi. May I give you the book to-morrow morning before we *go to shoot?* El. Glyn, The Reason why, Ch. XXVI, 236.
vii. In the meantime I'll *go to prepare* matters for our elopement. Goldsmith, She Stoops, IV, (207).
viii. He went straight from here purposing to *go see* his uncle. Mrs. Gask., Mary Barton, Ch. XXIII, 249.
Let Mary *go find* Will. ib., Ch. XXV, 265.
The reconstruction of the Ministry may *go hang*. Il. Lond. News.

Constructions after *to set*.

i. He busied himself with . . . making a specification of the expenses, that he might show it to Burge the next morning, and *set* him on persuading the Squire to consent. G. Eliot, Ad. Bede, IV, Ch. XXVII, 254.
It was perhaps this that *set* . . . Jem on *stealing* my own silver goblet. F. Picot, Strangest Journ., 188.[1])
ii. With the 5000 l. our office must be *set a-going*. Thack., Sam Titm., Ch. X, 131.
A wandering breeze *set* now and again the leafy breast a-*heaving*. Acn. and Eg. Castle, Diam. cut Paste, II, Ch. III, 141.
iii. With reference to your duties, I can *set* you *going*. Dick., Chuz., Ch. XXXIX, 309 b.
iv. She *set* herself *to make* as light of the whole affair as was possible Edna Lyall, A Hardy Norseman, Ch. XXV, 229.

Constructions after *to fall:*

i. And Enid *fell in longing* for a dress! All branch'd and flower'd with gold. Ten., Mar. of Ger., 630.
ii. It was not for nothing that my nose fell a-*bleeding*. Shak., Merch. of Ven., II, 5, 25.
At this we all *fell a-crying*. Dick., Cop., Ch. II, 11 a.
iii. After a while they *fell crying*. Kingsley, Herew., Ch. V, 36 b.
iv. He *fell* at once *to talking* about the Squire. Mrs. Ward, Rob. Elsm., I, 382.
v. The Queen desires you to use some gentle entertainment to Laertes before you *fall to play*. Shak., Haml., V, 2, 214.

[1]) Murray, s. v. *set*, 114. b.

The distinction was immediately approved by all, and so they fell again *to* examine. Swift, Tale of a Tub, (62b).
Upon this they *fell* again *to* rummage the well. ib., 63b.

Constructions after *to be*, etc.

i. I've been a turnin' the bis'ness over in my mind, and he may make hisself easy, Sammy. Dick., Pickw.
You're a-going to be made a 'prentice of. id., Ol. Twist, Ch. III.
Get some more port, Bowls, old boy, whilst I buzz the bottle here. What was I a-saying? Thack., Van. Fair., I, Ch. IV, 37.

ii. There was a bishop's lady in the shop, a-buying just such another (?) Aunt Jane at the Sea-shore, Ch. II.

iii. For he had one only daughter . . . and she lay a-dying. Auth. Vers., Luke, VIII, 42.

iv. You don't know how it pleases me, sir, . . . to hear you a-going on in that there uncommon considerate way of yours. Dick., Chuz., Ch. XLIII, 333a.

Constructions after *to burst out*.

i. After having looked at me earnestly for some time he *burst out a-laughing*. Smol., Humph. Clink., 112 (Tauchn.).
My uncle *burst out a-laughing*. Thack., Barry Lynd.

ii. He *burst out sobbing* and crying. Reade, It is never too late to mend, I, Ch. III, 49, T.

IX. Another survival of an ancient practice preserved in dialects and vulgar language is the use of the preposition *of* after the present participle of transitive verbs, when connected with the copula *to be*. This use of *of* goes far to show that in the majority of cases the periphrastical form of verbs goes back to a construction with the verbal noun (or gerund) in *ing*. Compare Jespersen, Tid og Tempus, IX, (412). See also Gerund, 33; and Expanded Form, 46.

In vulgar English the participle is also in this construction often preceded by the prefix *a*, which mostly represents an earlier *an* or *on*, but in some cases may also be a mere rhythmical insertion. Compare Fijn van Draat, Rhythm in Eng. Prose, Anglia, XXIV.

Observe also that such a sentence as *She was (a-)writing of a letter* corresponds to the Dutch *Zij was aan het schrijven van een brief*.

i. As she *was writing of it*. Shak., As you like it, IV, 3, 10.
Whom I left *cooling of* the air with sighs. id. Temp., I, 2, 222.
Both *warbling of* one song, both in one key. id., Mids., III, 2, 206.
My heart is *inditing of* a good matter, Auth. Vers., Psalm XLV, 1.
Coming out of another room and *seeing of* me . . . he said unto me, who is there, John Bunyan? Bunyan, A Relation of the Imprisonment, (109).
And verily at my return, I did meet my God sweetly in the prison again, *comforting of* me and *satisfying of* me that it was his will and mind that I should be there. ib., (113).

Suppose Baker was to come in and find you *squeezing of* my hand Thack., Lovel the Wid., Ch. III, 48.

ii. "They're a-twiggin' *of* you, sir," whispered Mr. Weller. Dick., Pickw., Ch. XX, 173.
Does the boy know what he's a-*saying of?* id., Barn. Rudge, Ch. III, 12b.
She fancied the bull was a-*chasing of* her again. Mrs. Alex., For his Sake, I, Ch. III. 49.

The vulgar use of this illogical *of* after other forms of the verb, as in the following quotations, seems to be rare.
If so be you *like of* the match, why, I am your man. Godwin, Caleb Wil., I, Ch. VII, 68.
Have I *offended of* your feelings? J. M. Barrie, The Admir. Crichton, II, 64.

X. In conclusion it may be observed that in vulgar language also the past participle is sometimes preceded by the prefix *a*.
If he hadn't a-*got* out time enough, I'd a-*let* him out for Sunday. Thack, Newc., I, Ch. XXVI, 291.
He said he "never could forget the kindness with which the Colonel have a-*treated* him". ib., 296.

SYNTAX.
The Verbal and Adjectival Character of the Participles.

7. As has already been pointed out (1), the participles hold an intermediate position between verbs and adjectives.

They are like verbs in admitting of the ordinary verbal modification by adverbial adjuncts and objects and, chiefly, in indicating an action or state with a more or less distinct time-association; i. e. a notion that the action or state they denote is thought of in connection with a certain length of time. They differ from the finite forms of the verb in calling forth this notion less clearly, and, besides, in being incapable of expressing the grammatical distinctions of person, number and mood, and in being less precise in marking those of voice and tense.

They are like adjectives in being applicable as adnominal modifiers and in admitting of the same modification as ordinary adjectives (22). They differ from adjectives in being associated with time-limitations, which are entirely lacking in the latter. Compare Wilmanns, Deutsche Gram., III, I, § 56; Paul, Prinz.³, § 254; Deutschbein, System, § 58; Mätzner, Eng. Gram.², III, 73, f. While, however, the participle in the majority of cases is intermediate between a verb and an adjective, we find it also in functions in which it has exclusively, or almost exclusively, the characteristics of either the former or the latter.

8. The past participle is now purely verbal when it is employed to assist in forming the complex tenses of the verb, as in *I have (had or shall have) come*.

In earlier stages of the language the participle in the complex tenses was distinctly felt as an adjective. Thus in Old English the past participle of transitive verbs, which was placed after the object, was often put in the accusative, e.g.: *hē hæfth ānne man ofslægene*¹) (= literally *he has a man killed*), while the past participle of such intransitive verbs, as were conjugated with *to be*, was always in concord with the subject, e.g.: *hie wǣron ā. farenne*²) (= *they were in a state of having departed*, Modern English *they had departed*).

This adjectival character more or less clings to the past participle in those constructions in which an intransitive verb is conjugated with *to be*, a practice which, although now obsolete, has left some traces even in the latest English.

Dickens is not merely alive: he *is risen* from the dead. CHESTERTON (Il. Lond News, No. 3844, 919 c).

It may be added that in French the adjectival character of the past participle in the complex tenses is still often shown by the variability of its written form, e.g.: Les fleurs, qu'il a cueillies. Mes soeurs sont parties. See also DEN HERTOG, Ned. Spraakk., III, § 95; PAUL, Prinz.³, § 253; JESPERSEN, Growth and Structure², § 206.

When a state resulting from an action is indicated by a combination of *to be* with the past participle of an intransitive verb, the latter may be said to be purely adjectival, *to be* having the function of a copula. Thus in

While I *am gone*, . . . I wish you to read over what I have marked in these books. DICK., Domb., Ch. XII, 109.

For further discussion see also Tense, 13 ff.

9. Both participles are virtually pure adjectives when the action they primarily imply is completely overshadowed by the notion of the quality of which this action is understood to be the manifestation, so that any time-association is absent from the speaker's or writer's mind. Thus in *a charming young lady* (= *an attractive or sweet young lady*), *a stolen interview* (= *a secret interview*). In its changed application the present participle often expresses an inclination or a cast of mind, i. e. a permanent attribute. Thus *a romping girl* may stand for *a girl given to romping*, *a grasping attorney* may have the meaning of *an attorney of a covetous cast of mind*. In the following quotation there are several instances:

A raging, ranting, cursing scold she is. FRANK HARRIS, The Women of Shakespeare, Ch. II, 42.

---

¹) BRADLEY, The Making of Eng., Ch. II, 65
²) SWEET, N. E. Gr., § 2166.

defiant = *defying*. i. She had started up with *defiant* words ready to burst from her lips, but they fell back without utterance. G. Eliot, Komola, II, Ch. XI, 310.

ii. His impetuous, adventurous and *defying* character. M⸺, Ess., Pitt, 509 1¹).
existent = *existing*. i. The quantity (sc. of gold) *existent* and in circulation. Rogers, Pol. Econ.³ III, 27¹).

It gives you types of *existent* Frenchmen ... of a very different class. Ruskin, Fors Clav., IV, Ch. XLIII, 153¹).

ii. The *existing* franchise may be virtually regarded as manhood suffrage. Mc Carthy, Short Hist., Ch. II, 18.

The question of machinery, or technical procedure, is not relevant, much of this ground having been covered by *existing* institutions. Eng. Rev., No. 113, 380.

It (sc. the essay) need to deal with the *existing* struggle. ib., 381.
repellent = *repelling*. i. Presently the rude Real burst coarsely in — all evil, grovelling and *repellent* as she too often is. Ch. Brontë, Villette, Ch. XII, 154.

ii. The wild steed's sinewy nerves still strain Up the *repelling* bank. Byron, Mazeppa, XV.
resistant = *resisting*. i. The *resistant* gravity about his mouth and eyes as he was being smiled upon made their beauty the more impressive. G. Eliot, Dan. Der., I, II, Ch. XVI, 251.

ii. But the *resisting* thoughts were not yet overborne. id., Komola, II, Ch. XI, 314.
resultant = *resulting*. i. A slip in the physical position has reacted upon the moral position or statesmanship with the usual *resultant* contusions. Eng. Rev., No. 113, 369.

We shall look for an expression of regret at the insufficient rainfall in India and the *resultant* famine. Times.

ii. There would either be a *resulting* trust or it would belong to the person who takes the estate. Jarman, Powell's Devises, II, 41¹).

A marked adjectival character is often evidenced by an ordinary adjective being placed in juxtaposition or contrast to the participle.

These are but wild and *whirling* words. Shak., Hamlet., I, 5, 133.
Such institutions are either public or private, free or *paying*. Murray, s. v. *hospital*, 3.
His manner was formal, but not surly and *forbidding*. Reade, It is never too late to mend, I, Ch X, 113.

ii. She was very weak and *reduced*. Lytton, My Novel, I, VII, Ch. XV, 467.

11. The verbal principle is distinctly prominent, i. e. the time-association is indubitable, in either participle, when it has the value of an undeveloped clause or is a constituent of an undeveloped clause. In the latter case the presence of ordinary verb-modifiers leaves no doubt of its predominantly verbal character. Also adjectives, indeed, may be used to form undeveloped clauses and may be accompanied by the same modifiers as verbs,

---
¹) Murray.

but they may be easily distinguished from participles by their being devoid of all time=association. Thus in the following sentences, in which the adjectives with their adjuncts represent different kinds of undeveloped clauses, the time=association does not attach to the adjectives, but to the verb *to be*, which becomes evident when the undeveloped clause is expanded into a full one.

The two races, *so long hostile*, soon found that they had common interests. Mac., Hist. I, Ch. 1, 15. (= *which had been so long hostile*.)

Ardent and intrepid on the field of battle, Monmouth was everywhere else effeminate and irresolute. ib., II, Ch. V, 100. (= *Although he was ardent and intrepid on the field of battle*.)

For a discussion of this function of participles and adjectives the student is referred to Ch. XX and XXI, where full details have been given.

12. The present participle is predominantly verbal in character when it is connected with the verb *to be* to form with it the expanded (often called the progressive) form of the verb, and also when it is used in a similar combination with the copulas *to remain* (or equivalent verb) or *to get* (or equivalent verb).

Also when purely adjectival, the present participle may, indeed, be connected with *to be* to form the nominal part of the predicate, but this construction bears only a formal resemblance to the expanded form of the verb, the meaning being essentially different. Compare, however, Expanded Form, 36.

It is not *surprising* that the public has become perplexed. Athen., No. 4627, 135 b. (= *strange*.)

A new ethic which hitherto *has been utterly lacking* among the nations. Eng. Rev., No. 113, 380. (= *absent*.)

13. The past participle is essentially verbal when it is employed to assist in forming the passive voice. Thus in:

Thousands of letters *are received* daily. Onions, Advanced Eng. Synt., § 116.
Fruit *was eaten* in large quantities. ib.

There is no passive voice in the strict sense of the word when the combination *to be* + past participle of transitive verb is used to denote a state resulting from an action. In this case the verb *to be* has the function of a copula and the participle is practically a pure adjective. Thus in:

The letter *is written* at last. Onions, Advanced Eng. Synt., § 116.

The young man's life is just beginning: the boy's leading=strings *are cut*, and he has all the novel delights and dignities of freedom. Thack., Pend., I, Ch. XVII, 172.

14. For the rest there is much uncertainty about the prominence of either the verbal or the adjectival principle in participles, especially when used attributively. As most participles admit of indicating either principle in various degrees, the context alone is often the only determining factor.

Thus *romping children* may mean *children engaged in romping*, but also *children given to romping*. In the first case *romping* is prominently verbal, in the second almost purely adjectival. The difference is much less marked in *boiling water* understood as *water bubbling up under the influence of heat* and *water at boiling temperature* (as opposed to *tepid water*).

In such a combination as *running footmen*, when taken by itself, *running* would on the first blush call forth to the hearer's mind the notion of a participle with a distinctly verbal character, but in the following quotation it reveals itself almost as a pure adjective:

At length, late in the afternoon, the Knight-Marshal's men appeared on horseback Then came a long train of *running* footmen. Mac., Hist. III, Ch. VIII, 99.

15. Present participles are often transferred from their proper subjects to others which are in some way related to them. The change is mostly attended by an obscuring of the time-association and by a substitution of a notion of a quality for that of an action in the speaker's or writer's thoughts. Compare

a paying guest with *a paying business*,
a blooming tree ,, *a blooming month*,
a flying bird ,, *a flying visit*.

The great range of subjects to which such a participle may be extended is aptly illustrated by the numerous applications of which the participle *running* is capable (See Murray, s.v.): *running* water (as opposed to stagnant water, or water obtained from a river, brook, etc.), *running* (i. e. fluid mercury, *running* sand (i.e. sand having no coherence), a *running* (i.e. leaky) water-tap, a *running* sore, a *running* lecturer (i.e. a lecturer not tied to one locality), *running* moss, a *running* metre, a *running* pulse, a *running* fire (i.e. a rapid and continuous fire), a *running* fight (i.e. a naval engagement carried on during a retreat or flight), a *running* hand, a *running* title (i.e. a short title placed at the top of the page), *running* (i.e. linear) *measure*, a *running* (i.e. continuous) *comment*, a *running* account (i.e. an account allowed to run on for a certain time), the *running* (i.e. current) *price*, the *running* gear (sc. of a mechanism), *running* tackle (i.e. tackle capable of moving when pulled or hauled), *running* rigging, a *running* loop, etc.

Further instances of transferred participles are afforded by the following quotations:

Be plain, good son, and homely in thy drift; | *Riddling* confession finds but *riddling* shrift. Shak., Rom. and Jul., II, 3, 56.

I observed your niece's maid coming forth from a *circulating* library. SHER
Riv., I, 2.
O *aching* time! O moments big as years! KEATS, Hyp., I, 64.
We see in him (sc. Burns) the gentleness, the *trembling* pity of a woman. CARLYLE.
A fresh and *blooming* month. DICK., Pickw., Ch. XVI, 137.
In the course of your *rambling* life. ib., Ch. XVI, 138.
He was only on a *flying* visit. G. ELIOT, Mid., IV, Ch. XXXVIII, 280
Sir James ended with a *pitying* disgust. ib., 282.
Then first, since Enoch's golden ring had girt | Her finger, Annie fought against
his will: | Yet not with *brawling* opposition she. TEN., En. Ard., 159.
His letters read full of a *sparkling* pleasure in the incidents of the tour. MAR.
BOWEN, The Rake's Progress, I, Ch. I, 2.

16. Also past participles are often transferred from their original
subjects, but this change concerns only their application as pure
adjectives. Compare

a *retired* gentleman with a *retired* spot.
a *learned* man ,, a *learned* book.
a *drunken* man ,, a *drunken* brawl.

in such word-groups as *faded* cheeks, *faded* powers, *faded* cheese, his *faded*
appearance, his *faded* eyes, *faded* metaphors, *faded* glories (see MURRAY,
s.v. *faded*),there is no transference of epithets in the sense indicated above,
but a predication of the participle to a variety of subjects likened to flowers

17. The character of the attributive participle is to a certain extent
shown by its place as to its head-word, a marked time-association
mostly entailing post-position. Thus it is easy to see a distinct
time-association in *He took all the letters written to the post*
and its absence in *He sent me a written circular not a printed one*.
Similarly the time-association is unmistakable in the participles
found in:

There is but one being *existing*, who is necessarily indivisible and infinite.
LEWIS, Hist. of Phil., 77.
It you cannot see the great gulf *fixed* between the two, I trust you will discover
it some day. KINGSLEY, Westw. Ho!, Ch. III, 23a.

But as the placing of an attributive word after its head-word
often implies increased relative stress of the former, it may be
assumed that also the latter principle may sometimes be held
responsible for a departure from the rule that attributive words
are normally placed before their head-words. See Ch. VIII,
§ 84 ff.

In the following groups of quotations it may be either or both of these
principles that may be assigned as having determined, consciously or
unconsciously, the different positions of the attributive participles.

The others had gone into the dressing-room *adjoining*. J. F. Benson, Arundel, Ch. XIV, 382.

ii. To step aside into some *adjoining* room. Mac., Hist., II, 506.[1])

i. On the *day following* he entered my room. Watts Dunton, Aylwin, IX, Ch. I, 270.
On the day *following* I entered upon my functions. Westm. Gaz., No 5376, 2c.

ii. On the *following day* appeared in the Gazette a proclamation dissolving that Parliament [etc.]. Mac., Hist., II, Ch. VIII, 99.
Early on the *following* day. Tynd., Glac., I, Ch. VIII, 57.

Note. It is remarkable that ensuing, a strict synonym of *following* as used in the above quotations, is always placed before its head-word.
Early on the *ensuing* morning. Dick., Pickw., Ch. XVI, 139.

i. Within memory of many people *living*. English was a feudal club without right of entry from without. Shane Leslie, The End of a Chapter, Ch. IX, 164.
No man *living* could do better. Conc. Oxf. Dict., s. v. *living*.

ii. The greatest *living* master of irony. ib.
The first of *living* artists. ib.

i. There are some litigations *pending*. Mrs. Ward, The Mating of Lydia I, Ch. IX, 181.

ii. A series of inquiries followed: as to the term of the proposed agreement; the degree of freedom that would be granted him; the date at which his duties would begin . . . passing on to . . . the nature of the *pending* litigations. ib., I, Ch. IX, 183.

i. The party *acquitted* should be released from confinement without delay.

ii. A portion of the public both inside and outside the building hurried towards the *acquitted* man. Times.

i. Shagram snorted . . . and refused to move one yard in the direction *indicated*. Scott, Mon., Ch. III, 66.

ii. The young man seated himself in the *indicated* seat at the bottom of the bed. Miss Brad., Lady Audley's Secret[2]).

i. The party *injured* growled forth an oath or two of indignation. Scott, Abbot, Ch. XIX, 198.

ii. The *injured* party applied to the magistrate for redress.

i. "The very thing," said Mr. Weller, who was a party *interested*, inasmuch as he ardently longed to see the sport. Dick., Pickw., Ch. XIX, 163.

ii. The evidence of *interested* persons is now received and its value estimated according to its worth. Williams, Real Prop., 207[1])

i. Among the guests *invited* were several foreigners.

ii. Mr. Asquith and the Home Secretary were among the sixty *invited* guests. Ill. Lond. News, No 3715, 6c.

i. There seemed to be nobody among his numerous friends who could give him the information *required*.

ii. Saying this, Mr. Brownlow looked round the office as if in search of some person who would afford him the *required* information. Dick., Ol Twist, Ch. XI, 105.

---

[1]) Murray.

[2]) Binger Palm, Place of the Adj. Attrib., § 29.

13*

In some cases, however, it is difficult to discern the application of either or any principle. Thus the position of the participle seems to be a matter of chance in:

i. He was a gentleman *born*. SCOTT, Mon., Ch. XXVIII, 301.
He's a liar *born*, and he'll die a liar. DICK., Great Expect., Ch. V, 46.
ii. The Boer is a *born* conservative. FROUDE, Oceana, Ch. III, 48.
She's a natural *born* nurse. WELLS, Britling, I, Ch. III, § 8, 94.

In not a few cases also the requirements of rime, metre or rhythm seem to have been the determining factor.

He that is strucken blind cannot forget | The precious treasure of his eyesight *lost*. SHAK., Rom. and Jul., I, 1, 237.
Now Romeo is beloved and loves again, | Alike bewitched by the charm of looks, | But to his foe *supposed* he must complain. ib., II, Chor., 7.
For what is wedlock *forced* but a hell, | An age of discord and continual strife? id., Henry VI, A, V, 5, 62.
And the country proverb *known*, | That every man should take his own, | In your waking shall be shown. id. Mids., III, 2, 458.

BIRGER PALM, in his admirable treatise The Place of the Adjective Attribute in English Prose, § 29, finds the test which is to decide whether a participle should be placed before or after its head-word, not in the absence or presence of a distinct time-association, but in the answer to the question whether or not the action expressed by it is connected in our thoughts with a "definite **acting person** (*operative force*)". (The writer has **acting person** printed in thick type, *operative force* in italic type.) He compares the two following quotations:

The young man seated himself in the *indicated* seat at the bottom of the bed. MISS BRADDON, Lady Audley's Secret.
This ... reflects an intimacy with the material *handled* which is unmistakable.

Now it seems difficult to see a difference between *indicated* and *handled*, so far as action by a definite acting person is concerned. In the above quotations the determining factor as to the position of the participle seems to be rather the stress of the latter relatively to its head-word. In the first the participle is subservient to its head-word, in the second the case is reversed.

If the theory were right, the order would have been reversed in:

They were content to pay the European trader the *agreed-upon* price. Westm. Gaz., No. 6483, 7 a.

a) It may here be observed that post-position of the participle is always impossible when its head-word is modified by a possessive pronoun or a genitive.

He heard his dear and *his doted-on* Mary Anne say ..., "Do you think I should care anything for that lame boy?" LYTTON, Life of Lord Byron, 14a.
He had been driven to ensconce the nest in a corner of *his already too well-filled* den. HUGHES, Tom Brown, II, Ch. III, 239.
His already wearied horse. SWEET, N. E. Gr., § 1788.

b) Mr. Birger Palm's principle seems to be more useful in deciding whether the verbal or the adjectival character is the prevailing one in an attributive participle. This will be brought home to the reader if he will take the trouble of comparing the groups of sentences given in Ch. VIII, § 104.

This is not the place to deal exhaustively with the various factors operating on the position of attributive participles. The subject has already been briefly discussed in Ch. VIII, treating of the place of attributive adnominal adjuncts in general, and has been incidentally touched on in Ch. XX and XXI, dealing respectively with participle clauses and nominal clauses. The student interested in this part of English Grammar may find ample discussion of the subject in Jespersen, Mod. Eng. Gram., Ch. XV, 15, 4 ff, and Birger Palm, The Place of the Adjective Attribute in English Prose.

18. In the following pages it is chiefly the attributive employment of the participles that will be dealt with, instances of their predicative use being only occasionally included.

From the following discussions will be excluded the application of the participles as constituents of undeveloped clauses, which has already found detailed exposition in Ch. XX.

The important use of the present participle as a constituent of the expanded (or progressive) form of verbs and of allied constructions with other copulas than *to be*, and with such words as *to lie*, *to sit* and *to stand*, has found adequate treatment in my treatise devoted to this interesting subject.

The employment of the past participle to form the passive voice of verbs will be done full justice to in a separate chapter.

Participles in which the time-association is distinctly perceptible may be called **verbal participles**, those in which it is highly weakened or entirely obliterated may be styled **adjectival participles**.

The Present Participle in Detail.

19. The present participle of practically all verbs can be freely used attributively.

The following quotations are roughly divided into two groups, according to the degree of purity in which the participle contained in them expresses the verbal principle. Only in the last group has the alphabetical order been observed. For illustration of adjectival present participles see also 22.

i. How silver-sweet sound lovers' tongues by night. Like softest music to attending ears! Shak., Rom. and Jul., II, 2, 166.

M. Charles Rivet, . . . in an *arresting* study, entitled The Last of the Romanofs, sets forth many things that needed to be said. Punch, No. 4005, 240 a.

The Eclogues of Virgil and Odes of Horace are each inseparably allied in association with the sullen figure and monotonous recitation of some *blubbering* school-boy. SCOTT, Old Mort., Ch. I, 12.
They ... profess no great shame in their fathers having served in the *persecuting* squadrons. ib., Ch. I, 22.
At this *affecting* appeal, Goodwin got up a little domestic tragedy of her own. DICK., Pickw., Ch. XVIII, 157.
Mr. Pott cast an *imploring* look at the innocent cause of the mischief. ib., 158.
Mr. Tupman, with a *trembling* voice, read the letter. ib., 160.
ii. May is a fresh and *blooming* month. DICK., Pickw., Ch. XVI, 137.
One would imagine that all Europe, Asia and America had rushed in a body to see this *compelling* drama (sc. Salome by Oscar Wilde). LORD ALFRED DOUGLAS, Osc. Wilde and myself, Ch. XXVI, 301.
They disturb the peace of mind and happiness of some *confiding* female. DICK., Pickw., Ch. XVIII, 160.
You may be an unfortunate man, sir, or you may be a *designing* one. ib. Ch. XX, 174.
Then the frown returned, redoubled in its *forbidding* scowl. TEMPLE THURSTON, The City of Beaut. Nons., III, Ch. VI, 255.
It's ... a base conspiracy between these two *grasping* attorneys. ib., Ch. XVIII, 161.
That was what the *knowing* ones call 'nuts' to Scrooge. id., Christm Car.⁵, I, 8.
As they say of a generous man, it is a pity he is not rich, we may say of Goldsmith, it is a pity he is not *knowing*. DOBSON, Life of Goldsmith. Ch. XII, 197.
It must have been of great service to you, in the course of your *rambling* life. DICK., Pickw., Ch. XVI, 138.
A *retreating* forehead and an equally *retreating* chin. AGN. AND EG. CASTLE, Diam. cut Paste, II, Ch. I, 109.
There was a very snug little party, consisting of Marie Lobbs and her cousin Kate, and three or four *romping*, good-humoured, rosy-cheeked girls. DICK., Pickw., Ch. XVII, 152.
He came to be known for his *seeming* eccentricities. TEMPLE THURSTON, The City of Beaut. Nons., III, Ch. VI, 256.
Well, it's a pretty spot, ... and one meets some fine *strapping* fellows about too, G. ELIOT, Adam Bede, I, Ch. II, 11.
He has written a *taking* song. EDNA LYALL, Hardy Norseman, Ch. XII, 98.
"A modest, *understanding* sort of man", was Honor's mental verdict. MAUD DIVER, Captain Desmond, V.C., Ch. III, 25.
He look'd and found them *wanting*. TEN., Ger. and En., 934.

20. Obs. I. In the case of objective verbs the object is often absorbed in the participle through being vague or indistinct, thus rendering them subjective. Thus in many of the above quotations: *this affecting appeal, attending ears, this compelling drama, some confiding female, a designing man, grasping attorneys, a knowing man, a taking song, an understanding sort of man*, etc.

II. Sometimes the object is implied in the head-word.
What a prodigy in God's world is a *professing* atheist. MANNING, Serm. Myst. Sin, I, 16¹). (= a man who professes atheism).

¹) MURRAY, s. v. *professing*.

The Church is the visible community of *professing* Christians founded by our Lord for the propaganda of the Kingdom. D. S. Cairns, The Mod. World, IV, 212[1]).

Intending passengers should book early, as the company reserves to itself the right to cease issuing tickets at any time. Notice, Great Western Railway. (= *persons who intend to be passengers*.)

III. In the majority of cases the head word of the attributive present participle is in the subjective relation to it. Thus in all the preceding quotations. Occasionally the relation is objective.

Tell him, from *his all-obeying breath* I hear | The doom of Egypt. Shak. Ant. and Cleop., III, 13, 77 (= *his breath, i. e. language, which all obey*.)

My gentle Caius, worthy Marcius, and | By *deed-achieving honour* newly named, — | What is it? — Coriolanus must I call thee? — id., Coriol., II, 1, 161. (= *honour achieved, i. e. won, by deeds*.)

Let *his unrecalling crime* | Have time to wail the abusing of his time. id., Lucr., 993. (*his crime which cannot be recalled, i. e. undone*.)

That hand shall burn in *never quenching fire* | That staggers thus my person. id., Rich. II, 5, 5, 109. (= *fire that will never be quenched*.)

Let me now conjure my kind, my condescending angel, to fix the day when I may rescue her from *undeserving persecution*. Sher., Riv., III, 3 (= *persecution which is undeserved*.)

IV. When used predicatively also adjectival present participles may govern a prepositional or non-prepositional object. The construction may be the same as that of the verb in the other applications, but not unfrequently is made to conform to that of synonymous adjectives. Thus we meet with *(un)becoming* and *(un)becoming to*.

    i. You've raised an artificial soul and spirit in him, ma'am, *unbecoming a person* of his condition. Dick., Ol. Twist, Ch. VII, 73.
    If Mrs. Nickleby took the apartments without the means of paying for them, it was very *unbecoming* a lady. id., Nich. Nick., Ch. III, 11b.
    ii. He was most strict in religious observances, . . . much more . . . than was *becoming to* his rank and age. Mottey, Rise, I, Ch. II, 76a. Sartorius assumes a jocose, rallying air, *unbecoming to* him under any circumstances. Shaw, Widowers' Houses, II, 36.
    i. What canst thou expect, but that . . . we deliver thee up to England as *undeserving* our further protection. Scott, Mon., Ch. XXVI, 285.
    ii. It sometimes happens that a person departs this life, who is really *deserving of* all the praises the stone-cutter carves over his bones. Thack., Van. Fair, I, Ch I, 4.

Observe also the prepositional object of the following participles corresponding to transitive verbs.

When at length they ran him to earth, he was *charming to* them, perfect in courtesy, and as kind as possible. Frank Harris, Contemp Portr., XVII, 300.

The proposal is *disturbing to* preconceived ideas. Westm Gaz, No. 6329, 1c.

---

[1]) Murray, s. v. *professing*.

He had his own code of what was *befitting* to a gentleman. GALSWORTHY, Beyond, III, Ch. V, 271.
The Allies are ... utterly *lacking in* sound revolutionary principles. Westm. Gaz., No. 7649, 1 b.

The following quotation affords a curious instances of a present participle forming a kind of compound with the reflexive pronoun that has the value of an adjective.

They looked so gay and *enjoying themselves*. EL. GLYN, Refl. of Ambr., I, Ch. IV, 52.

21. Present participles sometimes take the negativing prefix *un*. Such formations are devoid of almost all verbal force, the negativing *un* not being used in connection with verbs. See also the quotations with *unbecoming* and *undeserving* in 20 Obs. IV.

His name must bring *unpleasing* recollections. SCOTT, Old Mort., Ch. III, 34.
I must say it is very *unfeeling* of him to be running away from his poor little boy. JANE AUSTEN, Pers., Ch. VII, 55.
There is nothing very *unforgiving* in that. ib., Ch. XVIII, 177.
You are a female, and *unforgiving*. LYTTON, My Novel, I, VII, Ch. XI, 460.
(She) clench'd her fingers till they bit the palm, ! And shriek'd out 'Traitor' to the *unhearing* wall. TEN., Lancel. and El., 608.
People are so *extremely unthinking* about such a number of interesting things. EL. GLYN, The Reason why, Ch. XII, 109.
Missionaries have been as scurvily rewarded by our *unknowing* British Ministers of State as that other great body of public servants, the officers and men of the mercantile marine. Westm. Gaz., No. 7595, 15a.

22. Many also admit of being modified by the same intensives as are found with quality-expressing adjectives. Like the adjectival participles mentioned above (19), they are here arranged alphabetically:

(This), being only light, was *more alarming* than a dozen ghosts. DICK., Christm. Car.³⁹, III, 58.
The movement on the western front during the last week is one of the *most arresting* in the war. The Nation, XX, 22, 721a.
I'm a *very confiding* soul by nature. JEAN WEBSTER, Daddy-Long-Legs, 42.
Master Jervie is *very demanding*. ib., 234.
The other (sc. grandfather) was an earl, who endowed him with the *most doting* mother in the world. THACK., Pend., I, Ch. V, 55.
This is a *very entertaining* world. JEAN WEBSTER, Daddy-Long-Legs, 117.
She is *most forbidding*. EL. GLYN, The Reason why, Ch. XIV, 123.
He was told so by a companion ... one Tom Towers, a *very leading* genius. TROL., The Warden, Ch. X, 126.
After every outbreak of ill-humour this extraordinary pair became *more loving* than before. MAC., Fred., (691a).

But there are some delicious jam-sandwiches, which are *more quenching* than anything. BRADBY, Dick, Ch XII, 128.
Grant that they are a little *less saving*, have they not greater temptations to and excuses for improvidence. ESCOTT, England, Ch. XII, 219.
A *too, too smiling* large man ... appearing with his wife, instantly deserts his wife and darts at Twemlow. DICK., Our Mut. Friend, I, Ch. II, 11.
They were all ready to pay attention to that *deucedly taking* niece of Rashleigh's. MRS. ALEXANDER, For his Sake, II, Ch. II, 29.

Note. It is only in vulgar or colloquial style that adjectival present participles are at all placed in the terminational superlative. Instances of the terminational comparative have not come to hand.

Was not Wilkes the ... *charmingest* ... man. THACK., Catherine, II[1]).
Dolly might take pattern by her blessed mother, who ... was the mildest, amiablest, *forgivingest-spirited, long-sufferingest* female as ever she could have believed. DICK., Barn. Rudge, Ch. XXII, 86.
I have always found him the *bitingest* and tightest screw in London. id., Our Mut. Friend, III, Ch. XIII, 227.
Mr. Deane, he considered, was the *"knowingest"* man of his acquaintance. G. ELIOT, Mill, I, Ch. VIII, 64.
He once had a sister himself — the *rippingest* in the world. Westm. Gaz. No. 6975, 8 b.

23. Present participles are not, apparently, often converted, either wholly or partially, into nouns. A very common instance of partial conversion is afforded by *living*, which is used not only to denote a class of persons in a generalizing way, but also a single individual.

i. The land of the *living*. Bible, Psalm XXVII, 13; LIII, 5.
ii. Every night before I lie down to rest, I look at the pictures and bless both the *living* and the dead. BUCHANAN, That Winter Night, Ch. III, 27.

A class of persons in a generalizing way is indicated by the present participle in

The *sleeping* and the dead Are but as pictures. SHAK., Macb., II, 2, 54.

24. Present participles are not seldom used as intensives of either adjectives or adverbs. In the majority of cases they then denote an action which is caused by the excess of the quality expressed by the adjective or adverb.

I am afeard, Being in night, all this is but a dream, | Too *flattering-sweet* to be substantial. SHAK., Rom. and Jul., II, 2, 141.
I would have thee gone; | And yet no further than a wanton's bird, | Who lets it hop a little from her hand, | Like a poor prisoner in his twisted gyves, | And with a silk thread plucks it back again, So *loving-jealous* of his liberty. ib., II, 2, 181.

---
[1]) MURRAY

Her heart was so *aching-full* of other things that all besides seemed like a dream. Mrs. Gask., Mary Barton, Ch. XXI, 224.
It was a *pouring wet* day. Marj. Bowen, I will maintain, Ch. IX, 103.
She and I get on *rattling well* together. Shaw., Mrs. Warren's Profession, I, (174).

Note *a)* In the case of *passing* and *exceeding*, which are now used only archaically as intensives, there is some vague notion of an object implied in the participle. Thus *passing fair* seems to be understood as *so fair as to pass all others*. Compare Jespersen, Mod. Eng. Gram., II, 15.25.

Show me a mistress that is *passing fair*, | What doth her beauty serve, but as a note | Where I may read who pass'd that *passing* fair? Shak., Rom. and Jul., I, 1, 238—240.
I have a daughter that I love *passing well*. id., Haml., II, 2, 437.
A man he was to all the country dear, | And *passing rich* with forty pounds a year. Goldsmith, Des. Vil., 142.
Mr. Bromley guessed him to be in an *exceeding* ill-humour. Marj. Bowen, I will maintain, I, Ch. XI, 126. (*exceeding* modifies the adjectival part of the compound *ill-humour*.)

β) The participle may be understood as either an adverb or an adjective in:
Susannah's *glittering* brown hair was blown across her brow. Marj. Bowen, The Rake's Progress, I, Ch. I, 13.
One of her fair hands lay among the glasses on the *shining* white cloth. ib., 9.

γ) Also *running*, as used in such a combination as *three times running*, has an adverbial function.
He can speak seven hours *running* without fatigue. J. H. Newman, Loss and Gain, IV, VIII[1]).

25. Some present participles may assume the function of
   a) **conjunctions**, in this case often in connexion with *that*. Thus *being, considering, notwithstanding, providing (=provided), saving, seeing*. For illustration see Ch. XVII, §§ 46, 71, 77, 91, 156. Thus also *barring that* as in:
   Barring that she seldom says a word about anything but the way the rheumatism has her tormented, her Irish is as good as you'd hear. Birmingham, The Advent. of Dr. Whitty, Ch. V, 122.

   b) **prepositions**. Thus *bating, barring, according (to), concerning, considering, during, excepting (= excepted, except), failing, notwithstanding, pending, regarding, relating, saving, touching*.

---

[1]) Murray, s. v. *running*, 18.

Thus also the phrases *setting aside, leaving (or putting) on one side*. For discussion and illustration see Ch. XX, §§ 4, 7, 9. Compare also Onions, Advanced Eng. Synt., § 61 c, 4.

26. Present participles often enter into combination with other words, forming compounds with them which are written in separation, with a hyphen or in combination, according to the closeness of the connexion. In many of these compounds the verbal principle is considerably or wholly obliterated.

   a) with nouns,

   1) in the objective relation. These compounds can be freely made of any suitable combination, but are unfrequent in colloquial language: *pleasure=seeking gentlemen, holiday= making youths, a shop=keeping nation, the wage=earning classes, an epoch=making event.*

   She will not stay the siege of loving terms, | Nor bide the encounter of assailling eyes, | Nor ope her lap to *saint=seducing gold*. Shak., Rom. and Jul., I, 1, 216=8.
   Heart=piercing anguish struck the Graecian host. Pope, Iliad, XIV, 569[1]).
   The *heart=rending* sensation of seeing his children starve. Malthus, Popul., II, 45[1]).
   There are stories going about him as a *quill=driving* alien. G. Eliot, Mid., IV, Ch. XXXVIII, 280.
   Far as the *portal=warding* lion=whelp. Ten., En. Ard., 98.
   And on him fell, | Altho' a grave and staid *God=fearing* man … doubt and gloom. ib., 112.
   The … *painstaking* manner in which they superintend … this depart= ment. Law Times, XCIX, 544 2[1]).
   The trombones seemed … to drown everything else by their *ear=splitting* tones. Pall Mall Gaz.[1])
   Mary Fitton's lecherous, *change=loving* temperament … is not only ignored but is transmuted into tender loyalty and devotion. Frank Harris, The Women of Shak., Ch. IV, 77.

   Note *α)* Of a similar nature are compounds with words that have a substantival function.

   In those days there were pocket=boroughs, … a brawny and *many= breeding* pauperism, and other departed evils. G. Eliot, Fel. Holt, Intr. 2
   The great majority are Dutch born and *Dutch speaking*. Times, No. 2003, 447 a.
   Shakespeare is more like Marcus Aurelius than Goethe or Cervantes, but even Marcus Aurelius has not his *all=pitying* soul. Frank Harris, The Women of Shakespeare, Ch. II, 20.

---
[1]) Murray.

β) Some compounds are practically equivalent to present participle + object and are, accordingly, purely verbal.

It must have been Treherne who was *tree-felling*. J. M. BARRIE, The Admir. Crighton, II, 58. (= *felling trees*.)

2) **in an adverbial relation.** Although not, apparently, restricted to any particular adverbial relation, these compounds cannot be freely made and are met with only in literary language.

Home-keeping youth have ever homely wits. SHAK., Two Gent., I, 1, 2.
Who knows but this *night-walking* old fellow of the Haunted House may be in the habit of haunting every visitor. WASH. IRV., Dolf Heyl. (STOF., Handl., I, 145).
What housewife in Grimworth would not think shame to furnish forth her table with articles that were not *home-cooked*. G. ELIOT, Broth. Jac., Ch. II, (199).
Enoch's ocean spoil | In *ocean-smelling* osier. TEN., En. Ard., 94.
And Enoch's comrade, careless of himself, | *Fire-hollowing* this in Indian fashion, fell, | Sun-stricken. ib., 565.
Water-living creatures, which are always under water, wave the freely exposed gills by which they breathe in that water and extract the air dissolved in it. WELLS, Outl. of Hist., I, IV, § 1, 16 a.
Plant now *autumn-flowering* bulbs. Westm. Gaz., No. 7265, 22 a.
The English people, by losing their land, had been transformed into wage-earners, rural or *town-dwelling*. Bookmann, No. 316, 125 a.

b) **with adverbs.** These compounds can be freely formed of any suitable combination, but, save for certain fixed formations, such as *incoming, outgoing, outstanding, outlying*, etc. they are not particularly frequent and are chiefly met with in the higher literary style. The adverb may be one of

1) **place.** He thrice had pluck'd a life | From the dread sweep of the *down-streaming* seas. TEN., En. Ard., 55.
Until, the *forward-creeping* tides | Began to foam. id., In Memoriam, CIII, 37.
The *outgoing* tenant receives a certain sum from the *incoming* tenant. FAWCETT, Pol. Econ., II, VII, 240 [1]).
An English girl would not have told him that story in the same frank *upstanding* way. MRS. WARD, The Mating of Lydia, III, Ch. XVI, 328.
The *outstanding* event of the month at sea was the destruction of the Breslau. Rev. of Rev., No. 338, 88 a.
This great trunk cable once laid, branches still more closely connecting *outlying* portions of our dominions, will easily and naturally follow. Times, 1899, 264 b.
The last two coaches of the *incoming* train were thrown off the rails. Ill. Lond News, No. 3859, 450.

---

[1]) MURRAY.

Their being put out of action now suggests *far-reaching* possibilities. Rev. of Rev., No. 338, 88b.

2) time: Hedges, fields, and trees, hill and moorland, presented to the eye their *ever-varying* shades of deep rich green. Dick., Pickw., Ch XIX, 162.
She still took note that when the living smile | Died from his lips, across him came a cloud | Of melancholy severe, from which again, | ... There brake a *sudden-beaming* tenderness | Of manners and of nature. Tenn., Lanc. and El.; 326.
The *seldom-frowning* King frown'd. ib., 710.
Thus over Enoch's *early-silvering* head | The sunny and rainy season came and went | Year after year. id., En. Ard., 618.
Before these lines appear in print, a *long-standing* injustice will have been finally removed. Rev. of Rev., No. 338, 90a.

3) quality: Show a fair presence and put off these frowns, | An *ill-beseeming* semblance for a feast. Shak., Rom. and Jul., I, 5, 77.
A man of an *easy-going* disposition. Gord. Holmes, Silvia Craven, 18.
The *slow-moving* figure of the chair-mender. Marj. Bowen, The Rake's Progress, Ch. IV, 41.
The *finely* discriminating essay on Ben Jonson. Bookman, No. 316, 134b.

4) degree: He is a convinced and *thorough-going* Imperialist. Times, 1899, 296c.

c) **with adjectives or adjectival participles.** The participles used in these compounds are, naturally, only such as have been formed from verbs that do duty as faded copulas. See Ch. I, 5. Only compounds with *looking* are at all frequent:

i. Holland, to speak in a familiar phrase, was what we call a *good-looking* man. Davies, Garrick, II, 92[1]).
He was ... *well-looking*, though in an effeminate style. Dick., Little Dorrit, Ch. VI, 30a.
"Come in, d'ye hear!" growled this *engaging-looking* ruffian. id., O! Twist, Ch. XIII, 29a (John Dicks).
He was a *young-looking* man. id., Great Expect. Ch. XXIII, 224.
She is much too *striking-looking*. El. Glyn, The Reason Why, Ch. XIV, 123.
But such a *provoking-looking* type of beauty as she was did not long leave the men of the party cold to her charms. ib., Ch. XXI, 193.
She could not help owning to herself that he was extraordinarily *distinguished-looking*. ib., Ch. XVI, 149.

ii. He put on his cloak over his *bright shining* dress. Marj. Bowen, The Rake's Progress, Ch. III, 39. (*Bright* and *shining* may also be understood as two co-ordinate adjuncts.)
Autumn ... comes when we remember nothing but clear skies, green fields, and *sweet-smelling* flowers. Dick., Pickw., Ch. XVI, 137.
Could it be that he was poor — at least, not well enough off to live at a *good-sounding* address? Temple Thurston, The City of Beautiful Nonsense, I, Ch. XVIII, 153.

---
[1]) Murray.

Note α) The following is a formation of which it would be difficult to find a parallel in Present English:

(He) won to his shameful lust | The will of my most *seeming=virtuous* queen. SHAK., Haml., I, 5, 46.

Also the participial compound in the following quotation is one of very rare occurrence:

Then slowly climb the *many=winding* way. BYRON. Childe Har., I, XX.

β) When modified by *as* or *so*, a compound consisting of an adjective and a present participle is sometimes split up into its component parts, the indefinite article being placed between them. For similar formations with respectively past participles and adjectives in *ed* see 40, Obs. I and 43, Obs. V.

That, now to me, is *as stern a looking* rogue as ever I saw. SHER., School for Scand., IV, 1, (405).
I think it is *as honest a looking* face as any in the room. ib., IV, 1.
Monstrous handsome young man that — *as fine a looking* soldier as ever I saw. THACK., Pend., I, Ch. XI, 115.

Another curious construction is that instanced by:

What *sort of looking* man is Mr. Martin? JANE AUSTEN, Emma, Ch. IV, 28. T

27. Finally we call attention to some interesting periphrastic equivalents of present participles:

a) such as are made up of the stem of the verb and the prefix *a*, the worn=down proclitic form of the Old English preposition *an* (or *on*), Compare 6, Obs. VII.

"In these compounds the word governed by *a* was originally a noun, e. g. *life, sleep, work, float,* but being often the verbal substantive of state or act, it has been in modern times erroneously taken as a verb, and used as a model for forming such adverbial phrases from any verb, as *a=wash, a=bask, a=swim, a=flaunt, a=blow, a=dance, a=run, a=stare, a=gaze, a=howl, a=tremble, a=shake, a=jump.* These are purely modern and analogical." MURRAY, s.v. *a*, prep., 11. MURRAY, calls these compounds adverbial; they are, however, mostly adnominal. Some of those mentioned above would seem to be of only rare occurrence.

Why should these words, | Writ by her hand, so set my heart *adance*? BRIDGES, Hum. of the Court, I, 707.
Fathers and sons *agaze* at each other's haggardness. G. ELIOT, Dan. Der., III, VII, Ch. L, 114.
Here the monotonous round of life was already *astir.* MAUD DIVER, Captain Desmond, V.C., Ch. I, 10.
It (sc. Oxford) is a wholly congenial one (sc. environment) to Mrs. Ward ... *athrob* with causes never desperately forlorn. Westm. Gaz., No. 7277, 16 b.
With the above compare: Accordingly they were soon *a=foot* and walking in the direction of the scene of action. DICK., Pickw., Ch. IV, 30.

b) Such as are composed of a preposition and a noun, whether uniform or not with the stem of the verb, and preceded by either the definite or indefinite article or standing by itself. The word-groups may be passive in meaning, when the noun answers to a transitive verb.

1) word-groups with the preposition *at*, always without either article, always active in meaning. They can be freely formed, but only a few are in current use.

> We may see rabbits out *at feed* on the young grass. Hog Hutchinson (Westm. Gaz., No. 6011, 2c).
> See if you can take it (sc. my handkerchief) out without my feeling it, as you saw them do, when we were *at play* this morning. Dick., Ol. Twist, Ch. IX, 94.
> He was *at study* in the cell, or *at prayer* in the Church. Waldo H. Dunn, Eng. Biogr., Ch. I, 17. (also *in study*.)
> Old Gaffer Solomons who ... had been for the last ten minutes *at watch* on his threshold, shook his head and said [etc.]. Lytton, My Novel, I, III, Ch. XXV, 197. (more frequently *on the watch*.)
> Some one was also *at watch* by that casement. ib., I, VI, Ch V, 373.
> The oldest and youngest are *at work* with the strongest. Wordsworth, A Morn. in March.

Note α) The noun may be accompanied by a modifier.

> His active genius was always *at some repair or improvement*. Lytton, My Novel, I, II, Ch. X, 123.

β) The construction with the gerund, as in the following quotation, appears to be very rare:

> When he is drunk asleep, or in his rage, Or in the incestuous pleasure of his bed; At gaming, swearing, or about some act That has no relish of salvation in 't. Shak., Haml., III, 3, 91.

2) word-groups with the preposition *in*, with the definite or indefinite article or, which is mostly the case, without either article. See also 6, Obs. VII.

> i. Those who are *in the fight* need not professions and promises but concrete and definite acts before they can dream of laying down their arms. Westm. Gaz., No. 7577, 2a.
> It appears by his (sc. the moon's) small light of discretion that he is *in the wane*. Shak., Mids., V, 1, 254. (= Modern English *on the wane*.)
> ii. Figs, all whose limbs were *in a quiver*, and whose nostrils were breathing rage, put his bottle-holder aside, and went in for the fourth time. Thack., Van. Fair, I, Ch. V, 45.
> The story ... was sure to set the table *in a roar*. R. Add. King, Ol. Goldsm., Ch. I, 4 (= *on a roar*.)
> I am all *in a tremble*. Dick., Cop., Ch 1, 4a. (also *of a tremble*.)

iii. France's greater claims are not *in dispute.* Manch. Guard., V, No. 24, 482 c.
The Opposition are surprised to find the Government *in flight* before they brought up their guns. Westm. Gaz., No. 8333, 4 a.
The reaper once more stoops to his work: the cart-horses have moved on and all are again *in motion.* Dick., Pickw., Ch. XVI, 137.
The most prominent object was a long table with a table-cloth spread on it, as if a feast had been *in preparation,* when the house and the clock all stopped together. id., Great Expect., Ch. XI, 102.
If certain writers would regard journalism and authorship in a more business-like light than they usually do, they would soon find themselves *in receipt* of larger incomes. Westm. Gaz., No. 8121, 26 b.
The comedy ... had been *in rehearsal* for a week. Frankf. Moore, The Jessamy Bride, Ch. VIII, 66.
He is always *in study,* and must not be disturbed. Lytton, My Novel, I, VII, Ch. VIII, 453. (also *at study.*)
No one who has not experienced life on two dress-shirts — one *in wear,* the other in the wash — can quite understand what this will mean to me. Punch, No. 3811, 83 a.

3) word-groups with the preposition *of,* always with the indefinite article, chiefly met with in colloquial language.
"Oh, my dear, Caractacus is jealous," says your aunt all *of a flutter.* Agn. and Eg. Casile, Diam. cut Paste, II, Ch. II, 133. (also *in a flutter.*)
I was all *of a tremble:* it was as if I had been a coat pulled by the two tails, like. G. Eliot, Sil. Marn., I, Ch. VI. 42. (also *in a tremble.*)

4) word-groups with the preposition *on,* occasionally *upon,* with the definite article or without either article. Those with the definite article, always active in meaning, are very frequent, especially in colloquial language; those without either article are often passive in meaning, i. e. when the noun answers to a transitive verb.
i. The water was in the condition described by those learned in house-wifery as 'just *on the boil'.* (?), The Harvest of Sin, 31.
It was singing now merrily ... a soft effervescent melody, something like that of a kettle *on the boil.* John Ruskin, The King of the Golden River, Ch. II.
During the eighteenth century the influence of the Church of Rome was constantly *on the decline.* Mac., Popes, (562 b).
The malady is now pronounced to be *on the decline.* Graphic, 1891, 542.
Her brute of a husband was away *on the drink and gamble.* Rid. Hag., Jess, Ch. I, 6.
The importance of the House of Commons was constantly *on the increase.* Mac., Boswell's Life of Johns., (179 b).
Bee-keeping is declining, but silk-culture is greatly *on the increase* Harmsworth Encycl. s. v. *Servia.* (Note the varied practice.)
It is undoubtedly a fact that nervous disorders are *on the increase* in all countries. Westm. Gaz., No. 5231, 10 b.

"Of course you forgot him," said Osborne still *on the laugh*. Thack., Van. Fair, I, Ch. VI, 62.
Helen was *on the look-out* for this expected guest. Thack., Pend. I, Ch. VII, 79.
Next morning we were *upon the march*. Buchanan, That Winter Night, Ch. XIII, 102.
On the march to Mafeking. Graph.
Mountain-artillery *on the march*. Ill. Lond. News, No. 3882, 41.
Everybody seemed to be busy, humming and *on the move*. Thack. Pend., I, Ch. XXXI, 340.
He was *on the prowl* for what he could pick up. Wall. Besant, Bell of St. Paul's II, 15.
Where be... your flashes of merriment, that were wont to set the table on a roar? Shak., Haml., V, 1, 210. (also *in a roar*.)
He was famous there in his student days for setting the table *on a roar*. R. Ashe King, Ol. Goldsmith, Introd., 21.
But fortune was already *on the turn*. Mac., Hist.
Fine art is at a low ebb. But the tide is *on the turn*. R. H. Patterson, Es. Hist. Art., 329.
The strength of England was *on the wane*. McCarthy, Short Hist Ch. XIII, 176. (formerly also *in the wane*.)
In every direction we find British influence *on the wane*. Sat. Rev. (Westm. Gaz., No. 5394, 1bc).
The serpent was *on the watch*. Dick., Pickw., Ch. XXXIV, 509 (Compare: *at watch*.)
Mrs. Mountain is constantly *on the whimper* when George's name is mentioned. Thack., Virg., Ch. XII, 118.

ii.° I learned to hold my hands this way, when I was *upon drill* for the militia. Goldsmith, She Stoops, II, (178).
The Gaekwar of Baroda's wonderful Pearl Carpet, now *on exhibition* at the Victoria and Albert Museum. Graph., No. 2257, 319.
To-night, therefore, sherry was *on offer*. E. F. Benson, Mrs. Ames Ch. II, 42.
°° Six hundred and fifty thousand railway workmen were *on strike*. Rev. of Rev., CXCI, 500 b.
In a company that was nearly always *on tour* in those years, he could not have learned all that he did learn about the drama. Times, Lit. Sup. 990, 9a.
The plan of the poem (sc. The Traveller) was conceived, and some of it was written, while Goldsmith was *on tramp* through Europe. R. Ashe King, Ol. Goldsmith, Ch. XIV, 158.

Note: Sometimes the noun is preceded by a possessive pronoun:
Scopolamine (sc. a kind of drug) is still *on its trial*. Athen., No. 4567, 431 c.

5) **word-groups with the preposition *under*, always without either article and always passive in meaning.**

The Workers' Homes at Colon, with Storm-Sewer *under construction*. Graph., No. 2257, 327.
His thoughts... were occupied with other matters than the topics *under discussion*. Dick., Barn. Rudge, Ch. I, 3 a.

14

When the Military Service Act was *under discussion*, it was recognized that if the people knew that it must lead to industrial conscription, they would not acquiesce in military conscription. The Nation, Vol. XX, No. 14, 490 b.

c) Such as are composed of a prepositional phrase containing a noun and a gerund, noun of action, or infinitive.

1) *in the act of* + gerund, varying with *in (the) act to* + infinitive, now more or less archaic and unusual. The latter word-group, however, has an inchoative character, i. e. *in (the) act to* is equivalent to *about to*.

> i. Solomon Gills *is in the act of seeing* what time it is by the unimpeachable chronometer. Dick., Domb., Ch. IV, 27.
> When her mother was *in the act of brushing* out the reluctant black crop, Maggie suddenly rushed from under her hands. G. Eliot, Mill on the Floss, I, Ch. IV, 20.
> He had heard the sound of the approaching vehicle when he was *in the act of undressing*. Athen., No. 4481, 245 c.
>
> ii.² She was *in the act to turn away*, as a tear dropped on his forehead. Kingsley, Westw. Ho!, Ch. III, 21 a.
> ⁰⁰ (Atreides then) his massy lance prepares | *In act to throw*. Pope, Il., III, 349. (Thus frequently in Pope.)
> Sprung from a race whose rising blood, | When stirr'd beyond its calmer mood, | And trodden hard upon, is like | The rattlesnake's, *in act to strike*, | What marvel if this worn-out trunk | Beneath its woes a moment sunk? Byron, Mazeppa, XIII.
> (She) moved away, and left me, statue-like, | *In act to render thanks*. Ten., Gard. Daught., 160.
> He gazed so long | That both his eyes were dazzled as he stood, | This way and that dividing the swift mind, | *In act to throw*. id., Morte d'Arthur, 61.
> He was *in act to fire*. Buchanan, That Winter Night, Ch. III, 35.

2) *in course of* + noun of action. The meaning is always passive.

> Not even ... the great Oxford English Dictionary, now *in course of publication*, can be implicitly trusted in matters of pronunciation. Rippmann, Sounds of Spok. Eng., 4, footnote.
> The only other monument the church contained, that to the brothers Van Evertzen, ... was still *in course of erection*. Marj. Bowen, I will maintain, I, Ch. VII, 82.
> The last item of the local programme is *in course of performance*. Flor. Barclay, The Rosary, Ch. VI. 52.

3) *in process of* followed by an active or passive gerund or by a noun of action, which may be either active or passive in meaning.

> i.⁰ The Cape Colony is *in process of revising* its law affecting the use of the motor vehicle. Il. Lond. News, No. 3866, 760 a.

Sir Edward Carson is *in process of changing* the whole conception of Ulster which has prevailed in England hitherto. Westm. Gaz., No. 6341, 1 b.

⁶⁹ Conscription, he explained, was *in the process of being abolished*, and it was always intended that it should pass away. Westm. Gaz., No. 8144, 4 b. (The use of the article seems to be exceptional.)

ii.⁰ The enemy's rear-guards ... are *in process of orderly withdrawal* to a deliberately prepared new alignment. Eng. Rev., No. 101, 377.

⁶⁹ A cowslip-ball was *in process of manufacture*. Dor. Gir., The Eternal Woman, Ch. XXVI.

Mr. Asquith ... announced that a Coalition Government was *in process of formation*. The New Age, No. 1185, 73 b.

d) such as are composed of *busy* (or *employed, engaged*) + in + gerund.

The German was *busy in washing* his hands. Lytton, Night and Morn., 129.

Mrs. Boxer was *employed in trimming* a cap. ib., 291.

Two (sc. young gentlemen) ... were *engaged in solving* mathematical problems. Dick., Domb., Ch. XII, 103.

The Past Participle in Detail.

28. The past participle of practically all transitive verbs can be freely used attributively.

As in the case of the present participle, the following quotations are roughly arranged in two groups representing a decreasing scale of the verbal principle in the participles contained in them. In those of the last group, in which alone the alphabetical arrangement has been observed, almost every trace of the verbal principle may be said to have disappeared.

i. Prodigious birth of love it is to me, | That I must love a *loathed* enemy. Shak., Rom. and Jul., I, 5, 144.

Edward stepped forward with his *drawn* sword in his hand. Scott, Mon., Ch. XXVI, 283.

Slot = the track of a *hurt* deer. Webst., Dict.

He bent forward, with *parted* mouth and straining ear, to catch their conversation. Lytton, Night and Morn., 258.

Lady Spratt had taken a *discharged* servant of Mrs. Leslie's without applying for the character. id., My Novel, II, VIII, Ch. V, 40.

"Yes," said Leonard, between his *set* teeth. ib., I, VII, Ch. XIX, 189.

Not caring to go too near the door, until the *appointed* time, Mr Pickwick crouched into an angle of the wall. Dick., Pickw., Ch. XVI, 145.

Mrs. Pott smiled sweetly on the *disturbed* Pickwickian. ib., Ch. XVIII, 156.

A *plucked* man is a dismal being in a University. Thack., Pend., I, Ch. XXI, 220.

The *spread* supper-table. Hardy, Tess, V, Ch. XXXVI, 306.

"Like her audacity!" so Netta had understood his *muttered* comment. Mrs. Ward, The Mating of Lydia, Prol., Ch. II, 36.

The Budget deficit ... has been threatening for some years to become chronic, in spite of large and unexpected excesses of actual over *estimated* revenue. Westm. Gaz., No. 6240, 2 c.

ii. But in the *beaten* way of friendship, what make you at Elsinore? Shak., Haml., II, 2, 279.
The avenue was a *chosen* place for secret meetings and *stolen* interviews. Miss Brad., Lady Audley's Secret, I, Ch. I, 5.
Happily there were others of quite another stamp; notably Colonel St. John, C. B., a genuine soldier and a *cultivated* man. Maud Diver, Desmond's Daughter, II, Ch. I, 41.
Glaucus soon found himself amidst a group of merry and *dissipated* friends. Lytton, Pomp., I, Ch. VII, 29 b.
The meat was *done* on one side only. Webst., Dict.
The handsome lady regarded me with a *fixed* look. Dick., Cop., Ch. XLI, 398a.
Burns was an *inspired* peasant. Eng. Rev., No. 111, 127.
There was Jem Rodney, a *known* poacher, and otherwise disreputable. G. Eliot, Sil. Marn., I, Ch. V, 37. (may also be placed under 29, Obs. III.)
He was ... selected by the Commander-in-Chief for the command of the regiment because of his *known* influence over the Sepoys. Times.
The *practised* eye of Clive could perceive that both the men and the horses were more powerful than those of the Carnatic. Mac., Clive, (518 b).
Expert (n) = An expert, skilful, or *practised* person. Webst., Dict.
I could see no sign of any White Boys, real or *pretended*. Emily Lawless, A Colonel of the Empire, Ch. X.
Our own was a *stolen* match. Golds., Good-nat. Man, V.
She's engaged in ... organizing shop assistants and *sweated* work-girls. Bern. Shaw, Getting Married, (227).
An excellent start has been made in raising wages in certain *sweated* trades. Westm. Gaz., No. 6423, 1 b.

Observe that some past participles, such as *distraught, forlorn*, which are used only as adjectives, have lost all their other verbal forms.

The *distraught* father had appealed to the social worker. Eng. Rev., No. 63, 384.
This casts the glamour of a *forlorn* and lost cause on the personality of Doña Rita and her lovers. Westm. Gaz., No. 8149, 13 b.

29. Obs. I. In the majority of cases the attributive past participle, so far as it is of a distinctly verbal nature, is of a momentaneous or terminative character (or aspect). Thus in most of the preceding quotations. But it may also have a durative character, i.e. it may be capable of being expanded into an adnominal clause containing a passive present participle. Compare Kern, Part. Præt., § 9.

Heaven had placed her there for the safety and protection of the *persecuted* stranger. Scott, Mon., Ch. XXVIII, 301. (= the stranger *who was being persecuted*.)
He caused one of his attendants to mount his own *led* horse. id., Ivanhoe, Ch. II, 22. (= his own horse *which was being led*.)
Ellen and I will seek apart, | The refuge of some forest cell, | There, like the *hunted* quarry, dwell, | Till on the mountain and the moor | The stern pursuit be pass'd and o'er. id., Lady, II, XXIX, 24. (= the quarry *which is being hunted*.)

Two *led* horses, which in the field always closely followed his person, were struck dead by cannon shots. Mac., Hist., VII, Ch. XX, 220.

II. The relation between the participle and the noun modified is not seldom one for which there is no parallel in the relation between any of the other forms of the verb and its object. Thus in some combinations with:

born. He never was so delighted in his *born* days. Richardson, Pamela, III, 353.¹)
You shall rue it all your *born* days. Disraeli, Viv. Grey, VI, 1, 280.)
confirmed. The Englishman is a *confirmed* grumbler at the weather. Westm. Gaz., No. 6240, 2a. (= a man whose grumbling at the weather has become *confirmed*, i. e. firmly established.)
A confirmed invalid. Murray, s. v. *confirmed*, 2
destined. The *destined* combatants returned no answer to this greeting. Scott, Fair Maid, Ch. XXXIV, 358. (the men who were *destined* to be combatants.)
A *destined* errant knight I come, | Announced by prophet sooth and old id., Lady, I, XXIV.
past. Both are past=masters in the old diplomacy. Westm. Gaz., No. 7649, 1b. (Past=master = one who has filled, or passed, the office of 'master' in a guild, civic company, freemasons' lodge, club, and, by extension, the apprenticeship to any business.)
threatened. This had the effect of averting *the threatened misfortune*. Scott, Old Mort., Ch. III, 36. (= the misfortune with or by which he was threatened.)
At last he rose up from his bed, | That he might ponder how he best might keep | *The threatened danger* from so dear a head. Morris, The Earthly Par., The Son of Crœsus, IV.
The threatened railway strike. Times, No. 1807, 662d.

Compare the following combinations with the normal relation:

Threatened men live long. Prov. (= men that are *threatened*.)
He took his post near Louvain, on the road between two *threatened* cities. Mac., Hist. VII, Ch. XX, 213.

III. Sometimes the participle has been formed from a verb of declaring; the word-group, participle + noun, corresponding to a nominative + infinitive or to an accusative + infinitive.

i. The whole world is wondering at our stupidity in being thus misled by a man who is an *admitted* rebel. Eng. Rev., No. 111, 166. (= a man who is *admitted* to be a rebel.)
The hearing of the charge against *the alleged conspirators at Pretoria* has been postponed. Times. (= the men who are *alleged* to be conspirators.)
The Santa Casa is *the reputed house* of the Virgin Mary at Nazareth. Cobham Brewer, Reader's Handbook, s. v. *Loretto*. (= the house which is *reputed* to be the house etc.)

---
¹) Murray.

ii. The former (sc. young man) [is] *an avowed admirer of your ladyship*. SHER., School for Scand., I, 4, (364). (= a man who has avowed himself to be an admirer of your ladyship.)

He instantly arrested the *confessed culprit*. Times, 1898, 552a. (= the man who had confessed himself to be the culprit, or the culprit who had confessed.)

Mr. Cavaignac has done his duty ... in instantly arresting the *confessed culprit*. Times.

Nor can I pretend to guess under what wicked delusion it is that you kiss a *declared lover*. SCOTT, Fair Maid, Ch. XXV, 261. (= a man who has declared himself to be a lover.)

Dryden generally exhibits himself in the light, if not of a *professed misogynist*, yet of one who delighted to gird at marriage. SHAW, Hist. Eng. Lit., Ch. XII, 229. (= a man who has professed himself to be a misogynist. Compare: I have *professed me* thy friend. SHAK., Oth., I, 3, 342. Compare also: a *professing misogynist* = a man who is professing to be a misogynist.)

IV. A genitive or possessive pronoun modifying the head-word of an attributive past participle may in various ways be related to the verbal notion implied in the latter. Thus especially in combinations with:

appointed. And out he went into the world, and toiled | In *his own appointed way*. JOHN HAY, The Enchanted Shirt, XIX. (= the way which he had appointed for himself.)

He had taunted the Tories with *their appointed destiny* of "stewing in Parnellite juice". Times. (= the destiny which was appointed for them.)

Before long matters may develop in such a manner that a British Ambassador may again be in *his appointed place* in Petrograd. Rev. of Rev., No. 338, 94a. (= the place to which he has been appointed.)

decided. Mrs. Sowerberry was *his decided enemy*. DICK., Ol. Twist, Ch. VI, 65. (= a person who had decided to be his enemy.)

destined. To restore her to *her destined Husband*. STEELE, Tatler, No. 58. (= the husband that was destined for her.)

However much he yearned to make complete | The tale of diamonds for *his destined boon*. TEN., Lanc. and El., 91. (= the thing which he destined to be the boon to be offered to the Queen.)

devoted. They agreed with *his devoted sister* ... as to the prudence of keeping him out of England for a time. MERED., Lord Ormont, Ch. II, 29. (= his sister who had devoted herself to him. i. e. his sister who was zealously attached to him.)

limited. I'll make so bold to call, | For 'tis *my limited service*. SHAK., Macb., II, 3, 55. (= the service to which I have been limited, i. e. appointed.)

meditated. Wringing convulsively the hand of *his meditated father-in-law*, ... the ingenuous young suitor faltered forth [etc.]. LYTTON, My Novel, II, XII, Ch. XI, 814. (= the man whom he meditated making his father-in-law.)

presumed. Mr. Cross has voted twice with the Government for every time that he has voted with *his presumed friends*. Westm. Gaz., No. 5071, 1c. (== the members who were presumed to be his friends.)

threatened. He did not see *his threatened foe*. Morris, The Earthly Par., The Man born to be King, 43a. (= *the foe with or by whom he was threatened*.)
And that weak wailing of the child, His *threatened, dreaded enemy*. ib.

V. The past participle not unfrequently seems to have the value of a present participle, or, at least, to be exchangeable for a present participle, without much change of meaning. For illustration from Shakespeare see also Abbot, Shak., Gram³, § 294.

And, gentle Puck, take this *transformed* scalp From off the head of this Athenian swain. Shak., Mids., IV, 1, 67. (= *transforming* scalp, or, perhaps, scalp *with which he has been transformed*.)
Thus ornament is but the *guiled* shore | To a most dangerous sea. id., Merch. of Ven., III, 2, 97. (= *guiling*, or, perhaps, *full of guile*.)
"Away, harlot!" muttered Clodius between his *ground* teeth. Lytton, Pomp., V, Ch.VI, 146b. (Compare *grinding teeth* = grinders = molar teeth.)
Do we not while away moments of inanity or *fatigued* waiting by repeating some trivial movement or sound? G. Eliot, Sil. Marn., I, Ch. II, 15. (= *fatiguing*, or, perhaps, *full of fatigue*.)
With *hung* head and tottering steps she instinctively chose the shortest cut to that home. Mrs. Gask., Mary Barton, Ch. XX, 216.

Thus also in the following quotations from Shakespeare, in which the participle appears to indicate an inclination, a habit or an inherent capability to do whatever is expressed by the verb.

It is *twice blest*; | It blesseth him that gives and him that takes. Merch. of Ven., IV, 1, 186. (According to the Clar. Press editors = *endowed with double blessing*. Compare: In its injurious effects on both parent and child a bad system is twice *cursed*, a good system is twice *blessed* — it blesses him that trains and him that's trained. Spencer, Educ., Ch. III, 92b.)
Then, in despite of *brooded* watchful day, | I would into thy bosom pour my words. King John, III, 3, 52.
I was never *curst*; I have no gift at all in shrewishness. Mids., III, 2, 300. (= *given to cursing*.)
Here she comes, *curst* and sad. ib., III, 2, 439.
Yet time serves wherein you may . . . Revenge the jeering and *disdain'd* contempt Of this proud king. Henry IV. A, 1, 3, 183.

Conversely the transferring of the present participle from its proper subject may result in its assuming the value of a past participle.

I have seen the day That I have worn a visor, and could tell A *whispering* tale in a fair lady's ear. Shak., Rom. and Jul., I, 5, 27.
An old gentleman lying in a tiny room . . . his hands crossed upon his breast in *unbreaking* sleep. Temple Thurston, City of Beaut. Nons., III, Ch. XVI, 356.

VI. Some adjectival past participles formed from transitive verbs have the value of an active perfect present participle with pregnant meaning, so that the verb from which they have been formed may also be considered intransitive through having absorbed its object. Thus:

drunk(en) = having drunk (too much and, consequently, intoxicated), as in *the man is drunk(en), a drunken man.* Compare the Latin *homo potus.*

learned = having learned (much), as in *a learned man.*

mistaken = having mistaken (something), as in *the mistaken multitude, he is mistaken.*

read = having read (much), as in *to be read in the classics.*

Thus also *drawn* = having drawn (the sword), now only archaic, as in:

Why are you *drawn?* SHAK., Temp., II, I, 308.

VII. Sometimes, especially in SHAKESPEARE, we find past participles with the value of adjectives in *able* or *ible.* Compare ABBOT, Shak. Gram.³, § 375; FRANZ, Shak. Gram.², § 662.

Inestimable stones, *unvalued* jewels. Rich. III, I, 4, 27. (= *invaluable.*)
All *unavoided* is the doom of destiny. ib., IV, 4, 217. (= *inevitable.*)
With all *imagined* speed. Merch. of Ven., III, 4, 52. (= *imaginable.*)
You have displaced the mirth, broke the good meeting, | With most *admired* disorder. SHAK., Macb., III, 4, 110. (= *admirable* in the now obsolete sense of *to be wondered at,* as in: But, howsoever, strange and *admirable.* id., Mids., V, 1, 27.)
Full many a gem of purest ray serene, | The dark *unfathom'd* caves of ocean bear. GRAY, Elegy, XIV.
Mary was an *easily satisfied* little person. Eng. Rev., No., 61, 89.

Conversely adjectives in *able* or *ible* are sometimes equivalent to present participles.

There was a fire half-way up the chimney and roaring and crackling with a sound that of itself would have warmed the heart of any reasonable man. This was *comfortable,* but this was not all. DICK., Pickw., Ch. XIV, 120.
This was an *uncomfortable* coincidence. id., Cop., Ch. V, 35a.

30. Comparatively unusual is the attributive use of the past participle of verbs governing a prepositional object. In this case the preposition is regularly retained. Such a word-group is, indeed, frequent enough in post-position to its head-word, but in this case it is felt as (a constituent of) an undeveloped clause, i. e. the participle is fully apprehended as a verbal form. Some combinations are, however, of general currency; some appear especially when furnished with the negativing prefix *un.* See also 33, and compare JESPERSEN, Mod. Eng. Gram., II, 14.341; and DEUTSCHBEIN, System der neuenglischen Syntax, § 43, 3, Anm. 2.

Then there were the *much-talked-of* perils of the Tappaan-zee. WASH. IRV., Dolf Heyl. (STOF., Handl., I, 124).

He heard his dear and his *doted-on* Mary Anne say Do you think I could care anything for that lame boy?" Lytton, Life of Lord Byron, 14 a.
Was he not ... the most brilliant and most *sought after* young man in all England? El. Glyn, Halcyone, Ch. XI, 97.
They were content to pay the European trader the *agreed-upon* price. Westm. Gaz., No. 6483, 7 a.
The *longed-for* just and democratic peace. Rev. of Rev., No. 338, 93 a.

31. As to intransitive subjective verbs the attributive use of the past participle is confined to such as express a change of place or state. Even with this restriction the application has only a limited currency, some participles of this description hardly admitting of being employed attributively. Thus we could not say *a walked passenger, *a laughed girl, *a barked dog, *a slept child, these verbs implying no change of place or state.

Nor do we meet with such combinations as *a died man (compare however, a deceased man), *the started train, *a come guest, etc., although here there is a distinct reference to a change of some description or another. Also in some of the following quotations, marked with an asterisk, the attributive use of the participle has a somewhat incongruous effect. The fact is that the attributive use of these participles is mostly attended by a distinct fading of the verbal principle. Total loss of this principle may even render possible the attributive use of participles which do not imply any change of place or state. Thus in *a travelled man* (= a man experienced in travel), *a travelled air* (= an air wearing signs of travel). Thus also in such compounds as *a well-behaved man, a plain-spoken man*, which express a permanent habit or cast of mind. See 39, b, 2, and compare Wilmanns, Deutsche Gram., III, I, § 59; Deutschbein, System der neuengl. Synt., § 59.

The student may here be reminded of the fact that verbs which express a change of place or state can be easily told by their being conjugated in Dutch and German by, respectively, zijn and sein.

It may finally be observed that attributive past participles formed from intransitive verbs are regularly placed before their headwords, except in such combinations as *Mr. Jones, deceased, retired*, etc., in which the participle may also be understood as an undeveloped clause.

Here follow some quotations illustrating the attributive use of:

assembled. He was shortly afterwards elected, by the unanimous voice of the *assembled* company, into the tap-room chair. DICK., Pickw., Ch. XVI, 139.

deceased. They were contented to wish success to the son of a *deceased* presbyterian leader. SCOTT, Old Mort., Ch. III, 30.

He lived in chambers which had once belonged to his *deceased* partner. DICK., Christm. Car., I.

departed. Their talk was often about the *departed* mother. THACK., Pend., II, Ch. XXIX, 321.

escaped. Nobody thought for a moment that he was the *escaped* convict about whom such a stir had been made. Titbits.

Escaped prisoners. Morning Leader.

faded. The fields with *faded* flowers did seem to mourne. SPENSER, Colin Clout, 27.

fallen. The *fallen* and unfortunate King of France. DICK., Two Cities, III, Ch. I, 276.

foregone. The result was a *foregone* conclusion. PHILIPS, Mrs. Bouverie, 37.

moulder'd. A *moulder'd* church. TEN., En. Ard., 4.

retired. He was a *retired* servant, with a large family come to him in his old age. THACK., Sam. Titm., Ch. VII, 82.

returned. What would he say to the *returned* convict? DICK., Pickw., Ch. VI, 52.

shrunken. He had rather a *shrunken* appearance. G. ELIOT, Mill, II, Ch. IV, 154.

strayed. pin-fold. sheep-fold, but also a 'pound' for *strayed* cattle. Note to MILT., Comus, 7 (Clar. Press).

sunk. The *sunk* corners of her mouth. HARDY, Tess, V, Ch. XXXVI, 314.

sunken. He met her gaze with those yearning *sunken* eyes. MRS. WARD, Rob. Elsm., II, 266.

travelled. The phenomenon of *travelled* or perched blocks is also a common one in all glacier countries. WALLACE, Isl. Life, VII, 106.[1]

Like many a *travelled* man, (he) was not master of the English language. G. ELIOT, Brother Jacob, Ch. III, (543).

32. Obs. I. Sometimes the attributive past participle corresponds to a reflexive verb, or to an intransitive verb that goes back to a reflexive verb. Compare WILMANNS, Deutsche Gram., III, I, § 59, 2.

> Where is this *perjured* dancing girl of yours? ANSTEY, A Fallen Idol, Prol., 14. (from *to perjure oneself*.)
>
> Acting on information volunteered by a *surrendered* Boer, Captain Valentine left Pretoria this evening for the purpose of capturing a large herd of cattle. Times. (from *to surrender* < *to surrender oneself*.)

II. Only the participles of such intransitives as express a passing into another state appear to be capable of being used predicatively. In this application they are practically pure adjectives.

> Sir Henry came pottering in — oh, so *shrunken* in appearance. SARAH GRAND, Our Man. Nature., 31.

[1] MURRAY.

His cheeks were *sunken* and his eyes unnaturally large. Dick., Chuz. Ch. XXIX, 237 a.

The predicative use of participles formed from other intransitives, as in the following quotation, appears to be rare. Compare, however, 29 Obs. VI.

His valet-butler found him already *bathed*, and ready for a cup of tea at half past seven. Wells, The Soul of a Bishop, 89.

33. Derivatives with the negativing prefix *un* are freely formed from most adjectival past participles corresponding to objective verbs. Such as correspond to subjective verbs seem to be rare. Compare also Wilmanns, Deutsche Gram., III, 1, § 59, 4.

i.° The house was several centuries old, with a long *unbroken* family history. Sarah Grand, Our Manifold Nat., 31.
And thy sharp lightning in *unpractised* hands ! Scorches and burns our once serene domain. Keats, Hyp., I, 62.
White as the driven *unsullied* snow. Annie Besant, Autobiography.
Religion! what treasure *untold* ! Resides in that heavenly word! Cowper, Alex. Selk., IV.
Small dealers as they were, and grimy and *unwashen*, they had their regular avocations. John Oxenham, A Simple Beguiler.
⁰ Where was he to date from? Not from home, or the *unheard-of* arrival of letters there would arouse suspicion. ib.
One Saturday afternoon, at dusk, great consternation was occasioned in the Castle by the *unlooked-for* announcement of Mr. Dombey as a visitor. Dick., Domb., Ch. XI, 94.

ii. My heart *untravell'd* fondly turns to thee. Goldsm., Trav., 8.

34. Obs. I. Sometimes we find these derivatives with privative *un* followed by the preposition *by* (in Older English and, archaically, in Present English *of*) denoting a relation of agency, which shows that some verbal force may cling to them. It may, however, be observed that the word-group past participle + *by* (or *of*) + name of agency may sometimes also be understood as a kind of unit that has the value of an adjective denoting a state, to which *un* is affixed as a negativing prefix.

i. The board was *uncovered by a cloth*. Scott, Ivanhoe, Ch III, 24 (= bare.)
The arrival of the Force was quite *unexpected by* the public. Times, No. 1972, 1 a.
She thought herself *unloved by* him. Rich. Bagot., The Just and the Unjust, II, Ch. II, 43 (T.).
Thou merry, laughing sprite! ' With spirits feather-light, ' *Untouched by* sorrow and *unsoiled by* sin. Thom. Hood, Parental Ode.
A secluded region, *untrodden* as yet *by* tourist or landscape painter. Hardy, Tess, I, Ch. II, 10.

ii. And to this end (he) Had made the pretext of a hindering wound, That he might joust *unknown of* all. Ten. Lanc. and El., 581.

II. Also when no prepositional phrase with *by* (or *of*) follows, the verbal force may stand forth quite distinctly in such derivatives.
She had sat the whole evening through in the same chair without occupation, not speaking, and *unspoken to*. Trol., The Warden, Ch. VI, 80.

Thus even when used attributively, as in

If, after all, the *unhoped-for* son should be born, the money would have been thrown away. G. Eliot, Dan. Der., I, II, Ch. XV, 236.

35. The ordinary adjective intensives may also be found before adjectival past participles. Thus:

most. "Goldsmith," says Thackeray, "is the *most loved* of all authors." R. Ashe King, Ol. Goldsmith, Ch. XIII, 153.
Home Rule and the Insurance Act . . . remain the *most talked-of* subjects in the contest. Westm. Gaz., No. 6377, 2b.

much. "Tommy" looks far fitter . . . than the *much vaunted* soldiers of the War Lord. Graph., No. 2339, 439c.

rather. The tenth anniversary of the Tariff Reform movement . . . was kept in a *rather chastened* mood by the stalwarts of the movement. Westm. Gaz., No. 6228, 1c.

so. Our study is better than ever this year — faces the South with two huge windows — and oh! so *furnished*. Jean Webster, Daddy-Long-Legs, 164.

too. To-day he was *too roused* and angry to risk the chance of meeting . . M. de Witt. Marj. Bowen, I will maintain, II, Ch. VII, 189.

very. It may well be supposed that men who wrote thus to each other, were not *very guarded* in what they said of each other. Mac., Fred., (691 b).
He had a large, sallow, ugly face, *very sunken* eyes, and a gigantic head. Dick., Pickw., Ch. XVI, 140.
This is a *very interrupted* letter. Jean Webster, Daddy-Long-Legs, 42.

Note: Like adjectival present participles (22 Note), adjectival past participles are but rarely found in the terminational superlative. Instances of the terminational comparative appear to be non-existent.

Good fortune then! | To make me blest or *cursed'st* among men. Shak., Merch. of Ven., II, 1, 47.
Ay, be it the *forlornst* bodily tabernacle in which immortal soul ever dwelt. Miss Mulock, Noble Life, Ch. XII.¹)
The unfragrant and insanitary waif of its (sc. that of the Thames) *rottenest* refuse, the incomparable Rogue Riderhood, must always hold a chosen place among the choicest of our selectest acquaintance. Swinburne, Ch. Dickens, 61.
There never were such times for the working classes, and to recommend thrift to them as the *blessedest* of virtues. The New Statesman, No. 96, 433a.
The *staidest* opinions have modified or seek correction. Eng. Rev., No.103, 544a.
We couldn't see a thing, and then I got *loster* and *loster*. Hugh Walpole, Jeremy, Ch. X, 4, 261.

36. Some adjectival past participles, when used predicatively, may take a prepositional object like ordinary adjectives.

¹) Murray.

We found Ned panting and *bathed* in perspiration. Saiti, Old Chap.
The nation *unbroken to* such servitude began to struggle fiercely. Mac., Hist.
The book is *crammed with* matter, but never *burdened with* it. Bookman,
No. 316, 125 b.
Cicero never spoke better. Once more, and you are *confirmed in* assurance for
ever. Goldsmith, She Stoops, II, (189).
Somerset was very little *known to* the public. Mac., Hist., II, Ch. VIII, 98.
Marvell'd Sir David of the Mount; ' Then *learn'd in* story, 'gan recount ' Such
chance had happ'd of old. Scott, Marm., IV, XXII.
Sharp practitioners *learned in* the wiles of insolvency and bankruptcy. D.,
Little Dorrit, Ch. VI, 30 b.
I did not think you had been *read in* these matters. Congreve, Love for Love,
III, 4, (255).
He is deeply *read in* the writers, ancient and modern, who have treated on the
subject. Wash. Irv., Sketch-Bk., No. 21, 194.

Note *a)* Observe that *known to* varies with *known by*, in which the
verbal principle re-asserts itself.

Two women whom he loved and injured are *known by* every reader of books
so familiarly that if we had seen them, or if they had been relatives of our own,
we scarcely could have known them better. Thack., Eng. Hum., I, 41.

β) Sometimes an adverb apparently has the value of a prepositional object.
I found him *garrulously given*. Ten., Talking Oak., VI. (= *given to garrulity*).

37. When totally or partially converted into a noun, the past participle, to all appearance, never loses its verbal character entirely.

i. Some day she would . . . come back — to those *beloveds* who had given her
up — so tenderly. Mrs. Ward, Delia Blanchflower, I, Ch. VII, 189.
The Prison Chaplain entered the *condemned's* cell for the last time. Westm.
Gaz., No. 4983, 9 a.

ii.° It was at once our duty and privilege . . . to raise *the fallen*, seek *the lost*
and restore *the outcast*. Mrs. Wood, The Channings, Ch. I, 3.
The *self-taught* are keen and quick observers. Lytton, My Novel, I, VII,
Ch. VII, 449.
We justified our conquest to ourselves by taking away the character of the
conquered. Froude, Oceana, Ch. III, 43.

°° I nle into the old pew first, like a guarded captive brought to a *condemned*
service. Dick., Cop., Ch. IV, 26 b.
To the *Allied* cause the situation is more than hopeful. Eng. Rev., No. 74, 193.

°°° Ourselves will hear The accuser and the accused freely speak. Shak., Rich.
II, I, 1, 17.
Would God's anointed, accountable to God alone, pay homage to the
clamorous multitude? Mac., Bacon, (350a).

38. Some past participles may assume the function of prepositions. Thus in:

It's gone half *past* six. Mrs. Adynslow, For his Sake, I, Ch. III, 50.
He stayed till *past* two o'clock.
'Tis now *struck* twelve. Shak., Haml. I, 1, 7.

Now she knows she's to be married, *turned* Michaelmas. G. ELIOT, Sil. Marn. II, Ch. XVII, 132.

Note. *Provided* seems to be the only past participle that may assume the function of a conjunction. It is often found connected with *that* For illustration see Ch. XVII, 71. Observe also that it is sometimes either preceded or followed by *always*, in like manner as the Dutch *mits* is often connected with *altijd*.

i. Now my idea is that, if Englishmen advance the money for railway construction and other work, a certain proportion of the English money thus lent should be spent in buying English goods — *always provided*, of course, *that* we can supply them as cheap and good as any of our competitors. Rev. of Rev., No. 190, 369 b.

ii. He therefore informed them that he should not take it ill of them if they made their peace with the dynasty, *provided always* that they were prepared to rise in insurrection as soon as he should call upon them to do so. MAC., Hist, VII, Ch. XVIII, 1.

This question is likely to drag on for many months, *provided always* that Mr. Redmond can be induced to believe that Mr. Asquith is not playing with him. Westm. Gaz., No. 5243, 16 c.

39. Past participles enter into combination with various other parts of speech, forming compounds with them in which the verbal idea appears in various degrees of prominence. Partly depending on this and partly also in harmony with the supposed closeness of the connexion, these compounds are written in separation, with a hyphen or in combination.

a) with nouns, in some adverbial relation mostly one of agency. Instances with intransitive verbs seem to be rare. Although these compounds with participles of transitive verbs can be freely formed of any suitable combination, they are not common in colloquial language.

i.º At length Maria Lobbs, being more strenuously urged by the *love-worn* little man, turned away her head, and whispered her cousin to say . . . that she felt much honoured by Mr. Pipkin's addresses. DICK., Pickw., Ch. XVII, 152.

But Enid fear'd his eyes, | Moist as they were, *wine-heated* from the feast. TEN., Ger. and En., 351.

A luckier or a bolder fisherman | . . . did not breathe | For leagues along that *breaker-beaten* coast. id., En. Ard., 51.

The level rays poured dazzling between the tree-trunks; turning the *dust-ridden* air into a mist of dusky gold. E. F. BENSON, Arundel, Ch. I, 7.

The bank sloped away to a stream crossed by a *moss-covered* bridge. MARJ. BOWEN, The Rake's Progress, Ch. II, 17.

I believe he's spent his first few years in some *God-forsaken* hole. MAUD DIVER, Desmond's Daughter, II, Ch. II, 51.

The soil of an imagination like that of Keats is magically sensitive to *chance-blown* seed. Bookman, No. 316, 122 b.

The whole of this ... Res Publica ... has been seized by a peer-ridden or capitalist-controlled Parliament. ib., No. 316, 124b.
The railways are *State-owned*. Westm. Gaz., No. 6435, 2a.

Compare with the above compounds the combination illustrated by the following quotation:

The carpet and curtains were *faded by the sun*. LYTTON, My Novel, I, V, Ch. XXV, 288. (= *sun-faded*).

Helen Pendennis was a *country-bred* woman. THACK., Pend., I, Ch. VII, 81.
The master of that ship | Enoch had served in ... | Came ... Reporting of his vessel *China-bound*. TEN., En. Ard., 122.
Her pore (= poor) mother, not being a *Scripture-read* woman, made a mistake at his christening. TH. HARDY, Far from the Madding Crowd, Ch. X, 91.
Tongue-tied timidity is the best proof of sincerity. FRANK HARRIS, The Women of Shak., Ch. III, 54.

ii. No busy steps the grass-grown footway tread. GOLDSMITH, Des. Vil., 127.
He extended both hands to the *home-come* warrior. W. J. LOCKE, The Rough Road, Ch. XIX, 238.
There was not a shade of difference between ... the learned Scribes and the *world-travelled* warriors. CHESTERTON (Il. Lond. News, No. 3373, 48c).

Note. Thus we may also apprehend compounds with *self*, such as *self-made*, which admits of being analysed into *made by (one's) self*.

Helen says you are *self-taught*. LYTTON, My Novel, I, VII, Ch. XIX, 489.
Regularly, every morning after he had finished his breakfast, she performed her *self-appointed* task. JACK LONDON, The Call of the Wild, Ch. IV, 123.

b) with adverbs, the participle corresponding to

1) a transitive verb. The adverb may be one of

α) quality. Such compounds can almost be formed ad libitum. See MURRAY, s. v. ill, 7. Note especially *ill-bred, well-bred, ill-advised, ill-disposed, well-disposed*.

An *ill-advised* and unfortunate insurrection. WORDSWORTH.
Mark many *rude-carved* crosses by the path. BYRON, Childe Har., I, XXI.
You are an honest man, and *well-affected* to our family. LYTTON, Eugene Aram, Ch. IX, 60.
The influence of the season seems to extend itself to the very waggon, whose slow motion across the *well-reaped* field is perceptible only to the eye. DICK., Pickw., Ch. XVI, 137.
There were a few *well-disposed* natives who saw them and were sorry for them. MCCARTHY, Short Hist., Ch. XIII, 187.
Nor can I ever be persuaded that the *so-called* hardening is necessary in a world which ... requires softening down rather than stiffening up. Eng. Rev., No. 113, 343.
Tennyson pieces *exquisitely observed* detail into a *delicately wrought* picture. Bookman, No. 316, 122b.

β) degree. He saw the Jew with his *half-closed* eyes. DICK., Ol. Twist, Ch. IX, 89.

The street of labour before the war was a street of starvation — of *badly-fed* women and *under-fed* children. The New Statesman. No. 250, 372a.

γ) place. He came up with *outstretched* hand. THACK., Pend., I. Ch. XXX, 321.
He exhorted them to show their *inbred* superiority as Dorians. GROTE, Greece, V, 237.
Jane arrested her with an odd, shy motion like that of an *out-flung* claw. AGN. and EG. CASTLE, Diam. cut Paste, II, Ch. I, 117.

δ) time. Local tales and superstitions thrive best in these sheltered *long-settled* retreats. WASH. IRV., Sketch-Bk., XXXII, 365.
This is, perhaps the reason why we seldom hear of ghosts except in our *long-established* Dutch communities. ib.
The *before-mentioned* hamper. DICK., Pickw., Ch. IV, 33.
It is not our purpose to describe this *oft-travelled* tour. THACK., Pend., II, Ch. XIX, 199.
The "Ode to Psyche" was not ... the *last composed*, but the first of the five famous Odes. Bookman, No. 316, 122b.
But if it was the *earliest composed* [etc.] ib.
She (sc. Japan) watches Imperialism trampling the *new-born* Russian State. Eng. Rev., No. 113, 373.

For further instances of participial compounds with *new* see especially JESPERSEN, Mod. Eng. Gram., II, 15.31. Observe also that in these compounds *new* varies with *newly*. Thus JESPERSEN, quotes:

Some bright spirit *newly born*. SHELLEY.
The *newly married* pair. THACK., Pend.

Constructions like that illustrated by the following quotations seem to be rare:

The master told me to light a fire in the *many-weeks-deserted* parlour. EM. BRONTË, Wuth. Heights, Ch. XIII, 69b.
She that ever kept | The *one-day-seen* Sir Lancelot in her heart. TEN., Lanc. and El., 742.

2) an intransitive verb. Instances are not very common, being practically confined to certain fixed combinations. Of particular interest are the numerous compounds with *behaved* and *spoken*. This latter participle has the value of the adjective *speeched*, formed from the noun *speech;* but compounds with *speeched* are, apparently, non-existent. See also **31**, and compare JESPERSEN, Mod. Eng. Gram., II, 15.36.

A very *pretty-behaved* gentleman. SHER., Riv., 5, 1, (275).
Hussy — an *ill-behaved* women or girl. WEBST. Dict.
David was very *well-behaved* to his mother. G. ELIOT, Broth. Jac., Ch. I, (473).

Lord Roberts declares he has the *best-behaved* army in the world. Times
I don't consider myself at all a *badly-behaved* woman. BERN. SHAW,
Overruled (Eng. Rev., No. 54, 182)
Compare: Some rich peasants in a village in Brunswick used to meet at
the village inn about the time *well-conducted* people entered the church
STOU., Handl. I, 58.

ii. The Captain . . . was at least a *civil-spoken* gentleman. LYTTON, My
Novel, I, III, Ch. X, 161.
Mrs. Hazeldean, though an excellent woman, was rather a bluff,
plain-spoken one. ib., I, III, Ch. XIII, 171.
He's a nice, *fair-spoken*, pretty young man. THACK., Pend., I, Ch. V, 64
A *free-spoken* young man. FLOR. MARRYAT, A Bankrupt Heart, II, 75

Thus also *outspoken*, as in:

She had always been remarkably frank and *outspoken*. EDNA LYALL,
We Two, I, 43.

iii) Again the *long-fallen* column sought the skies. GOLDSM., Trav., 136
In honour of this toast Mr. Weller imbibed, at a draught, at least
two thirds of the *newly-arrived* pint. DICK., Pickw., Ch. XXIII, 206
"I must have gone about the world with closed eyes," was the remark
of a *well-travelled* man after he had completed only half the Course
Eng. Rev., No. 111, Advert

Note *α)* In some compounds the adverb stands after the
participle.

Those years of too early and too heavy toil . . . made her (sc. Octavia
Hill) prematurely *grown-up*. Athen., No. 4465, 515 b.

β) Sometimes the compound contains two adverbs.

Shelley's "Hymn to Intellectual Beauty" . . . is *more long-drawn-out*
Bookman, No. 316, 123 a.

c) **with adjectives**,

1) such as denote a place of origin.

A *foreign-born* resident of a country. WEBST., Dict. s. v. alien.
The great majority are *Dutch born* and Dutch speaking. Times,
No. 2003, 447 a.
The percentage among the "*foreign-born*" is higher than among the native
born. WELLS, The Future in America, 156.)

In some combinations of a similar nature the origin-denoting word
is rather adverbial than adjectival. Thus in:

She was a stout, round, *Dutch-built* vessel. WASH. IRV., The Storm
Ship (STOF., Handl. I, 84).
The Opposition propose a *Canadian built* and *Canadian manned* Navy
Westm Gaz., No. 6101, 1 b.
American-made boots, *foreign manufactured* goods. Times.

2) such as denote the result of the action implied in the
participle.

---
¹ JESPERSEN, Mod. Eng. Gram., II, 15.32.

Thou sure and *firm-set* earth, | Hear not my steps, which way they walk.
Shak., Macb., II, 1, 56.
Clearshaven was he as a priest. Longf., Tales of a Ways. Inn. Prel.
He purchased a sufficiency of *ready-dressed* ham. Dick., Ol. Twist,
Ch. VIII, 82.
Breakfast . . was *ready-laid* in tempting display. id., Pickw., Ch. V, 39.
His small bundle of clothes was *ready-packed*. G. Eliot, Brother Jacob,
Ch. I, (487).

40. Obs. I. When modified by such adverbs of degree as *as, so*, the component
parts of the compound may be separated by the indefinite article.
See especially A. Schmidt, Shak. Lex., I. For similar formations
with respectively present participles and adjectives in *ed* see 26, c.
Note β; and 43, Obs. V.

There's no man is so vain | That would refuse so *fair an offer'd* chain.
Shak., Com. of Er., III, 2, 186.
I hold myself *as well a born* man as thyself. Scott, Abbot, Ch. XV, 140.

II. Occasionally we find a group of two participles connected by *and*
used attributively. Some of these compounds are quite common.

He would certainly have struck a stranger as a *born and bred* gentleman.
Em. Brontë, Wuth. Heights, Ch. XIV, 75b.
Their speculative faculties seem only to be able to run into *cut-and-dried*
channels. Ei. Glyn, The Reason why, Ch. XII, 109.
The rather stout lady was no other than the quondam relict and sole
executrix of the *dead-and-gone* Mr. Clarke. Dick, Pickw., Ch. XXVII, 240.
(*Dead* has the value of an adjectival participle.)

The Participles compared with allied Forms.

41. Attributive present participles are distinguished from attributive
gerunds by being differently stressed: word-groups with the
former having double stress (often called level or even stress),
those with the latter having strong stress on the gerund and
weak-stress on the head-word. Thus *falling sickness* (= illness
in which the patient falls) has double stress, while *training-
college* has strong stress on *training* and weak stress on *college*.
In some cases the nature of the verbal in *ing* in these compounds is uncertain, causing the stressing of the word-group
to be variable. Thus, for example, *reforming days, retiring
pension, working man*. For further discussion and illustration
see Ch. XXIII, § 13, Obs. VII; and Gerund, 15. Compare
also Mätzner, Eng. Gram.², III, 73.

42. Attributive past participles should not be confounded with
adjectives derived from nouns by means of the suffix *ed*, such
as *aged, crooked, gifted, skilled, talented*, etc.

Thus also *stringed*, as in *stringed instruments*, which is sometimes erroneously given as a variant of the participle *strung*. But *bended*, as in *on his bended knees*, is a real participle; in Middle English it was superseded by *bent*. (See MURRAY, s.v. *bended*.)

In these formations the suffix is distinctly used with the sense of *possessing, provided with, characterized by* (whatever is expressed by the preceding word or word-group). This meaning is considerably weakened in certain words similarly formed, such as *bigoted, crabbed, dogged*. See MURRAY, s.v. *-ed*, suffix, 2.

Some forms in *ed* admit of a twofold interpretation; i.e. they may be apprehended as adjectives derived from nouns by means of the suffix *ed*, or as past participles of verbs which are derived from nouns.

I found this a *limited* source of information. SCOTT, Old Mort., Ch. I, 21.
There were great, round, pot-bellied baskets of chestnuts, *shaped* like the waistcoats of jolly old gentlemen. DICK, Christm. Car., III, 60. (best understood as formed from the noun *shape*).
From earliest times the Waganda have been a *clothed* people. Graph., No. 2271, 962 b.

Sometimes there is an adjective with the prefix *be*, similarly furnished with the adjectival suffix *ed*, mostly adding to the notion expressed by the above adjectives that of surrounding, covering or bedaubing. See MURRAY, s.v. prefix *be*, 6. Also these forms can in many cases be regarded as participles, i. e. when there is a verb with the prefix *be* used in all the forms of an ordinary verb. When, however, there are no such variations, the form in *ed* is best considered as an adjective. MURRAY, accordingly, somewhat misses the point in observing that "some are used only in the passive voice".

In the high-road, he saw a man he knew, a member of his club, top-hatted and *befrocked*. TEMPLE THURSTON, The City of Beautiful Nonsense, Ch. XI, 79.
He was in a state of *befogged* memory. W. J. LOCK., The Rough Road, Ch. XVII, 204.
Encouraged by certain *be-monocled* war-correspondents, they picture us all grouped round Salonica. Westm. Gaz., No. 8179, 11 a.

43. Obs. I. Adjectives formed from nouns by means of the suffix *ed* are very common, may indeed be freely formed of any noun, although only a limited number have found general currency. Thus *a chimneyed house, a storied room, a hatted man* and a host of other such formations would hardly be tolerated, and some writers have found occasion to exclaim in rather strong terms against the free coining of such adjectives, which poets in particular are apt to indulge in. Thus JOHNSON, commenting on GRAY's poetry writes, "There has of late arisen a practice of giving to adjectives derived from substantives, the termination of participles; such as *the cultured plain,* ... but I was sorry to see, in the lines of a scholar like GRAY, *the honeyed spring*"

COLERIDGE delivers himself in Table-Talk, 171 as follows, "I regret to see that vile and barbarous vocable *talented* ... The formation

of a participle passive from a noun is a licence that nothing but
a very peculiar felicity can excuse".

DEAN ALFORD appears to have been positively shocked by the
frequent occurrence of the adjectives in *ed*. In his The Queen's
English §§ 218—21 he registers a vehement diatribe against the
adjectives *talented* and *gifted*, words which every educated English=
man, himself perhaps included, uses every day in literary com=
positions. He writes à propos of *talented* and *gifted*, "We seem
rather unfortunate in our designations for men of ability. For
another term by which we describe them, *talented*, is about as bad
as possible. What is it? It looks like a participle. From what
verb? Fancy such a verb as *to talent!* COLERIDGE sometimes cries
out against this newspaper word and says, 'Imagine other participles
formed by this analogy, and men being said to be *pennied, shillinged*,
or *pounded*. He perhaps forgot that, by an equal abuse, men are
said to be *moneyed* men, or, as we sometimes see it spelt (as if
the word itself were not bad enough without making it worse by
false analogy) *monied*".

"Another formation of this kind, *gifted*, is at present very much
in vogue. Every man whose parts are to be praised, is *a gifted*
author, speaker or preacher. Nay sometimes a very odd transfer
is made, and *the pen* with which the author writes is said to be
gifted, instead of himself".

Among the following instances some may, in a manner, be regarded,
as nonce-formations. For illustration from SHAKESPEARE see ABBOT,
Shak. Gram., § 294.

He had not the self-command necessary for addressing his brother with
a sufficiently *honeyed* accent. G. ELIOT, Brother Jacob, Ch. I, (488).
Many a night from yonder *ivied* casement, ere I went to rest, | Did I
look on great Orion sloping slowly to the west. TEN, Lock. Hall, 7.
Dixon creeping past the door of the sick room on his *stockinged* feet, could
hear the moaning. MRS. WARD, The Mating of Lydia, I, Ch. IV, 93.
Can *storied* urn or animated bust | Back to its mansion call the fleeting
breath? GRAY, Elegy, 41.
It (sc. Windsor Castle) is a place full of *storied* and poetical associations.
WASH. IRV., Sketch Bk., X, 82.
The *verandahed* bungalow. GALSWORTHY, Beyond, III, Ch. VI, 275.
Brick houses with *walled* gardens behind them. G. ELIOT, Felix Holt,
I, Ch. III, 64.
Within a *windowed* niche of that high hall | Sate Brunswick's fated chieftain.
BYRON, Childe Har., III, XXIII.

Adjectives of this kind may, of course, also be formed from com=
pounds, e. g. *great-coated* from *great-coat*.

About an hour afterwards (Henry) came *booted* and *great-coated* into the
room. JANE AUSTEN, North. Abbey, Ch. XXVI, 202.

11. Like ordinary adjectives the forms in *ed* may take the privative
suffix *un*; e. g.: *unskilled*.

She that has that (sc. chastity), is clad in complete steel, / And like a quiver'd nymph, with arrows keen | May trace huge forests, and *unharbour'd* heaths. MILTON, Comus, 423.

They descended the flights of *uncarpeted* wooden stairs and passed outside his door. TEMPLE THURSTON, The City of Beautiful Nonsense, Ch. XVI, 122.

Do you think I am absolutely *ungifted* that way? ib., I, Ch. XVIII, 154.

III. Also such compounds as *clear-headed, good-natured, kind-hearted, strong-minded*, etc., in which an adjective and a noun are joined together by the adjectival formative *ed*, are very numerous and frequent, and can be made of practically any suitable combination.

This is the *even-handed* dealing of the world. DICK., Christm. Car.^s, II, 51.

A creepered, *plain-fronted* little brick house. GALSWORTHY, Beyond, Ch. X, 227.

The Russian Democracy in its *single-handed* struggle with Prussian Junkers. Rev. of Rev., No. 338, 93a.

Also *party-coloured*, in England more usually spelled *parti-coloured* or *particoloured*, belongs here, *party* being an adjective adapted from the French parti, Latin partitus = divided.

Similarly such combinations as *half-hearted, double-edged* may be included among compounds of this description.

I always say a *half-breakfasted* man is no good. GALSWORTHY, The Country House, I, Ch. II, 20.

Winton was *triple-proofed* against betrayal of feeling. id., Beyond, I, Ch. I, 10.

These compounds should be distinguished from those in which an adjective in *ed* formed from a noun, is modified by an adverb, e. g. *well-intentioned, well-mannered*.

"Count, Count," screamed Mrs. Leo Hunter to a *well-whiskered* individual in a foreign uniform, who was passing by. DICK., Pickw., Ch. XV, 133.

When there is a verb uniform with a noun, it is difficult to tell whether in these compounds the suffix *ed* is a verbal (participial) or an adjectival formative. Thus, for example, in the case of *beautifully-coloured, well-conducted, well-shaped*.

Shakespeare... was himself, not only handsome and *well-shaped*, but very gentle and courteous, with most ingratiating manners. FRANK HARRIS, The Women of Shak., Ch. I, 3.

Horsen stared fixedly at that *perfectly-shaped* face. GALSWORTHY, Beyond, III, Ch. IX, 301.

The uncertain nature of the suffix *ed* is also responsible for the fact that the language sometimes has two kinds of compounds, one with an adverb, one with an adjective. Thus we meet with *well-sized* and *good-sized* (the ordinary word).

Thus also we find *absent-minded, high-minded, noble-minded, strong-minded*, etc. by the side of *cruelly-minded, justly-minded, cheerfully-minded*, etc.

For comment on and illustration of these and many other similar formations see especially JESPERSEN, Mod. Eng. Gram., II, 15.34 ff. There is no difficulty in distinguishing the above compounds in which one of the component members is a noun or may be understood as a noun, from such as are made up of an adverb + past participle, e. g. *ill-bred*, *ill-advised*, etc., discussed higher up (39, b). It may, however, be observed that in the compounds *long-lived* and *short-lived* made up of a noun *live* (for *life*) — *ed*, the form *lived* is often, erroneously, apprehended as a past participle and, consequently, mispronounced as the past participle of the verb *to live*. See MURRAY, s. v. *long-lived* and *short-lived*.

IV. On the plan of such compounds as *blue-eyed*, *left-handed*, we also find such as have for their first member

a) a noun, e. g.: *eagle-eyed*, *lantern-jawed*, *leather-aproned*, etc. Instances are quite common, any suitable combination, indeed, being capable of developing such a compound.

[These] facts and circumstances ... are beheld by every one, but our *mole-eyed* contemporary. DICK., Pickw., Ch. XVIII, 156.
There were great, round, *pot-bellied* baskets of chestnuts. id., Christm. Car.^{III} III, 62.
He was dressed in a *plum-coloured* velvet. MARJ. BOWEN, The Rake's Progress, Ch. IV, 43.

b) a definite or indefinite numeral. As to compounds with the latter, instances are at all common only with *many*; e. g.: a *four-footed animal*, a *many-coloured carpet*.

i. It was late in the afternoon when the four friends and their *four-footed* companion turned into the lane leading to Manor Farm. DICK., Pickw., Ch. V, 43.
Miss Arrowpoint and Herr Klesmer played a *four-handed* piece on two pianos. G. ELIOT, Dan. Der., I, I, Ch. V, 65.
They (sc. women) do not ... know how terribly *two-edged* is their gift of loveliness. MEREDITH, Ord. of Rich. Fev., Ch. XXVII, 212.

ii. *few*. Men and women and children, who, guided by hope or by hearsay, | Sought for their kith and their kin among the *few-acred* farmers | On the Acadian coast. LONGFELLOW, Evangeline, II, 2, 9.
many. Entering then, | Right o'er a mount of newly-fallen stones, | The *dusky-rafter'd*, *many-cobwebb'd* hall, | He found an ancient dame in dim brocade. TEN., Mar. of Ger., 362.
Tulips and petunias, marigolds and flame-flower, morning glory and bougainvillæa made a jubilance of *many-coloured* carpet. E. F. BENSON, Arundel, Ch. I, 9. (Thus also *multi-coloured*, as in: It (sc. his love) burned with a steady and unwinking flame, without rockets and *multi-coloured* stars. ib., Ch. I, 7.)
The sun of late June is warm upon the *many-charioted* streets. GISSING, A Life's Morning, Ch. XX, 272.
We have seen *many-sized* rooms since then. TEMPLE THURSTON, The World of Wonderful Reality, Dedic. (= *largely varying as to size*.)

Note especially *the many-headed beast* or *monster* (after Hor. Ep. I, 1, 76: Belua multorum es capitum) = *the populace*.
Then there came a turnip, then a potato, and then an egg: with a few other little tokens of the playful disposition of the many-headed. DICK, Pickw., Ch. XIX, 170.
no. He was a brown-whiskered, white-hatted, no-coated cabman DICK., Sketches by Boz, XVII.
several. It is a several-chorded lute on which they play. SYMONDS (Macm. Mag., XLV, 325) [1]

c) different pronouns. Instances occur only occasionally.
  i. She's got *thy* coloured eyes. G. ELIOT, Adam Bede, 161. [2]
  ii. *This* shaped eye or that. MEREDITH, Ord. of Rich. Fev., 231. [2]
  iii. Both are printed in the *same* sized paper. COLLINGWOOD, Life of John Ruskin, 348. [2]

V. When modified by such adverbs of degree as *as*, *so*, *too*, the compound is sometimes split up into its component parts, the indefinite article being interposed. Such a word-group as *so honest a face* appears then to be moulded into a compound adjective through taking the suffix *ed*. See ALEX. SCHMIDT, Shak. Lex., I. For similar formations with, respectively, the present and the past participle see 26, c, Note β; and 40, Obs. I.

Let me live here ever; | *So rare a wonder'd father and a wife.* Makes this place Paradise. SHAK., Temp., IV, 123 (= *so rarely wondered a father*, i.e. a father endowed with such a rare power of working miracles. AL. SCHMIDT.)
In this the antique and well-noted face | Of plain old form is much disfigured, | ... It makes the course of thoughts to fetch about. | ... Makes sound opinion sick and truth suspected, | For putting on *so new a fashion'd robe*. SHAK., King John, IV, 2, 27.
I have known *as honest a faced* fellow have art enough to do that. SCOTT, Kenilworth, Ch. XII, 141.

Similarly such a word-group as *such a colour* may take the adjectival suffix *ed*, resulting into the compound *such a coloured*.
Her hair is auburn, mine is perfect yellow: | If that be all the difference in his love, | I'll get me *such a colour'd* periwig. SHAK., Two Gent., IV, 4, 196.

VI. The non-repetition of the modifying element in the second of a succession of such compounds as in the following quotation appears to be very rare:
What false Italian, | *As poisonous tongued as handed*, hath prevail'd | On thy too ready hearing? SHAK., Cymb., III, 2, 5.

VII. The unaltered noun is sometimes used where the meaning intended seems to require the adjective with the suffix *ed*. Thus *edge-tool* varies with *edged-tool* (for the different application see MURRAY);

---
[1] MURRAY.
[2] JESPERSEN, Mod. Eng. Gram., II, 15.351.

barefoot with *barefooted*. Scott (Old Mortality, Ch. II, 25) has *a wheel carriage*, instead of the ordinary *wheeled carriage*.

Thus not unfrequently compounds whose first element is a numeral, through contamination with similar compounds which denote a measure, such as *four-foot ruler*, a *five-act comedy*, a *thirty-mile walk*, a *three-day visit*, etc. discussed in Ch. XXV, 31 ff.

The Elliot pride could not endure to make a third in a *one-horse* chaise. Jane Austen, Pers., Ch. X, 92.

His poor old mother had the happiness of seeing . . her beloved John step into a close carriage, a *one-horse* carriage, it is true, but [etc.]. Thack., Pend., I, Ch. II, 17.

The *four-horse* stage-coach by which I was a passenger. Dick., Great Expect., Ch. XX, 193. (Compare: They drove to the Town-Hall in a *four-horsed* carriage. Graph. No. 2276, 55.)

A very nice *four-wheel* chaise. Dick., Pickw., Ch. V., 51. (Collins' Clear-Type Press; other editions have *four-wheeled*, and this seems to represent Dickens's ordinary practice.)

A comfortable *four-post* bed. Jean Webster, Daddy-Long-Legs, 234. Here's a *four-leaf* clover. ib., 213. (Murray has only *four-leaved*.)

Observe that *seven-league* boots varies with *seven-leagued* boots. With the above compare:

i. Tom's *two-word* reply. G. F. Bradby, For this I have borne him., Ch. VII, 83.

ii. An old *eight-day* clock . . ticked gravely in the corner. Dick., Pickw. Ch. V., 44.

The *eight-hour* day. Rev. of Rev., No. 214, 332a.

iii. His *ten-mile* walk. Hardy, Return III, Ch. VI, 260.

iv. A *three-years'* child. Coleridge, Anc. Mar., IV.

v. The race has been a *two-days* event. Il. Lond. News, No. 3856, 360a.

44. SHAKESPEARE has also forms in *ed* derived from adjectives, mostly in the sense of *made* whatever is expressed by the adjective. Such forms differ, as to their grammatical function, in no way from ordinary past participles.

The painful warrior *famoused* for fight, [. .] Is from the book of honour razed quite. Son., XXV.

Shall that victorious hand be *feebled* here? King John, V, 2, 146.

Look here, what tributes wounded fancies sent me, | Of *paled* pearls and rubies red as blood. Lover's Compl., 198.

Lo, all these trophies of affections hot, | Of *pensived* and subdued desires the tender. ib., 219.

Addenda and Corrigenda.

An incorrect numbering of the sections in the treatise on the Infinitive in the manuscript stage has, unfortunately, led to an incorrect numbering in the 'Order of Discussion' prefixed to this treatise. To set the matter right, the reader is recommended to alter 6-33 into 6-34; 34-41 into 35-43; and to increase each following number by two.

Further Comment on

The Infinitive.

§ 21, c: The quotations given seem to show that the use of *to* before the infinitive after *dare* as a present indicative is especially frequent in emotional utterances. Thus also in:

You *dare to tell* me that I have no imagination! Galsw., Silv. Box, II, (68)

§ 40, c: According to Murray (s. v. *make*, 53) the use of an infinitive with *to* after *to make* is now archaic.

§ 54: In the following quotation the non-repetition of *to* seems to be due to the negative:

How can you expect four women to dine every day and not *quarrel*? Wilk. Col., The Woman in White, I, 36. (A change of *not quarrel* into, for example, *live in perfect harmony* would, apparently, entail the repetition of *to*.)

§ 72, a: In the following quotation the retention of the active voice seems to be due to the requirements of the metre.

Who has not seen it will be much *to pity*. Byron, Don Juan, I, VIII

§ 77: The alternative practice would seem to be impossible in:

i. There was also plenty *to eat*. Lyt., Paul Clif., Ch. XXI, 249
There is not any plot *to speak of* in Lesage's "Gil Blas" Marr..., Life of Ch. Dick., Ch. VII, 87.
There was much *to learn*. Wells, Kipps, III, Ch. I, § 3, 135. [almost *There was much (left) that had (yet) to be learned*. Dutch Er moest nog veel geleerd worden. *There was much to be learned* would suggest *There was much that could (or might) be learned*. Dutch Er kon nog veel geleerd worden.]

ii. There was no sound *to be heard*. Dick., Nick., Ch. V, 27b
There is no more *to be said* about it. id., Hard Times, Ch. XIX, 171

§ 79, f: Also in the following quotations substitution of the passive for the active infinitive would be impossible:

Needn't keep this shop, if I didn't like. But it's something *to do*. Wells, Kipps, III, Ch. III, § 7, 329.
I thought — I'd like to keep a bookshop anyow, jest for something *to do*. ib., III, Ch. III, § 3, 316.
What it must have cost *to build*! ib., II, Ch. IX, § 2, 267

81, Obs. III: It should have been observed that in such sentences as *The horse is quiet to ride* the adjective does not express a quality of the action denoted by the infinitive, but of the thing indicated by the subject. This accounts for the fact that expansion is impossible.

The Gerund.

§ 13, b Note α: The use of the definite article before the gerund after *worth* appears, after all, to be common enough. Here is another instance.

Such a risk was certainly not *worth the running*. MARZIALS, Life of Ch. Dick., Ch. II, 37.

β: It is not only adverbs in *ly* which may be found before gerunds, also certain adverbs of indefinite time are sometimes met with in this position.

It was impossible, even before dinner, to avoid *often walking about* in the pattern of the carpet. DICK., Hard Times, III, Ch. II, 102 b.

He could do nothing but tenderly express his regret at parting and speak vaguely and almost mysteriously of their *soon meeting*. DISR., Syb., III, Ch. X, 207.

His *long wooing* her. TEN., En. Ard., 703.

It should, however, be borne in mind that not a few adverbs are not unfrequently used adnominally. On the strength of gerunds being partly substantival in character the adverbs in the above quotations may, therefore, in a manner be apprehended as adnominal modifiers. We quote a few curious examples of adnominal adverbs.

The amount and regularity of the cheques from Messrs. Bradbury and Evans, the *then and still* owners of that happy periodical, made him aware that he found for himself a satisfactory career. TROL., Thack., Ch. I, 22.

Raleigh's half=scientific declamation, and his *often* quotations of Doctor Dee, the conjuror, have less effect on Osborne than on Cumberland. KINGSLEY, Westw. Ho,, Ch. XVI, 126 b.

At *nearly* Christmas the foliage was as brilliant as when the outrage was committed. MISS MITFORD, Our Village, Ch. 1, 15.

19, b: The alternative construction with the preposition *of* is impossible when the object is a reflexive pronoun, and also when it otherwise forms a kind of unit with the verb.

It is *the thinking ourselves* vicious then that principally contributes to make us vicious. GODWIN, Cal. Wil., II, Ch. VI, 188.

This made *the taking offence* impossible. ib., I, Ch. IV, 31.

26, b: To the verbs requiring, or at least preferring the active voice of the gerund, notwithstanding its passive meaning, may be added *to repay*.

(This) book published twenty years ago ... will repay *studying* in these times. Westm. Gaz., 21 10, 1922, 8 a.

d: Also *past*, which is closely synonymous with *beyond*, distinctly prefers the active voice.
> i. He was *past rousing*. Wilk. Col., The Woman in White, 1, 152.
> He would have been *past saving*. ib., III, Ch. XI, 448.
> That we can come out of it with credit or dignity is *past hoping*. Westm. Gaz., 7 10, 1922, 7 a.
> ii. I tried vainly to soothe her and reason with her, she was *past being soothed*. Wilk. Col., The Woman in White, I, 152.

37, b: The desire of giving particular prominence to the originator of the action may even give rise to the nominative of a personal pronoun being used instead of the objective. Thus Jespersen (*De to hovedarter av grammatiske forbindelser*, 33) mentions the following curious, as yet exceedingly rare, construction:
> Instead of *he converting* the Zulus, the Zulu chief converted him.

With this sentence compare the following, in which *it*, on account of its particularly strong stress, could hardly be changed into *its*:
> She sat with her own back and the back of the large chair toward it (sc. the window), screening the fire, as if she were sedulously keeping it warm, instead of *it keeping her warm*. Dick., Cop., Ch. V, 38 a.

37, f: The word-group in construction B may even contain an entire clause:
> All peoples are not equally prepared. It is not a question of ascendency it is a question of *those who are able doing* the task they alone are prepared to perform. Manch. Guard., V, 25, 515 c.

46, a, 1: *Robbery* and *assassination* are, respectively, equivalent to *being robbed* and *being assassinated* in:
> His accidental presence ... assisted Sir Percival's escape from *robbery* and *assassination*. Wilk. Col., The Woman in White, I, 167.

64: For the infinitive having been, in part, the source of the gerund see also Murray, s. v. *ing*, 3; and *to*, B, 22.

The Participles.

3, c. Note α: Instances of a present participle implying a time-sphere posterior to that of the predication with which it is connected are occasionally met with.
> Miss Tyrell regarded her for a moment in silence, and then quitted the room, *coming back again from half-way up the stairs to answer a knock at the door*. Jacobs, A Master of Craft, Ch. XVII, 87 a.
> Belinda rose noisily and gathering up her untidy books, thrust them back in a heap on the shelf, and putting on her hat stood at the door *commenting undutifully upon her parents and shrilly demanding of the small Wheelers whether they were coming or whether she was to stay there all night*. ib., Ch. XVII, 85 b. (The context imparts a momentaneous, or rather ingressive character to *stood*, so that it is equivalent to *went and stood*. Dutch ging staan.)

Of a different nature are the following examples, in which, however, there is the same posteriority of time-sphere:

The King (sc. Leodogran) | Sent to him (sc. Arthur), *saying*, 'Arise, and help us thou! | For here between the man and beast we die'. TEN., Com. of Arth., 45.

Then quickly from the foughten field he sent | Ultius, and Brastias, and Bedivere, | His new-made knights, to King Leodogran, | *Saying*, 'If I in aught have served thee well, | Give me thy daughter Guinevere to wife'. ib., 137.

It is of some interest to compare the above examples with analogous constructions in other languages.

In German the practice seems to be as unusual as in English. The following instances have come to hand:

Von allen Inseln kamen sie, | Und horchen von dem Schaugerüste | Des Chores grauser Melodie,

Der streng und ernst, nach alter Sitte, | Mit langsam abgemessnem Schritte, | Hervortritt aus dem Hintergrund, | *Umwandelnd* des Theaters Rund. SCHILLER, Die Kraniche des Ibykus, XIII.

Die (i. e. die Jagdgesellen) kamen hin, befanden die Sache als wahr und richtig, und ritten heim mit großer Verwunderung dem Könige Bericht *erstattend*. L. BECHSTEIN's Märchenbuch u. s. w.²³, pag. 8 ima sq.

CURME (A Gram. of the Germ.-Lang.², § 182, 3), without, however, referring to its relative infrequency, mentions the following example:

Ada war in die Gesellschaft zurückgetreten, den Dank derselben *entgegennehmend*. SPIELHAGEN.

In Latin the use of the participium præsentis instead of the participium futuri seems to be common enough. SPEYER (Lat. Spraakk.², § 719, Aanm. 2) quotes:

Legati a Saguntinis Romam missi auxiliam *orantes*. LIV., XXI, 6, 2 (= qui orarent, not qui orabant.)

Another instance is found in:

Suspensi Eurypylum *scitantem* oracula | Phoebi mittimus. VERG., Aen., II, 114.

Thus also in Greek, e. g.:

ἐς τὴν ἄλλην Σικελίαν ἀξιοῦμεν πρέσβεις δηλοῦντες ὡς κοινὸς ὁ κίνδυνος. THUCYDIDES, VI, 34, 1. (Let us send ambassadors to the rest of Sicily, *representing* that the danger is common.)

There is a similar difference as to time-sphere in the actions expressed by the verbs in such constructions as *to go out hunting*, in which, however, the present participle goes back to an earlier gerund (6, Obs. VIII).

Likewise in the curious construction employed in:

Her morning dress was dimity, | Her evening silk, or, in the summer, muslin, | And other stuffs, with which I won't stay *puzzling*. BYRON, Don Juan, I, XII.

17: In sentences like *The Boer is a born conservative*, the participle is practically divested of all verbal characteristics, as appears from its being placed in the same position of the adjective *high* in:

This good lady is a *born* lady, a high lady. Dick., Hard Times, I, Ch. XI, 31 b.

Thus also *born and bred* in:

There are apartments at the Bank where a *born and bred* lady, as keeper of the place, would be rather a catch than otherwise. ib., I, Ch. XVI, 47 b.

Placing *born* after the noun hardly affects its grammatical character. In *She's a natural born nurse* post-position is, of course, impossible.

27, b, 4: A solitary instance of a word-group consisting of *on* — def. art. — stem of transitive verb has come to hand.

My lady, there are few more impressive sights in the world than a Scotsman *on the make*. J. M. Barrie, What every woman knows, II, (55).

Further Illustration of
The Infinitive.

§ 11, a: It was hinted that perhaps they *need not* always make so much smoke. Dick., Hard Times, II, Ch. I, 49 C.

Apparently he (sc. Mr Lloyd George) assured Dr. Wirth in quite general terms that he *need not* be anxious for the future. Manch. Guard., VI, 22, 451 a.

§ 12, a, 2: We *need* express *little* surprise. Westm. Gaz., 14 10, 1922, 1 a.

§ 65, c: The countess of Marney held a great assembly at the family mansion in St. James' Square, which Lord Marney *had intended to have let* to a new club. Disr., Syb., IV, Ch. XI, 264.

§ 66, Obs. I, a: "I'm glad to see you so well, Miss Cardinal," he said, "I *had been afraid* that it *might have exhausted* you." Hugh Walpole, The Captives, I, Ch. III, 46.

§ 71, Obs. III: *'Tis to be done* again at three (sc. the dressing of the wounds) and then she may be left till morning. Dick., Hard Times, Ch. XIII, 88 a.

§ 72, a, s.v. *to do*: "I have come here to learn something of their condition," said Egremont, "That *is not to be done* in a great city like London." Disr., Syb., III, Ch. VI, 184.

The wretched ignorance with which Jupe clung to this consolation ... filled Mr. Gradgrind with pity. Yet what *was to be done*? Dick., Hard Times, I, Ch. IX, 24 a.

§ 72, b: "Why pet," said Trotty, "what's *to do*? I didn't expect you to day, Meg." Dick., Chimes?, I, 15.

§ 75, a, i.: He would stop to examine the nature of the soil, till my pockets (not his own) with great lumps of clay, stones and rubbish, *to analyse* when

he got home, by the help o' some chemical apparatus he had borrowed from Mr. Squills. LYT., Caxt., II, Ch. II, 38.
The clergyman exhorted him that whatever his hand found *to do*, he was to do. WELLS, Kipps, I, Ch. II, § 4, 47.

 ii.: A neighbouring butcher presented me with a choice morsel of steak, not *to eat*, but *to wear*. JER., Paul Kelver, I, Ch. III, 32 a.

 i. and ii.: It is she who wants somebody *to protect*, *to help*, *to work for* — somebody to give her children *to protect*, *to help*, *to work for*. SHAW, Cand., III, (178).

 b: The other things included books *to read* and books *to give away*. WELLS, Kipps, I, § 1, 13.

§ 76, Obs. I: All schemes of social progress . . . require money *to be expended*. Westm. Gaz., 28 20, – 22, 2 a.

§ 83: We passed through glittering joyous streets, piled high each side with all the good things of the earth – toys and baubles, jewels and gold, things good *to eat* and good *to drink*, things good *to wear* and good *to see*. JEROME, Paul Kelv., I, Ch. I, 18 b.

§ 55, Obs. III: I find myself looking over my sketches as I used to look over my lessons when I was a little girl, and when I was sadly afraid that I should turn out not fit *to be heard*. WILK. COL., The Wom. in White, I, Ch. VIII, 51.

§ 88: It would appear from this unexpected circumstance of to-day . . . as if something had crept into Thomas's and Louisa's minds . . ., which *had never been intended to be developed*. DICK., Hard Times, I, Ch. IV, 9 a.
The marriage was *appointed to be solemnized* in eight weeks' time. ib., I, Ch. XVI, 48 a.

The Gerund.

19, b: I protest you have made my blood run cold with *the very mentioning the top of that mountain*. FIELD., Tom Jones, VIII, Ch. X, 148 b.
It was necessary to *the realizing his project* that he should pass for a god. GODWIN, Cal. Wil., II, Ch. I, 153.
The civilities that had once or twice occurred in the bustle of a public circle, the *restoring her fan*, which she had dropped, or *the disembarrassing her* of an empty tea-cup, made her heart palpitate. ib., I, Ch. VI, 55.
In those parts they call it Lonesome Ford. That is better than just *the giving it* of a good name TEMPLE THURST., The Flower of Gloster, Ch. XXVII, 157. (The alternative construction would be *the giving to it*.)

20: *This crossing the Alps* is a trial. DISR., Lothair, I, Ch. VI, 31.
It is a bad thing — *this beating the police*. id., Syb., V, Ch. I, 292. (The alternative of-construction would give rise to ambiguity.)

22: *The not being troubled* with earnestness was a great point. DICK., Hard Times, II, Ch. VII, 74 a.

25: My wounds will not bear this perpetual *tampering*. GODWIN, Cal. Wil., II, Ch. III, 163.

52, b, 1: Waste not a sigh on *fortune changed*... On thankless courts or *friends estranged*. Scott, Lady, II, III, 15–16.
   2: Such a prince as our Henry the Fifth would have been the idol of the North. The follies of his youth, the selfish ambition of his manhood, the Lollards roasted at slow fires, the prisoners massacred on the field of battle, the expiring lease of priestcraft renewed for another century... everything is forgotten but the victory of Agincourt. Mac., Macch., (36 b)

The Participles.

5, b: By this time a whole village was up and windlasses, ropes, poles, candles, lanterns, all things necessary, were *collecting* and being brought into one place to be carried to the Old Hell Shaft. Dick., Hard Times, III, Ch. VI, 119 a (The quotation shows that some verbs are more adaptable to the old practice than others.)
The clergyman's wednesday Evening Lectures are *publishing* there by subscription. Wilk. Col., The Woman in White, III, Ch. IX, 417.
Staying only long enough to drink the watchman's coffee, which was *heating* on a gas-jet, they left it (sc. the office) and began to search the wharf. Jacobs, A Master of Craft, Ch. II, 11 b.

6 Obs. VII: The Holborn Viaduct was then *in building*. [from] Paul Kelv., I, Ch. VIII, 67 a.

26, a, 2: You've been on *foreign-going* ships, then. Jacobs, A Master of Craft, Ch. I, 8 b. (*Foreign-going* = going to foreign parts.)
A hundred and thirty political offenders have been *hunger-striking* for one week in the prison at Lichteburg. Manch. Guard., V, 21, 406 c.

Errors of the Press.

Page 3, line 20 from top: change area into areas.
  „ 3, „ 24 „ „ „ he „ be.
  „ 13, „ 12 „ bottom: scarcely „ scarcely
  „ 20, „ 20 „ „ „ Bronte „ Brontë.
  „ 92, „ 5 „ „ place a full stop after 'adverbially.

An Apology.

In conclusion I have to say a few words about my references to the Oxford English Dictionary. Throughout my grammatical work I have consistently indicated my obligations to this famous monument of English scholarship by "Murray". This was unexceptionable in the initial stages of my work, when the deeply lamented lexicographer bore the undivided responsibility of his grand undertaking. But as time went on and other scholars joined the staff as responsible co-editors, the term became less appropriate and a more comprehensive name was needed. Some writers began to quote the Dictionary under the abbreviation H. E. D. (Historical English Dictionary), many preferred the somewhat jovial N. E. D. (New English Dictionary), and this appears to be the most widely favoured designation to this day. More recently the more accurate O. E. D. (Oxford English Dictionary) has come into vogue. As for me I have not, hitherto, seen my way to change the indication of my references to the Dictionary, because I thought it undesirable, if not misleading, to do so while I was engaged on one and the same work. However, since it has come to my knowledge that it is the desire of the present editors to have the work entrusted to their care referred to by the last-mentioned initials or the fuller description, Oxford English Dictionary, I have, in deference to their wishes, made up my mind to use the same indications in any grammatical work which, after this, I may commit to the press. I sincerely hope that they will accept my apology for not having done so at an earlier stage of my grammar in the same friendly spirit in which I offer it.

Lightning Source UK Ltd.
Milton Keynes UK
UKHW010641090820
367908UK00001B/211